PUVIS DE CHAVANNES: THE FISHERMAN'S FAMILY

MODERN PAINTING

BY FRANK JEWETT MATHER, Jr

GARDEN CITY   NEW YORK

GARDEN CITY PUBLISHING CO., INC.

SET UP AND ELECTROTYPED BY T. MOREY & SON

PRINTED IN THE
UNITED STATES OF AMERICA

TO IRVING BABBITT

DEAR BABBITT: Except for certain talks with you among the Berkshire Hills and those that rim the Arno, this book either would not have been or would have been something quite different. I was painfully extricating myself from the false æsthetic of the 1890's. Through Whistler I had learned that art was a lucky accident. Painter friends had insisted that it was technique. As a young writer, I believed firmly that my art lay solely in graceful and unexpected ordering of words and phrases. Most of my intellectual seniors and betters had proved that art could have nothing to do with life in general.

The eloquence with which you opposed these views did not fully convince me at the time, but started a growing distrust of theories that left art in a vacuum. Your successive books, particularly "The New Laokoön" and "Rousseau and Romanticism," when, alas! talks with you were rarer, taught me that enjoyment of art is a responsible act in a life, that its tendency is a function of the work of art and as such proper subject of criticism, finally that this modern age has witnessed a progressive exaggeration of individualism which, apparently enriching, actually has confused and impoverished all the arts. Not satisfied with defining the malady of our times, you have indicated a remedy in a revived humanism which shall give to the artist's imagination some worthier discipline than any single individual experience affords.

It is largely your example that has heartened me to extend to the field of modern painting that criticism of ideas and ideals which you have so brilliantly applied to modern literature, morals and politics. So in this book alongside of much with which you will disagree you will find more of your own. You will find me more indulgent than yourself towards the pleasanter by-products of error, less hopeful, perhaps, of truth's prevailing through polemic, but you will also find me fighting beside you for such art as is humanistic, traditional and socially available. It is with pleasure and gratitude, Dear Babbitt, that I now return to you much that I borrowed as we strolled thirty-odd years ago under the elms about Williamstown or along the cypress rows above Fiesole.

FRANK JEWETT MATHER, JR.

PRINCETON, N. J.
NOVEMBER, 1926.

NOTE

THE substance of this book was delivered as Lowell Lectures in 1916. Everything has been much expanded and rewritten and the two chapters on Modernism are new.

CONTENTS

LIST OF ILLUSTRATIONS

LIST OF ILLUSTRATIONS

MODERN PAINTING

INTRODUCTION

A SURVEY of the art of modern times is an adventure. One feels like the explorer who from a mountain top begins to sketch the features of some vast uncharted land. All he can hope to do is to express the generalities of the scene. Here is mountain, here forest, here lake or river valley. What counts in such a report is accuracy of compass bearings. We must know whether he had a good compass, or roughly estimated his north from woodmen's signs. So in our survey of modern art nothing is more important than those standard terms by which we find our way in what were otherwise confusion. The reader will bear with me then if at the outset I tell what I mean by certain terms which I must constantly employ—classic, romantic, pseudo-classic.

All will agree that the moving power of every artist is vivid sensibility, impulsiveness. He feels more deeply than most men. Genius is to madness near allied—such commonplaces express the truth that art arises in a kind of turbulence. But art ends in a highly organized product—painting, sculpture, stately monument, the complicated perfection of which implies disciplined toil. Then the artist is not merely the favored child of impulse, or at least the great artist is not; he is on the contrary the stern

3

master of himself, the austere critic of his own emotions. What is conceived in expansive joy is brought forth in travail and restriction. About the well-balanced artist there is a kind of double personality; he is a working partnership between an epicurean and a stoic. The artist who attains this just balance between creative impulse and executive discipline is a classic.

He is, then, a classic not by reason of especial technique or subject-matter, but because of the inner harmony of his being. And just as he solves the inner conflict between the yea and nay in his own heart, so he usually reconciles with equal success those perpetual outer conflicts, between the past and the present, between the individual and society. The past—he uses and reveres it without letting its hand rest too heavily upon him; society—he studies and serves it, making aids of its restrictions, and of its compulsions a source of athletic strength. The classic artist may for good reason be a recluse; he is never a rebel. He never conceives the world as hostile to him, or conditions as too unmanageable. In short, the classic temperament in the artist is merely a sublimation of that humanity and common sense which we value in a layman. As the great romantic painter Delacroix insists: "Genius is merely the capacity for being reasonable in a superior degree."

If moderation, compromise, and lucidity are the watchwords of the classic spirit, excess, revolt and mystery are the countersigns of romanticism. Your true romantic is an isolated titan. Restraint, the social bond, tradition—these irk him. He does not accept the common lot, he prefers not to be understood, but to wreak for its own sake an imperious need of self-expression. He creates, not in disciplined joy, but in frenzy, perhaps in anguish. Reverie is his realm, remote pasts, or exotic lands are his refuges from the vulgarity of the present. His battle cry is the freedom of the artist, by which he often means license. He admits no values except values of temperament. He is prone to push vehemence to the point of incoherence.

Clearly I have described what in a man who was not an artist would be regarded as a morbid excess of individualism. French criticism, being that of a lucid and compromising race, almost invariably treats romanticism as a disease. German criticism, being that of a cloudy and uncompromising race, generally treats romanticism as the highest artistic virtue. Now is not the moment for us to take sides. We can do so better after we shall have seen the fruits of the two ideals as manifested in art. But let me say at once that it is a very narrow view of human temperament which regards the instinctive restraints and self-disciplines of the soul as less natural and worthy than its instinctive desire for unlimited expansion.

So far, for the sake of clearness, I have purposely exaggerated the contrast between the classic and romantic spirit. Actually they often blend in the most confusing way. And evidently your classic artist, unless he lead a deep emotional life, can have nothing to give. Lacking passion, his restraint and discipline have nothing to work upon. The mills of his intelligence powder only chaff. As evidently, the wildest romantic must have at least discipline enough to carry through the difficult technical processes of his art. Or rather, it was so until very recently, when masterpieces were first achieved in an instantaneous fury of creation without taking thought of any kind. But more often your avowedly anarchical genius has a way of being quite restrained and classic, on the sly, as it were. Many a wild-eyed titan of the studios manages to attract and retain the bounty and the affection of his pious maiden aunt. He merely does it shamefacedly, where a classic would do it candidly.

Since romanticism in its multiform phases and disguises is the prevailing note of the nineteenth century, we shall have to study it with great thoroughness. It is enough now to admit that these classifications apply best to artists safely dead. Your romantic of to-day is often the classic of to-morrow. We have merely learned to accept his new scale of values. A superficial novelty of subject-matter or technique blinded us to his fine equipoise. Millet, the lover of the old Italians, of the Bible and Virgil, passed for a revolutionary vulgarian. It was his critics who were unbalanced, not the quiet, great soul at Barbizon.

These distinctions matter more to the layman and critic than to the artist. The classic artist will take care of himself—human wisdom is his gift; and so will the romantic artist manage to get along in some irresponsible way of his own, if only in a fool's paradise. What we really need to guard against is the false classic and the false romantic, types that unhappily abound. The pseudo-classic artist—he who draws a mean discipline from narrow traditions and applies this discipline only to negligible emotions; the pseudo-romantic artist—he who affects a vehemence which he does not really feel, and pays you off with specious sensationalisms—these are the enemies; these it behooves us to know. And even here we shall do best to work by indirection, to study not the pretenders, that were waste of time, but those elect spirits who whether in serene self-discipline, in stormy revolt or in rapturous dreaming have created the great painting of our own times.

THE ACADEMIC BACKGROUND

THE ACADEMIC BACKGROUND
(1664–1815)

SINCE for better or for worse, the art of the Renaissance ended and the art of to-day began in the academic style (or in pseudo-classicism as it is more technically called), that must be the somewhat ungrateful theme of this first chapter. Let me invite you to visit a salon the French Royal Academy of Fine Arts held in 1785, just four years before the Revolution. You will find the walls of the Hall of Apollo in the Louvre hung with what the Parisian art student of a less reverent age calls "machines." Here are huge canvases full of carefully posed figures enacting great historical parts, mostly from classical or religious literature. The great Vien offers you Priam's Return from the Tent of Achilles—a frigid transcript from Homer; the only less great Peyron contributes a bit of Euripidean pathos in the Death of Alcestis; the ingenious Suvée is Virgilian in Æneas preparing to return to Battle about Troy; the austere Berthélemy draws from Livy the stern episode of Manlius Torquatus, condemning his own son to death; the veteran Lagrenée is Plutarchan in the Death of the wife of Darius; mortuary and Plutarchan again is Ménageot with his moving Cleopatra and the Asp; even the frivolous Drouais draws from the

11

Bible the idyl of Christ and the Woman of Samaria. A promising young artist, Jacques Louis David, mark him well, for he is the only one of the exhibitors of whom you are ever likely to hear again, is sternly Roman in his Horatii most resolutely swearing their blood feud before their weeping women.

You are probably bored at the mere enumeration, and a modern art student would have fled at the first sight of any of these stilted and colorless designs. Paris was not bored but delighted. The Academy was more than delighted, for it had worked a full hundred years to effect this revival of a classic and noble style. The spectacle is odd. Here are the contemporaries of Rousseau and Voltaire playing solemnly at being the contemporaries of all the Greeks and Romans, and doing so not merely with the public approval but also at the public expense— the spectacle is so odd I say that we must try to explain it. And this involves a brief retrospect.

In 1664 the Académie Royale des Beaux-Arts, a languishing voluntary association since 1648, was put on a solid official basis by Louis XIV, through his great prime minister, Colbert. From 1666 its best students were accredited to the new Government School at Rome. The King intended not merely to encourage art by training artists but also to dictate the kind of art they should produce. To this end the Academy was to conduct lectures. The painters were to associate with men of letters, who in their turn were to serve as censors of taste. The King and his treasurer, Colbert, and his artistic director, Charles Le Brun, knew perfectly the kind of art they wanted: it was to be decorous, noble, historic, classic. Above all it was to be literary, vindicating those consecrated traditional ideas which should make for the stability of the best of monarchies. The King and his counsellors knew equally well the kind of art they did not want. Except for a minor branch, the necessary portraiture of prosperous or aristocratic personages, there was to be nothing contemporaneous. Antiquity must supply the themes, at least older literature. Common life must be avoided. Light-mindedness of all sorts must be eschewed.

There were withal notable rewards for following the right classic way. The state would buy otherwise wholly unsalable pictures which measured up to the academic specifications. The Gobelins factory accepted only orthodox designs, and paid well. Docile pupils of the Academy passed delightful years at the cost of the State at the Villa Médicis at Rome. The historical painters constituted the highest class in the Academy, and were especially favored in the exhibitions. The critics indeed regarded the historical painters as the only ones worthy of attention. Neglect and contumely, on the contrary, were the lot of those artists who from defect of nature or training could not attain to the grand style. For them no association with men of letters, no prizes, no State purchases, no presentations at court, and—extremest of all privations—no lectures. For support these

RUBENS: JUDGMENT OF PARIS

POUSSIN: EURIDYCE STUNG BY THE ADDER

unfortunate outsiders depended on the caprice of the untutored throng. One would have expected them to starve. They did not, they even throve in their own unregulated way. They maintained their humble rival Academy of St. Luke, a descendant of the mediæval painters' guild, they produced painters of the force of Watteau and Chardin, they even enlisted a few critics, worse yet they sold their pictures. The Academy had to work hard for the victory it finally achieved in the Salon of 1785.

Since the century of controversy between the Academy and the outsiders has determined all critical opinion about art ever since, we cannot neglect it. Perhaps the briefest statement of the issue would be that it was between warm art and cold art. The fight was waged most appropriately in the names of the nobly vehement Fleming, Rubens, and the nobly decorous Frenchman, Poussin. Bring a fine Rubens into a room, and the temperature is immediately raised, bring a fine Poussin in, and the temperature will be lowered. Do you wish to be excited go to Rubens; would you be soothed, there is Poussin. A liberal taste might well like both experiences, not so the highly classicized taste of seventeenth century France. The inordinate vitality of Rubens's hurtling nudities seemed not only indelicate—which they certainly are, but positively vulgar—which they emphatically are not. After all, the French Academy merely took Rubens as priggish folk have taken him ever since. There is nothing that troubles your prig

like heartiness, and Rubens's beefy heroes and heroines are portentously hearty. So the century that
was extolling the gentle melancholy of Virgil against
the barbaric excesses of Homer, by the same token
found in the serene, well pondered, slightly frigid
idyls of Nicholas Poussin its beau-ideal of the painter's art. One cannot say that it was an unworthy
ideal, merely a very limited one.

How the anxious academicians put their big wigs
together and concocted an orthodox doctrine of
official painting I can only suggest. The painter
pedant François Du Fresnoy had codified it all in the
smooth hexameters of his Latin poem "De Arte
Graphica," 1665. It was translated into every civilized tongue, and remains still the fountainhead of all
pseudo-classic dogma for the art of painting. Let me
abridge to the essentials its numerous articles of faith.
And to show that this short credo was no sudden
growth, let me here and there illustrate the articles
from the views of older artists and critics.

(1) Art must treat only important and noble subjects preferably from classical antiquity. Nicholas
Poussin had written in that letter which is his artistic testament: "A noble subject matter should be
chosen, and one free from workaday grime."

(2) Hence art must be public, a function of the
State, avoiding the merely private and trivial.

(3) Nature must be used by the artist only with
circumspection. One must avoid the commonplace
and vulgar subjects which unhappily nature produces.

Imitate only *belle-nature*. As early as the middle of the 15th century the Florentine artist-critic Leon Battista Alberti had written: "We must take the things we paint from nature, but choosing always their most beautiful and distinguished aspects."

(4) Belle-nature cannot, however, be discovered with your own eyes. It is an error to use them too freely. Use instead the eyes of the ancient poets and sculptors who have already sifted out all that is fairest in nature.

(5) Painting should not merely be heroic, national, select, and classically tempered, but it should also be as literary as possible. Painting is like poetry, *ut pictura poesis*—went the indisputable maxim. It would be a futility for the painter to invent his own themes, a degradation for him just to pick them up here and there from observation. Let him take them from the great repertory of the older poets.

(6) Since the main business of painting is to tell impressively and with clearness some action of classical antiquity, the clarity of the drawing is what counts. Color is confusing—Rubens's makes your head swim—be sparing of your color then, and make your painting simulate the naked majesty of antique sculpture. Here the painter of Toulouse, Hilaire Pader, in his poem "La Peinture Parlante," 1657, sums up the views of two generations of censors.

> "Mille et mille tableaux d'excessive valeur
> Ont pour tout fondement l'éclat de la couleur.
> Qui n'est qu'un accident qui peut ou ne peut être
> En un même sujet sans qu'il change son être."

One is glad to recall that Poussin snubbed Pader savagely for his foolish book.

To show that I do not exaggerate the pseudo-classic programme let me quote a little from Du Fresnoy's poem in John Dryden's English.

"The principal and most important part of painting is to find out, and thoroughly to understand what nature has made most beautiful, and most proper to this art." The choice must be guided "according to the taste and manner of the Ancients; without which art is nothing, is a blind and rash barbarity." That is to say, "according to the statues, the basso-relievos and the other ancient pieces, as well of the Grecians as of the Romans. Ancient or antic is that which has been made from the time of Alexander the Great to that of Phocas, during whose empire the arts were ruined by war. These works from their beginnings have been the rule of beauty."

Such was the doctrine that the Royal Academy of Fine Arts and its literary allies preached for a century. The great archæological discoveries and publications of the middle of the 18th century came to reinforce the teaching. Herculaneum (1757) and Pompeii made antiquity palpable. Wincklemann's great work on Greek sculpture (1764) put at the disposal of the classical creed a rare philosophy and eloquence. Even Lessing, the champion of Shakespeare against the French dramatists, tacitly admits the incomparable superiority of the ancient marbles. The current was irresistible. Goethe, in youth the celebrant of the

Gothic sublimity of the Cathedral of Strasbourg, in middle age, at Rome, declares all beauty to be measured by that of Greece and Rome. Even in fashion, antiquity tyrannizes. The tall powdered wigs come down in favor of hair parted simply like that of the marble goddesses; feminine furbelows give way to clinging draperies; public men are sculptured either in the virile toga or even in the heroic "altogether"; the frivolous bowed legs of rococo chair and couch stiffen, straighten, acquire massiveness, achieve plinths and capitals. Sober Louis Seize has succeeded frivolous Louis Quinze, the grand style has come to its own.

Now the trouble with the grand style will already be apparent. It presupposed an infinite process of copying the ancients. "What did the Greeks do without any antiques?" Delacroix was soon scornfully to ask. Evidently this difficulty had not occurred to the Academicians. Moreover they not only required slavish copyism, but copyism of inferior examples. Note that terrible betrayal in the passage from Du Fresnoy in which he dates the antique between Alexander the Great and Phocas. That is he calmly ignores all the greatest periods of Grecian sculpture. And all these zealots of antiquity really never saw the glory that was Greece, they caught at best only its attenuated echo in the commercial garden statuary of imperial Rome. They copied what were only bad copies. Olympia, Delphi, even Athens, were closed books to those eager souls who expatiated amid that mass ' of second-rate Hellenistic marble cutting which clutters the museums of the Capitol and the Vatican.

Not merely did they subject art to mediocre examples as regarded the past, but they intrusted her to equally mediocre custody as regarded the present. The official teaching of art in France was put in charge of a distinguished succession of Professors. Such custody, however delightful to the Professor, is almost invariably fatal to the wildling, art. Eventually the Professors did kill the grand style with kindness, and they would have done so earlier, had not the French Revolution given the style a respite and at last a more heroic taking off than it really deserved.

Happily the devotees of the grand style remained only a favored official oligarchy. The Academicians from the first had to face the deplorable fact of a world that did not want its art too cold, or too serious, but on the whole preferred it amusing, frivolous and a bit warm. For this sub-academic world were painted, largely under the influence of the suspect, Rubens, those deliciously artificial pastorals now greatly desired of the museum director and the auctioneer, the playful or wistful masterpieces of the *École galante*. The pleasure-loving nobles, and prosperous merchants and great ladies, the amateurs and the new race of picture dealers had no objection to Rubens, or to any art that stirred and charmed. Many painters took the superiority of the Academy humorously, or ignored it entirely.

WATTEAU: GATHERING IN A PARK

FRAGONARD: THE BATHERS

Thus Watteau counsels his pupil Lancret to quit masters and consult "the master of all masters—nature—to go and sketch some landscape in the suburbs of Paris, afterwards to sketch some figures, and thus to compose a picture after his own choice and imagination." And the academician Boucher warns young Fragonard bound for the School of Rome not on peril of disaster to take "*ces messieurs,*" his masters, too seriously. Why indeed go back to cold marbles, when one can study the whimsical grace of the Italian comedians, why confect a sham Arcadia, when one can see the satin-clad lovers of our own day in languorous dalliance beside our own fountains and in the shadow of our own plane trees?

So must have argued Antoine Watteau, if he argued at all. At any rate, the cherry and azure and amber of Rubens reappear, more pensively, more moderated, in his *fêtes galantes.* So do his followers Lancret and Pater, so do the good portrait painters Largillière, Nattier, Drouais really stem from Rubens. François Boucher, improvisor, stage manager of a powdered and rouged Olympus, not without its attractiveness, is a kind of diminished society Rubens. Greuze with his demurely coquettish maidens, and his sentimental family scenes is technically merely bleached out and devitalized Rubens. Fragonard, on the contrary, with his blisses and kisses, and eager swains and panting nymphs is like a rather little Rubens more than a little tipsy. He carries the warm and frivolous style down to the chill days of the Terror.

It should be understood that the Academy had no quarrel with this popular and playful art so long as its own superiority was admitted. The gravest academicians were glad to welcome Moreau le Jeune and Fragonard as their book illustrators. I suppose the houses of the straitest classicist admitted rosy cupids, fancifully draped shepherdesses, and completely undraped nymphs as agreeable decoration. Thus things went along in France past the middle of the eighteenth century under a very human agreement to disagree. Even under the stricter orthodoxy of the Empire, it was permissible to buy the seductive little paintings of the old Fragonard and the young Boilly, provided you praised the official sublimities of David. The Academy was entirely tolerant of the minor art so long as that art advanced no claims. The stricter orthodoxy of the end of the century, grew largely from fear of competition. When, in the early 1770's the Academy of St. Luke began to hold successful exhibitions, condescension changed to intolerance.

After an outrageous campaign of persecution, in 1776 the Royal Academy obtained the legal suppression of its rival. It had perhaps been well frightened when an intrepid young critic, Dénis Diderot, claimed a measure of greatness for the genre painting of Greuze. It was alarming to hear him appeal from taste to passion. Had he not written in his critique of the salon of 1765—"First touch me, astound me, tear me to bits, make me tremble, weep, shudder, rage, then please my eyes if you can." It was against such romantic insurgence that the Academy made its last and most successful stand.

Taking the eighteenth century, in France, as a whole, both discipline and impulse had lost ground. Discipline, without attaining style, had sacrificed charm and beauty, running out in empty formalism; impulse, in the painting of the *École galante*, had achieved great charm and skill at the expense of seriousness.

England characteristically made a fair compromise between the restrictive and expansive principle. In England, where the Royal Academy was not founded till 1768, and art had to take care of itself undandled by professorial arms, Rubens and his follower Van Dyck remained the great exemplars. The peculiar poetry of Gainsborough in portraiture and landscape is expressed in the idiom of Rubens and Van Dyck. Sir Joshua Reynolds, though in the famous "Discourses" which as President of the Royal Academy he delivered between 1769 and 1790, he constantly advocated the imitation of the ancients, was far too wise to practice what he preached. He drew much from Rubens and Van Dyck, even more from Titian and Correggio. He advised the severities of the historical style for his students, for himself the loveliness of the women and children of the best of aristocracies was world enough. "The Discourses" have a genuine liberalism. Sir Joshua does some lip service to the doctrine of the supremacy of the ancients, but he includes among the ancients Raphael,

Michelangelo, Rubens, Rembrandt, Correggio. Perhaps the greatest defect of the "Discourses" is the failure to admit the greatness and variety of Hogarth.

It was hard for Sir Joshua Reynolds to be quite fair to the peppery vulgarian who had invented the term "portrait manufacturers." The greatest of "portrait manufacturers" could not be expected to extol a talent which he honestly believed trivial and disorderly. Indeed the full greatness of Hogarth had to wait until the Romantic revival for recognition. Oddly the English have generally underestimated their popular great artists. Hogarth, admirable portraitist, consummate narrator, delicate as a technician even for an age of technical *finesse*, was immensely admired and liked, but very much taken for granted. He was not exotic enough to seem a great artist. His extraordinary little genre pieces, the joyous Shrimp Girl, with scores of austere and characterful portraits, won him popularity but not fame. Perhaps it is really a nice modesty in the English, an avowal of their limitations, that it has always been hard for them to see that anybody so like themselves could really be a great artist. So Hogarth fretted and stormed in vain against Sir Joshua's vested interest in elegance, and his influence has possibly been greater on the Continent than in England. Meantime the prints of "Marriage à la Mode," and the "Idle and Industrious Prentice" were scattered through Europe, preparing the way for the realism of the new century.

I have evoked the isolated, premature figure of

Hogarth to show a certain lack of actuality in the "Discourses." Possibly Sir Joshua at times was saying less what he thought himself than what as a teacher he thought it was profitable for his pupils to hear. When, however, he advocated a historic style of painting as the highest, it was doubtless with a genuine and modest sense of the limitations of his own delightful genius. He was socially minded, like his friend Dr. Johnson, and wished to see art serve the State. His own art was frankly the luxury of a class, and his dissatisfaction with that state of things does him only credit. Later we must consider the tragic effect of the "Discourses" in particular cases. Now it is enough to say that upon normal spirits Sir Joshua's practice was more influential than his preaching. The florid tradition of Rubens continued to thrive until the early Victorian period. The portrait painting of England, in Romney, Beechy, Hoppner, and Lawrence; and of America, in Gilbert Stuart, Trumbull and Thomas Sully kept singularly true to the fresh, candid, and vital tradition of the diplomat painter of Antwerp. The fact that this normal and delightful style died out naturally in England, becoming inadequate as men cared more for character and less for decoration, is perhaps a sign that it would similarly have declined in France. But there its end was sharp and tragic, as was the end of many a fair and frail survivor of the *ancien régime*.

From the point of view of art criticism it would be an open question whether the French Revolution occurred to produce the painting of Jacques Louis David, or whether he occurred to express its Roman accent. There never was a closer harmony between man and hour. Four years before the Revolution, he had exhibited in the salon of 1785, the Oath of the Horatii. The Horatii with rhetorical swagger might already be vowing the death of an aristocrat. David was a testy, suspicious person, and a formidable patriot. When denied the Prix de Rome, he attempted suicide. Later, in a quarrel with the sculptor Houdon, he planned revenge in a legal homicide which was with difficulty thwarted. The old Royal Academy fell with the kingship, but the new Institut de France, in 1795, took over many of its functions including the École des Beaux-arts and the Roman school. David naturally became the leading mind in the reorganization.

He was a truculent Jacobin and a convinced terrorist. For the Republic he planned and organized the fêtes to the Nation and to the Supreme Being. When Marat fell under the dagger of Charlotte Corday, David painted the grimmest of modern pictures, the friend of the people stark dead in his tub, the heavy face dreadfully fixed, the half-divined pose, for only the head and the massive hand are visible, wholly majestic. This severe and truthful character David invariably had in portraiture. Whether in the delightful Mme. Recamier, in the subtle portrait of the Captive Pope, Pius VII, or in a score of sullen beauties who are mere names to us, David

Louvre

J. L. DAVID: RAPE OF THE SABINES

Louvre

J. L. DAVID: CORONATION OF NAPOLEON

reveals an extraordinary intensity and passion. In curious contrast to this work are such frigid and declamatory compositions as the Horatii, 1784, and the Rape of the Sabines, 1799, and the insipidity of such pictures as the Paris and Helen of his last years. It is significant of the man that he cared little about his own masterpieces of portraiture, and ruthlessly imposed upon a generation of students the frigidity and pretentiousness of his Roman mode.

David's classical mode is best studied in the great canvas The Rape of the Sabines. It exemplifies if not his best practice, at least all his theories. The taste of the moment responded to it with enthusiasm. From its exhibition in France and the United States the painter made a fortune. We see it to-day, much as Théophile Gautier saw it about 1860. With him we feel its general picturesqueness of effect, its tact in arrangement, its supreme elegance in details. But certain things which the famous Romantic critic accepted we no longer accept. It is a singularly life-less picture. No spear will ever fly, no pose ever change; the graceful forms are locked and frozen in theatrical relations and attitudes. After a long look one feels sympathy with them, shares their fatigue and longs for some merciful curtain to fall. A modern eye though it may accept the pleasantly united colors, again will find them unrelated, while the uniform smooth finish brings an element of monotony. The whole thing, though well thought out, is not felt at all, and the decorum with which the savage theme

is uttered comes perilously near to insipidity. Its
failure is that of its school. Grandeur is not to be
attained merely through taste, nor will even taste
thrive on the exclusive pursuit of grandeur.

Yet we must remember that these great compositions, so empty and tedious to us, were thrilling to a
generation that was making all things new with old
Plutarch as its guide. In swift succession France
relived all phases of Republican and Imperial Rome.
The Mirabeaus, Dantons, Marats, Robespierres felt
themselves reincarnations of the Ciceros, Cinnas,
Mariuses, Brutuses, and a young Corsican Lieutenant
of Artillery already had his dreams of reinacting
Cæsar on a wider stage. When the Republic dwindled
to the Triumvirate—how Roman the devolution—
and vanished before the guns of Thermidor, David
made no more difficulty than the other Jacobins in
following the star of Napoleon. We need not accuse
him of insincerity, he admired the savior of France,
and the overtures were all on Napoleon's side. He
divined great utilities in the turbulent painter. He
gave him his confidence. "Why paint defeated people?" he hinted before David's Leonidas and his Spar-
tans. "Paint me very calm on a very excited horse,"
was the order for Napoleon crossing the St. Gothard.
A statesman rarely so opens his heart to a mere artist.

For Napoleon, David was to do a series of splendid
pageants—Napoleon setting the crown on his own
head with the rapt court about and the Captive Pope
an interested spectator. Napoleon delivering the

eagles to the legions of France—these are the best. They are very modern, and yet in their ceremoniousness and restraint very classic. Not quite great pictures—having neither the richness nor delicacy with which a Veronese or Tiepolo would have endued these Imperial pomps—they are yet a lucid and manly art, in every way a notable sort of memorial. We must later face the paradox that David felt these great canvases were not historical painting. It was historical painting to pretend the Rape of the Sabines, but not to record honestly the Coronation of a Napoleon. For now it is enough to say that when Napoleon fell, in 1815, David fled to exile in Brussels where he painted excellent portraits and insipid mythologies, still dominated the École des Beaux-Arts, by proxy, at arm's length, feverishly resisted all the modern coloristic movements, and died in an unblessed disconsolate old age in 1825.

Except in his classical aberrations, he was an excellent painter, lacking in color, but energetic and characterful. What is unqualifiedly bad about him is not his art, but his artistic dictatorship. Inheriting the rigid pseudo-classicism of the Academy, he enforced it with all the authority of the Republic and the Empire. The old dualism by which the academicians and the amateurs had lived in tolerable disagreement for a century was no longer indulged. The frivolous graces of the École galante, the fresh and candid tradition that had come down through Rubens from Venice, this was officially stifled. One must imagine one of those shocking judicial drownings, *noyades* of Revolutionary days, the victims being all the nymphs and shepherdesses, and swains and serenaders from Watteau to Fragonard, all the coquettish and petulant nudities of Natoire, Lagrenée and Boucher. Under they go while a sullen little man gloats on the bank and gives thanks to the Supreme Being.

Thus in most Revolutionary fashion David cleaned the artistic slate. It is time to reckon the gain and loss. It was gain to establish the doctrine that art should be heroic in theme and monumental in style. Much of the best painting of the century was thus made possible. It was gain to break through the dilettantism of the *École galante* and to magnify the civic function of art.

It was loss to limit art to its public aspects, to disapprove its slighter and more exquisite triumphs; it was loss and positive error to hold up an ideal of monumental painting which wholly disregarded decorative quality. It was loss to annul those beautiful traditions of decoration and composition which, however enfeebled, had come down through Rubens from the Italian Renaissance. It was loss to set up an ideal of painting which utterly disregarded charm and richness of color. David's own timid and sleek and bleached-out technic has more or less devitalized academic painting ever since. It was loss to set up a purely linear tradition of draughtsmanship, by which the cold, unbroken, descriptive line was regarded as the only meritorious way of drawing. This was to ignore the actual shimmer and appearance of a Nature which explains herself not in hard contours but in balanced and vibrating areas of color and light and shade.   It was further loss to emphasize the more discursive and descriptive methods against those more spontaneous methods which convey action, balance, mass, and ultimately the passions of the soul.   It was loss to confine painting to a conventional, almost geometrical lighting, based on the toplight of the studio.   This was to neglect the subtle witchery of actual light and shade.   It was loss and gravest error to point men from the inexhaustible variety of natural appearances, to the cold monotony of second-rate antique sculpture.   It was worse error yet to regard the reintegration of the classic past as the highest function of the artistic imagination.   And finally it was most deplorable error to suppose that art can be compressed within the small logic of a single practice and of a single mind, that art can be calculated, that art can dispense with passion, mystery, and dreams.

If we have read David's teaching aright, the balance lies pretty heavily against him.   There is no need to resurrect the on the whole well forgotten names of his most faithful followers, Girodet, Gerard, Guérin— all men of a certain competence, but feeble and frigid souls.   His greatest follower, Ingres, had the good sense to go back to Raphael and to nature.   Inheriting the colorless and linear method of David, he enlivened it, made it more tense, subtle and exquisite.   He is the incomparable model of the academic painter, and his

Morgan Memorial, Hartford, Conn.

BENJAMIN WEST: RAISING OF LAZARUS

Louvre

BARON GROS: PEST HOSPITAL AT JAFFA

precepts and example kept the orthodox academic theory a potent influence through the century.

How the typical academic style of the century— with its solid merits and grave defects—grew out of David and Ingres is the theme of another chapter. Before leaving David and considering the lesser pseudo-classics outside of France, I wish to make concrete the real formidableness of David's tyranny. And to that end I will take the tragic case of his pupil and successor as Director of the École des Beaux-Arts, Baron Gros.

Gros was a born painter, a splendid colorist, a master of the expressions of the human form and face, a sensitive observer of the moods of nature, an intense and somewhat melancholy spirit, a just and human sympathy. Fortune gave him precisely the experiences and subjects that his genius required. He went over the Alps with Napoleon, was the first artistic eye that ever scanned and measured the thrilling spectacle of a generous folk in arms. On his great colorful canvases he set down the throbbing truth of those great days. Napoleon moving with Olympian detachment among the pest stricken soldiers at Jaffa, Napoleon leading the rally that took the Bridge at Arcola, Napoleon grim and resolute among his despairing leaders, amid the snows of Eylau. It is in those great canvases, which combine the clarity and immediate thrill of the panorama with the variety and *finesse* of the easel picture, that the Napoleonic epos to-day chiefly lives. Yet Baron

Gros drowned himself in the despairing conviction that he had failed to master the true historical style. What a tragic paradox! What a light it casts upon the great pseudo-classic deception!

When David fled to Brussels, Gros, famous, beloved, prosperous, reigned in his stead. A modest and loyal man, he apologized for his own departures from the orthodox style, and proclaimed himself David's personal representative in the École des Beaux-Arts. His chief worry was lest David might think the standards were being relaxed. Meanwhile David from Brussels kept urging Gros to do a real historical picture—Gros the creator of the Jaffa Pest Hospital, of the Arcola, and the Eylau! David subtly reminds Gros that he has as yet only undertaken "futile subjects." His great canvases are after all only "topical pictures" based on contemporary events of little importance. Since his inclination is military, let him consider Themistocles.

These repeated suggestions worried Gros. He undertook one or two classical subjects which he did rather badly. He came to regard his glorious career as a failure. The State urged him to paint a great picture on the Battle of the Nations, Jena. Gros refused, writing, "I feel the need of resting up with subjects more proper to the study of art." His depression passed into a melancholia. One day he walked up the Seine, carefully placed his cane and top hat on the bank, waded out into three feet of water, bent under and stayed under. Remember

J. L. DAVID: MLLE. C. DUVAL D'OGNES

SIR JOSHUA REYNOLDS: NELLY O'BRIEN

Baron Gros when men tell us that what art needs is
the authority of dictators and academies.

It remains only to show briefly how universal the
pseudo-classic mode was in Europe, and to discuss its
value. We are inclined to regard the greatest of the
pseudo-classics, David, as the only considerable figure.
He merely represents the most complete embodiment
of a general tendency. Everywhere the adoration of
the inferior classics—for such the museum marbles
are—wrought the same results. In England the
colonial American, Benjamin West, from the early
'60s illustrated the historical style as later advocated
by Sir Joshua Reynolds. And his great canvas of
1765, Agrippina landing at Brundusium with the Ashes
of Brittanicus, was the sensation of its day, and still
remains one of the more stately and impressive examples of orthodox academism. With an amazing
inventiveness and a noble perseverance which almost
atone for his weakness in significant mass and action
and his deficiency of color, West composed his great
versions of classical legend, Bible story, and contemporary history. Death on the White Horse, or the
death of the contemporary hero, General Wolf, it
was all in the day's work to the industrious President
of the Royal Academy. To-day we marvel that such
high endeavor could result in work so mediocre.
Another colonial American, John Singleton Copley, a
loyalist driven to London by the Revolution, ended
his days in great contemporary stories, The Capture
of Gibraltar, the Death of Chatham, and did them

quite extraordinarily well, with a material grasp which West never attained. A younger American, Washington Allston, poet and painter, again aimed at the historic style, with an eye not merely on the ancients but on the color of Titian and the sublimity of Michelangelo. How far he fell short of an almost impossible synthesis such pictures as Christ raising the Dead Man, and the Prophet Elisha sufficiently attest.

In England the ideal of a grand historic style tortured the sensitive mind of Benjamin Haydon, wrung from him a few ambitious canvases of a singular emptiness, and finally drove him to a suicide's grave. It is a dreadful fallacy to suppose that one can attain sublimity by intending it. It seems to be a rather unconscious by-product of favored times and gifted individuals. In particular it implies a background of training. Here was the defect of most of the successors of West and David—they had been trained in insipid habits of draughtsmanship, and they never learned to paint at all. Instead of intelligence of their art, they offered their ambition and highmindedness. Naturally the public could consider not their laudable intentions but their pretentious and anæmic work. The wonder is that such tragedies as poor Haydon's were not more common than they were.

The dogma of the historic style, often diminished to a harmless anecdotage of common life, has prevailed in England until very recent times. In the

'30s it produced in the frescoes of the New Parliament
Houses, by Armitage, Watts, and Dyce, a very competent if not inspiring success.   Transformed, in
mediæval or romantic guise, it has done something to
steady the course of British Pre-Raphaelitism.

How widely the pseudo-classic notion prevailed in
Europe at the opening of the nineteenth century may
be suggested by a quick geographical survey.   In
sculpture Canova, Thorwaldsen and Flaxman represent at its best an ideal of mannered grace more
tolerable in the simplicity of marble than in painting.
The Dane, Carstens; the Belgian, Navez, the Italians,
Appiani, Hayez and Benvenuti; the German illustrator
Retsch, and the frescoist Cornelius—all represent so
many hapless attempts to galvanize the grand style.
David's influence was preponderant even in the Italy
of Guardi and Longhi and in the Spain of Francisco
Goya.   Everywhere the doctrine of the grand historic style wrought the same havoc, everywhere it
cut off the Renaissance tradition, everywhere it
reduced the variety of art to a uniformity based on
bad classic models, everywhere it substituted a cold
and stilted workmanship for the old fervor.

Yet when all is said I think it unwise to follow the
critics of the Romantic school in regarding pseudo-
classicism merely as so much stupid error, and its
effect as valueless and wholly harmful.   Let us grant
its narrowness, let us concede that it deserved to be
overthrown.   All the same there was value in setting
against the casual picturesqueness of the eighteenth

century a more Spartan standard of art. There was value in restoring to art the public and civic function which it had too readily sacrificed. There has been, I believe, a limited value in the rather dull and un-inspired standard of academic painting which the École des Beaux-Arts and the other academies have transmitted to our times.

If it is France that has produced all the more fruitful movements in the art of the nineteenth century, whereas England, Germany, Italy, America, have originated few new artistic ideas, and present in their art chiefly varieties of copyism or disorder, this has been because France has had a central official style. Let us admit that academic patronage is a very sorry substitute for that normal coöperation and interchange between artist and public which char-acterized ancient Greece and Renaissance Italy. But in a society where this *entente* between public and artist has lapsed, academies with all their pedantries have their place. Just as a strong central government befits a democracy, so this kind of standardization befits an individualistic period of art. From this notion of central authority liberty itself learns the direction its expansion must take, and the just meas-ure of revolt. Considered in this light, the pseudo-classicism of which David is the sinister archangel, will seem not so much a stupid or ignoble doctrine, as a necessary, if reactionary, phase in the readjustment of the human spirit to the conditions of democracy.

And it should be remembered also that the art

which pseudo-classicism destroyed on the whole hardly deserved to live, while the new art that did deserve to live owed much to that effort which had made the state not merely the custodian of taste but also the teacher and the patron of the artist. I am firmly convinced that any future harmonizing of artist and public, any relief from the prevailing small anarchy and individualism, will draw something from the example of David and Napoleon. Pedants they were, but of heroic type, sparing themselves not at all, and sincerely if somewhat narrowly, desiring the best things for art. Surely it behooves us rather to admire their potent manhood and their positive achievement, than to scoff at their obvious limitations. We may disagree with them, but we can only express our disagreement by those terms which they have stamped indelibly upon the thinking of the modern world.

THE ROMANTIC MOVEMENT

THE ROMANTIC MOVEMENT

(1822–1863)

MODERN art takes its character from the doctrine that the artist is free. Romanticism at bottom means nothing other than this. Drive the doctrine to the extreme, and you make the artist more or less than a man. Nobody else is free; we are all trammeled not merely from within, through the bodies and minds we have inherited, but also from without, through the pressure of public opinion, the weight of custom, the compulsion of law. Now the first Romantic artists did not press the ideal of freedom to the extreme. Such men as Géricault and Delacroix, the true pioneers of modern painting, merely wished exemption from what we have seen was the quite unreasonable tyranny of official pseudo-classicism. Without programme or manifesto, they quietly took the risk of dissent. From the coldness and monotony of the pseudo-classical style they appealed to the warmth and variety of life; from the closed canon of the classical dictionary they appealed to the wide-roaming imagination.

Romanticism, then, as a conscious movement has its definite beginning, about the year 1830, in the France of Chateaubriand, Géricault, and Delacroix, but, as is usually the case, there were earlier flickering

premonitions. Alongside of the heroic art of David,
throve a vivacious popular art in illustration and
caricature. Making no pretensions, it created no
offense. Indeed much of the sentimental narrative
of Greuze and the domestic idyllism of Fragonard and
Boilly bespeaks an emotional freedom very far from
the prevailing academic decorum; and through the
frigidities of the Empire, Prud'hon pursued his quest
of the poetry of passion. Because he was so charming
he escaped rebuke. Since he habitually veiled his
mystical eroticism in mythological forms, he carried a
sufficient classic warrant. These are the timid song-
sters of the twilight before the dawn.

But the sinister precursor of Romanticism appears
appropriately not in classic France but in the desert of
decadent Spain, in the figure of Francisco Goya. For
fifty turbulent years he pursued an unabashed course
of raw emotionalism in both life and art. The
proudly languid men, the moodily sensuous women
of Spain, he painted them, not heroically, but as they
were. He caught the sharp tang of contemporary
events—the impotent rising of Madrid against the
bayonets of Murat—shrieking, trembling citizens
ignobly confronting the French firing squads. All
that you have in his grim picture in the Prado, May 3,
1808. It is the unrestrained note, the harbinger of
coming romanticism. In his great albums of aqua-
tints, the "Caprichos" and the "Miseries of War,"
he let loose a veritable hell of violence and nightmare.
Upon the walls of his house on the Manzanares he

GOYA: MAY 3, 1808

GÉRICAULT: THE RAFT OF THE MEDUSA

spread foul visions of witchcraft, rendered with incomparable power. Take his picture of the Three Fates in mid-air debate over the misshapen form of a human fetus. For his recreation he watched the bloody spectacle of the bull ring, and set down all its savage phases on the copper plate or lithographer's stone.

Not merely did Goya's practice affront the prevailing theories of decorum, but also in theory he attacked the academic cult of a colorless linear precision. "They talk to me about lines, always lines," he petulantly exclaimed, "but I don't see these lines in nature, only lighter or darker masses." His guides he affirmed, were nature, Velasquez, and Rembrandt. No word of Poussin or Raphael. In 1824, Goya, being very old and crotchety and deaf, made a flying visit to Paris. If, as is likely, he visited the Salon where Constable's Hay Wain and Delacroix's Massacre at Scio were first shown, he must have taken a sardonic pleasure in witnessing the to-do made over a "new" kind of painting which he himself had been practicing for a matter of thirty years, as one may see in his fantastic Landscape with Flying Men. Yet Goya was born before his time, and the true leadership of modern painting fell to a very robust and to a very sensitive young man, Théodore Géricault and Eugène Delacroix.

Géricault was a lover of the ordinary color, energy, and passion of life. A sportsman, in a degree an Anglo-phile, he loved the spectacle of the race horses plunging towards the finish, the balance of a beefy hussar controlling a rearing charger; the pounding of cannon and caisson wheels over rock and turf. The man was a wholesome materialist. Obviously such a man could do nothing with the slow unbroken line of David, which, by the way, he had mastered; he sensibly chose the more sketchy and colorful methods of Gros. Up to a certain point his military and race-course pictures seemed harmless enough. They really did not compete with the big machines of the Institute painters. Then he made what was to be the most portentous machine of the century, the Raft of the Medusa, and his name at once was anathema.

As one studies this great faded canvas, it is hard to recall the scandalized state of mind of the visitors to the Salon of 1819. We see to-day a thrilling, solemn apparition. A great raft piled with ragged, staring, drenched, miserable men, heaves mightily on the back of a huge roller. A sail has been sighted and the stronger men stretch in a tense mass to make their signal seen. The weaker crouch or lie stolidly behind. In the water at the near edge of the raft lies the splendid nude body of a dead or dying youth. The great lift of the thing, a nobility in its grimness, a deep hot color which is a very symbol of storm and stress— this is what still compels in this great picture.

The story of the suffering of the survivors of the frigate Medusa was recent and vivid, and the canvas may be regarded as a bit of inspired journalism. That was the unpardonable thing. Had it been an illustration, all would have been forgiven, but a salon picture, as big as the usual historical masterpiece, in as massive a gold frame; a genre picture masquerading as a masterpiece, and, admired, and talked about, and hint of its purchase by the State—the thing was intolerable. More sensitive and humorous critics averred that it made them seasick.

Géricault, a robust and unreflective person, hardly realized the revolutionary character of his own work, and resented a notoriety that brought little benefit and much abuse. Yet he had at a blow shattered the pseudo-classic molds, by asserting the artist's right to represent with the most passionate energy whatever has deeply moved him. Against the exclusiveness of the Institute, he showed that the whole world is open to the artist. He died untimely in 1824, only thirty-one years old. He did not end the academic régime in France, but it has never lived comfortably since the Raft of the Medusa hove into view. It was from then put on the defensive, projected into a formidable world whose very existence it had ignored.

The work which Géricault merely began was extended and defined by a far subtler and more self-conscious person, his friend and devout admirer, Eugène Delacroix. In a very real sense Delacroix is modern painting, personally the fullest and finest expression of the artist's new freedom; in his art, so universal that little has since been developed except within the scope of his activity. This universality

Louvre

DELACROIX: MASSACRE AT SCIO

is his main trait.   In such paintings as the Ceiling of
Apollo and the Python in the Louvre, and Trajan
halted by the Widow who claims Justice, at Rouen,
or Medea meditating the slaying of her Children,
he showed himself more at home in classical antiquity
than the painters of the Institute.   His antiquity had
warmth, and life and persuasiveness.   Up and down
the Middle Ages his imagination ranged free.   His
first success was Dante and Virgil ferried across the
Styx, in the Salon of 1822.   History or Fiction alike
served him.   The Templar carrying off Rowena,
from Scott's "Ivanhoe," is no less vivid than the
cavalcade of the Crusaders through Constantinople.
Current events stirred him as they had Géricault.
The whole tragedy of the hard-won redemption of
Greece lives in the great canvas, The Massacre of
Scio.   That passion for liberty which built the barricades of 1830 and finally threw the heavy hand of
monarchial Europe off from Republican France,
where can it be so readily grasped as in the Liberty
leading the People of the Louvre?   Let us dwell a
moment on these heroic pictures.

The Massacre at Scio was shown in the Salon
of 1824, and a conservative critic pronounced it the
Massacre of Art.   To-day it is hard to understand
such a verdict.   Borrowing much from Gros' The
Pest Hospital at Jaffa, Delacroix has expressed every
emotion of despair, resignation, and weakness, keeping such expressions always noble, and enduing the
cruelty of the ravagers with a kind of impersonal

force and splendor. The swinging movement of the whole group, the sense of battle-reek passing over a lovely country side—all this magnificently seen. How far it all is from the elegant immobility of the academic style! The whole conception draws much from the athleticism of Rubens, though tinged with a pathos most personal to Delacroix himself. The vaporous landscape owed much to the Englishman, Constable, who exhibited in the same Salon of 1824. Delacroix, eagerly grasping the superior luminosity of Constable's broken color, repainted the entire background. It is a work of great learning; and better yet of great passion and sincerity. The ease and spontaneity of the workmanship and the free and painterlike quality of the color may best be appreciated by recalling a really very similar subject, done in the pseudo-classical style, David's Rape of the Sabines, painted in 1799, just twenty-five years earlier. The contrast between the two styles speaks for itself.

In the Scio, Delacroix had the advantage of a subject which, while of thrilling interest, for all Europe watched with horror these birth-pangs of a new Hellas, was also exotic and remote. That Delacroix had equal vision and energy in a near-by theme is shown in the magnificent Liberty leading the People, July 28, 1830. It was the moment when Republican France suddenly and forever shook off the Bourbon dynasty which Europe had foolishly re-throned. The barricades rose in every avenue. The veterans of Napoleon's campaigns and their sons

Louvre

DELACROIX: LIBERTY LEADING THE PEOPLE

Louvre

DELACROIX: ALGERIAN WOMEN

sprang to arms. Delacroix imagines one of the many barricades. For a moment Liberty has come down to grasp the tricolor, and lead the heroic mob over their own dead to victory. How amazingly he carries off the mixture of reality and symbolism! How akin to these exalted bourgeois is the stalwart genius who grasps the musket of a fallen soldier, how worthy of her that striding boy with his two pistols, and that grim and cautious citizen who has grasped the flintlock without relinquishing his top hat! All of the indomitable democracy of France is in that picture, the determination that in blackest days has never yet failed to clear the road towards liberty.

Delacroix was a patriot and much more. With a fervid cosmopolitanism he made images for the masterpieces of foreign literature. Hamlet, Faust, Mephistopheles, it was he who best gave them visible form in his lithographs. The sinister heroes and heroines of Byron take form at his touch. His ready admiration goes out to foreign artists. He copied scores of the drastic designs of the Spaniard, Goya. He was the friend and admirer of the brilliant Englishman, Bonington; the eulogist of the candid portraiture of Sir Thomas Lawrence; the public champion of the neglected art of John Constable. He first of modern artists fathomed the immemorial fascination of the East. From Morocco he brought back a series of gorgeous sketches, the memories that later refined themselves in half a dozen great pictures, and the conviction that he had lived to see the men of the

Homeric age. Hellas became palpable to him through Morocco. Man and history by no means exhausted his sympathy and curiosity. A favorite recreation was to visit the Jardin des Plantes and surprise the beasts of prey in their characteristic moods and attitudes. Except his friend, the sculptor Barye, no one has so vividly expressed the ferocity of the mood carnivorous. His fecundity was as amazing as his scope. From the tiny water color to the monumental fresco, he was always the master, always vehement, always discreet.

A somewhat superior and disillusioned person, in his late years a recluse, the creative passion in him never for a moment flagged. And it was reinforced by a magnificent intelligence. A fastidious aristocrat by birth and habit, he was a fine critic both of art and music. His essays collected from the *Revue des Deux-Mondes*, in which he interprets those artists Gros and Prud'hon, who through the pseudo-classical decline kept alive some ideal of vitality and loveliness, that paper in which he treats of the notion of the beautiful—these are classics of criticism and models of French prose. His diaries and letters are a mine of intellectual treasures.

To painting, in the narrower technical sense, his contribution was considerable. His line was fluent, a thing less of contours than of accents. It surged and broke and resumed its course in the very cadence of the great emotions of his pictures. His color was brilliant, fairly prismatic. The critic Charles Baudelaire remarks Delacroix's predeliction for sinister reds. From Rubens he learned to combine impetus with equilibrium in audacities of balanced thrusts; Veronese and Titian helped to clarify his coloring. Nor did he hesitate to learn from the calculated symmetries of the alien Raphael. Always an experimenter in color, he initiated, partly under Constable's inspiration, the modern method of painting in broken color. He found that the eye at the proper distance blended the strokes of frank color, and that the color thus obtained was far more brilliant and vibratory than any that could be mixed on the palette. He observed the complementary colors, the blue shadow in yellow light, before Chevreul had demonstrated it scientifically. The whole movement which we call Luminism or Impressionism owes much to him. In his forty years of unrelenting and ever intelligent activity he gave most of the valuable precedents of the art of our day.

In his expansive sympathy, his mediævalism, his exoticism, he is akin to the literary Romantics—to his adored Byron, to Victor Hugo whom he adored not at all, to the German apostles of temperament and whim. Where he is the superior of nearly all of his literary contemporaries is in his taste and balance. It was in every way fortunate that the perilous doctrine of the freedom of the artist was first most fully embodied in a genius who combined with the scruples of a fine gentleman, the conscience of a scholar, and the regulating experience of a citizen of the world.

It was the distinction of Eugène Delacroix to bring over into a century of increasingly bitter nationalism something of the lucid cosmopolitanism of the eighteenth century. There never was a more fastidious taste or one more free from unworthy prejudice. The inner checks were adequate in such a person. In many another liberated artist they were inadequate.

In his famous essay "Considerations on the Beautiful" Delacroix writes, "We must find beauty where the artist puts it." Obvious to us, this was not obvious at all to a generation trained to find beauty only where academies put it. And all the art of modern times has been built on this axiom that the artist is the sole judge of beauty. All the strength and all the weakness of our art is comprised in this programme of individualism. Elsewhere in the essay Delacroix writes, "A ragged Jew by Rembrandt is as beautiful as a sibyl by Michelangelo." The beauty in either case is not in the subject-matter, but in the depth of the feeling and the competence of the work. Such a maxim was a death warrant to an already declining pseudo-classicism. Beauty is not pigeonholed in schools. For the artist, it is where he surprises it in life and nature and in his own soul; for the person of taste, beauty is where the artist puts it. The whole law and gospel of Romanticism are in these words, and it is time we looked more narrowly into what this freedom of the artist implies.

First of all, the highest value is no longer reflection, restraint or nobility but spontaneity. What counts is solely the artist's feeling. "Feeling is everything," *Gefühl ist alles*, Goethe had proclaimed, significantly through the mouth of Mephistopheles. It was the very battle cry of the Romantic artist. And it is highly important to note that this new feeling was rarely such as could be shared by many people; it tended to be recondite and uncompromisingly personal. The glory of the pseudo-classical artists was their representative character; their pride was in being widely understood. The glory of the Romantic artist, on the contrary, was usually just his unrepresentative character; his pride was often in being misunderstood. His vision was too exquisite, too personal, to be communicated generally. His public was a few elect and kindred souls. The coterie becomes the support of an art becoming ever less civic and popular. The tragedy of the misunderstood artist, unexampled in all great ages of art, becomes common. This enforces upon many of the finest artists a sort of amateurism or an approach to mendicancy. Delacroix, Corot, Diaz, Puvis and Manet, living on their inheritances or allowances are types of the amateur. Monticelli leaving his pictures to pay the tavern keepers, Whistler jaunty in the Sheriff's hands, Millet tided over starvation by the bounty of artist friends—these are various aspects of the tragic comedy of the artist in an indifferent or hostile world.

Neglect often breeds pride and resentment. The artists become to themselves a separate, superior class amid their inferiors, the philistines or bourgeois. The artist is driven in on himself, lives in an ivory tower of his own fashioning, breathes the thin, high air of his own fancy, and loses robustness, sympathy, and understanding of his fellow men. The typical artist of the century is a rebel or a pure dreamer, through no fault of his own, in most cases, but from the decline of the old art loving aristocracies, the sudden rise of an unrestrained middle class with an inborn preference for bad art, the lack of intelligent civic support. The new commercialism surged ahead without regard for the artist, who had to make the best of a sadly changed world. That great art was nevertheless produced shows merely how imperishable is the instinct to create beauty. But art in a time when society gives no satisfactory place to the artist, represents merely the successful evasion by which the artist makes some tolerable place for himself in the sun. The story of Romantic art then is the story of so many personal escapes from the chill oppression of an unfeeling world. Let us see how this simple formula of escape includes every important movement and artist.

The artist may escape into remote happier pasts, into exotic lands; or more humbly into near-by nature; he may escape in vehement self-assertion, and in the excitement of freely indulged passion; he may escape into himself and become pure dreamer; he may escape by becoming pure spectator and dilettante, cool observer of a life which he declines to share.

Escape into remote happier times or into exotic lands is a form of primitivism. That the present world is bad is the assumption, earlier times were better; innocent, barbarous people are our moral superiors, simple people are better than complicated people—you will readily recognize the formulas that have prevailed ever since the great romantic philosopher Rousseau. Since we must avoid the finished and sophisticated, classical antiquity can be of little use to us; the artless fervor of the Middle Ages may make us once more young and blest. Such was the teaching that pervaded, I may say infected, the second quarter of the nineteenth century. The German Romantics, and Victor Hugo, are its champions. John Ruskin made of primitivism and neo-mediævalism the basis of a comprehensive æsthetics, morals, and even political economy. The new Socialism in its warfare against capitalism—that is to say against the more highly trained and competent minority—is in some degree primitivistic. Completely so, is the group of modern eccentric artists who find their keenest joy and inspiration in the negro sculpture of the African west coast.

Mediævalism has been one of the most important forms of modern primitivism. It was supported not merely by the Romantic Revival in European literature, but by all the neo-catholic movements, including that of the Anglican High Church.

Delacroix's universal genius touched the mediæval themes with great success. In the Crusaders in

Constantinople, he seized much of the color and splendor of bygone chivalry. But Delacroix expended upon his mediæval themes all the resources of the most modern art, as did Victor Hugo in his mediæval poems and novels. The true mediævalists pursued a more logical and less artistic course. They wished to feel and be like the pious and exquisite artists that preceded the pagan Renaissance. If you had been in Rome in the 1820's you would have found an unkempt and enthusiastic band of German students living together in the old monastery of S. Isidoro. They were all intense Christians, pious Catholics, enemies both of the pagan frigidity of the pseudo-classic school, and even more of the frivolity and sensuality of the moribund Renaissance tradition. They proposed nothing less than to glorify God and His Son and the Blessed Virgin, with the simplicity of the early Italian artists. The ideality of a Fra Angelico, the serenity of a Perugino were their models. It was a sincere but quite impossible enterprise. No one can safely imitate an archaic art, for no one can recover the state of mind that produced it. These Nazarenes, as they were jestingly called, were after all merely academically trained youngsters playing earnestly at being primitive. Very few of them in any sense survive. Overbeck, their leader, enjoys at best a pale and dubious immortality from the fact that his wall paintings are in one or two famous tourists' resorts in Italy, as in St. Mary of the Angels at Assisi. All the work of the Nazarenes is similarly timid and bloodless and imitative. It has the graver defects of its pietism.

A more famous and successful group of Romantic mediævalists is the English Pre-Raphaelites. You will recall that the facile tradition of Rubens persisted in England alongside of the pseudo-classicism of Benjamin West and Haydon. There were in the early years of the young Queen Victoria certain artists who felt vividly the defects of both manners. William Dyce sought to recover the monumental simplicity of Raphael and his predecessors. In this he relatively succeeded where the German Nazarenes had failed. Ford Madox Brown strove for a more precise and intense expression and a fuller color than either of the British schools had attained. At bottom his desire was to vitalize the old notion of historical painting. In such works as King Lear and his Daughters, Christ Washing the Disciples' Feet, and the Historical Paintings in the Manchester City Hall he very fairly succeeded. His influence was potent upon a very serious and opinionated young man, William Holman Hunt, and a prodigiously clever boy, John Everett Millais, who in 1838 were sharing a studio in London. They felt the staleness of both English traditions, they wanted a more honest art. On the one hand the stolid precision and sincerity of Ford Madox Brown attracted them, on the other hand the freshness and variety of the Italian artists before the pagan Renaissance,—Gozzoli, Botticelli, Ghirlandaio.

Soon the Cleveland St. studio became a rallying ground where the whole theory of a new painting was wrangled out. To the councils came an impressive apparition, Dante Gabriel Rossetti, son of an Italian political refugee. Rossetti carried with him the air of romance, mystery, genius. He wrote beautiful poetry as naturally as he breathed, his casual designs were full of power and charm. The banded friends formed their little fraternity, the Pre-Raphaelite Brotherhood, and very soon the pictures signed P. R. B. were the occasion of mirth or vituperation according to the temper of the critic. When we recall such pictures as Millais' Isabella's Feast which was exhibited in 1849 it is hard to see why such fresh and charming and eminently thoughtful work should have provoked a good man like Charles Dickens to unmannerly abuse. The programme of these young men was nature and sincerity—surely a good one. They would present nothing that they had not studied, tell nothing that they did not know. Every person in their pictures was to be done from a particular model, every accessory was to be painted from the actual object. All the persons in the picture of Isabella's Feast are thus actual portraits of the Pre-Raphaelite group. Everything was to be honestly explained in all its details, nothing shirked, improvised, or merely suggested. Their ideal was frankly microscopic, and they achieved most of the merits that are within the compass of the microscopic eye.

It seems as if they must have read the old Italian

OVERBECK: ANNUNCIATION

Liverpool

J. E. MILLAIS: ISABELLA'S FEAST

painter Cennino Cennini, who gives the most precise instructions as to "The Way of Drawing a Mountain." "If thou wishest to get a good style of mountain, and one that should seem natural, take big stones which should be rough and not smooth; and draw them from nature, giving their lights and shadow, as reason shall permit thee." Plainly the scale and grandeur of those mountains which are bathed in air and flecked by passing cloud shadows would escape the artist who worked after this manner.

What counted, and still counts, in the Pre-Raphaelites was their delicacy and humility, and the feminine taste with which they filled their pictures with ideal expressions and pleasant incidentals. Much of their work has a gentle spirituality. It is both sensitive and penetrating in such rare masterpieces as Rossetti's Annunciation, but too often the Pre-Raphaelite work is devoid of the character of great and lasting art. The juvenilia of those men are their best work: Millais' Isabella, and Christ in the Home of His Parents, Rossetti's Annunciation and Vision of Dante. Holman Hunt was never anything but a bad painter. The overstrain in all his pictures must be positively painful to a sensitive person. With dogged fidelity he stuck to his big ideas and microscopic workmanship until his death in the early years of this century. The clever Millais gradually settled down into a fashionable portrait painter in the conventional British tradition. Rossetti, the most considerable figure and only genius of the group, drifted away from them into a fanciful type of mediævalism, comparable in its fashion to that of Tennyson's "Idylls of the King." Burne-Jones, with greater professional ability, made notable decorative application of Rossetti's wistful primitivism. With the Tractarian movement, high church, and the Gothic revival of the mid-Victorian age, Pre-Raphaelitism is assuming the pathos of distance in a rather obscure historicity. It remains the classical example of futile escape into the past.

Exoticism, the craving for remote picturesque scenes, escape into barbarism, is so clearly a Romantic tendency, that it need not detain us. The artist may be guided by curiosity of a naturalistic sort, or by love of barbarism and hatred of civilization. The love of color and mystery of the East has been strong in many artists of the century. Delacroix found in Morocco stimulus for his passionate creativeness. John La Farge fortified himself by idyllic voyages amid the South Seas for the amazing decorative achievements of his old age. It would be idle to enumerate the regular or occasional orientalists— even the term has become standard; Marilhat, Decamps, Fortuny, Fromentin, Schreyer, Gérôme, Besnard, and our own Edward Lord Weeks are among the more distinguished. In leaving exotism I need not insist that it is one of the most normal romantic activities, corresponding to that curiosity and love of adventure which humanity is never likely to deny itself.

The shortest road of escape from a too hard world
is into oneself—to lead the life of imagination and of
dream. Escape into the tower of ivory, Sainte-Beuve
has poetically named this sort of evasion. At all
times artists have been prone to find sufficient kingdom in their own minds. Botticelli, Giorgione, El
Greco, Watteau will occur to you as so many adepts
at reverie. The Spanish dramatist Calderon builds
one of his most poetical plays about the theme of
"Life as a Dream." But in older art and literature
the dream mood was exceptional. It has remained
for our own time to make it standard, so that the
basis of pictures might be hallucination; of poetry,
the wandering mind. The endeavor has led to much
affectation; it has also produced pictures and poetry
of a strange and haunting loveliness. That has been
so much the characteristic of our art, that the fine
English critic Theodore Watts-Dunton sums up our
specific achievement in letters as a Renaissance of
Wonder. The phrase surely applies as distinctly to
the painting of William Blake, of Adolphe Monticelli,
and Thys Maris, as it does to the poetry of Coleridge,
Rossetti, James Thomson, and W. B. Yeats. Naturally
the mood of dreams is highly individual. Classification
among visionaries is on the face of it absurd, and I shall
not attempt it. It will be enough to summon from their
Ivory Towers just a few of the great dreamers, leaving
you from your own favorites to complete the roll.

William Blake is the most various and imposing.
There is nothing of the softness of reverie about him.

D. G. ROSSETTI: MARY MAGDALENE *Drawing*

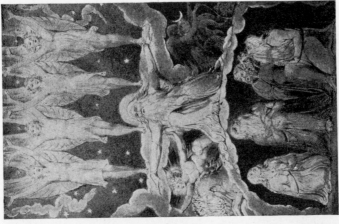

From the original watercolor in the J. P. Morgan Library

WILLIAM BLAKE: THE MORNING STARS

The hallucinations which daily presented themselves
to his inner eye, were crystal clear. He spoke in
familiar converse with the Apostles and with the
long dead English Kings and Queens. He had visions
of the future. In strange prose poems, interwoven
with his own powerful sketches, "The Book of Thel,"
"America," "The Marriage of Heaven and Hell," he
expressed an anarchical morality. He actively hated
the painters of the Renaissance, for their conven-
tionality—in short for their civilization. During a
long and laborious life he toiled steadily and sensibly,
though ever on the verge of madness, and his visions
have not merely a strange power and beauty, but also
complete lucidity. There is in this art the clarity and
hardness of the genuine mystic—a quality very unlike
that of the soft and self-indulgent dreamer.

Let us consider one of the etchings which he made
in 1823–25 to illustrate the Book of Job. The text is
"The Morning Stars Sang Together." Remember
that it is a little plate only a few inches square, yet
it has the monumentality of some great fresco. Mark
too the complete precision and clarity of the method.
When Blake is most mystical he is least vague. He
commands his dream. It is this capacity to maintain
a kind of calm and a remarkable executive probity on
the brink of frenzy and in the face of actual hallucination that makes William Blake spiritually and æs-
thetically the superior of most artists of the dreamer
type. There is no weakness, no casual reverie in his
exalted art.

HOLMAN HUNT: STRAYED SHEEP

MONTICELLI: MUSICALE

William Blake must stand to us for the mystical type of Romantic. There have been many others, some of remarkable quality like the Belgian, Ferdinand Knopf and the recently departed Parisian, Odilon Rédon and the Norwegian adept of tragic hallucination, Eduard Munch. Indeed the true and the false mystic have greatly abounded in a century that has deliberately cherished the fallacies of the cave. I can only say that none of the other mystics seem to me in any way comparable in power or in attractiveness to Blake, and that most of the would-be mystics in art have, in my opinion, been at the best sentimentalists and at the worst charlatans.

But generally speaking the Romantic mood of reverie, so persistent through the century has been honest enough. The critic must concede its sincerity, and its value as the inspiration of certain exquisite phases of art. One of the most delightful day-dreamers was Adolphe Monticelli, a joyous, vagabond painter, who tramped up and down his beloved Rhone valley, drinking deeply of its generous wines, living himself back into Watteau's world, dreaming of a beautiful no-man's land inhabited by satin-clad charmers and their suitors, and leaving the little pictures wherein such visions took form in payment of his tavern bills. I recall especially one of his pictures, a garden of love, haunted by lightly clothed, languorous beings, whose white forms shimmer amid vaguely defined foliage and through palpable air, as the bulging coral masses bloom uncertainly amid moving

sea weeds when your boat moves over tropic shal-
lows. The very essence of this art is indecision. It
comes out of that twilight of the soul between sleep
and waking, in which image succeeds image, none
fixing itself clearly in consciousness. A delicious kind
of blurring is the result. It has been the chief defect of
Romantic criticism to confuse this sort of reverie
with the genuinely athletic processes of artistic
creation. We are readily taken by the sheer charm
and spontaneity of the mood. America has produced
something quite analogous in quality in the coruscating idylls of the late Maurice Prendegast.

Now it seems to me that there is no reason why
we should not accept and enjoy this art for what it
has to give. It would be a poor life that had not its
moments of sweetly roving fancy, that could not
build up its gardens of love, that had no capacity for
beautiful makebelieve. Yet we do well to remember
that the greatest art has ever laid hold of the larger
issues of life, that it has scorned to be merely charming, that it has never really been vague. There is
something so ingratiating about the gipsy painter
dreaming of goddesses and fair women in his pot-
houses, that we have to shake ourselves a bit, to see
that such art ought to be exceptional. Technically,
Monticelli grows out of Watteau and Delacroix, but
as you see he is a Delacroix, so to speak, with his
brains knocked out, and nothing left but an exquisite
lot of nerve terminals vibrating with the eternal
intoxication of woman's grace.

D. G. ROSSETTI: BEATA BEATRIX

Both in his life and in his art he is so much the type of the romantic dreamer, that we might safely let him represent the class. Yet there are those who have dreamed to deeper and better purpose. Rossetti, whom we have already considered among the Pre-Raphaelites, has made particularly his own a heavy and moody type of beauty. Under many names the same drooping head, deeply shadowed by the dark hair that canopies the intense eyes, reappears in his pictures. She is of a tragic sensuousness. We know that the model was his wife, Elizabeth Siddall, and that the memory of her was saddened and intensified both by her early tragic death, and by the depression that came from narcotics. These heads are saturated with a kind of sterile desire, infinitely pathetic, just a little monotonous. They are products of stagnation and obsession. We may grasp Rossetti more truly in certain little drawings which express his really great and largely unfulfilled powers, for example, the drawing of the repentant Magdalen approaching the House where Christ is Feasting. It is a real masterpiece of what used to be called, perhaps too mockingly, "intense" art. The superb movement of the repentant woman, the splendor of her beauty, the frank sensual attractiveness of the companions she is quitting—all this is very masterly, as is the psychological condensation of the theme within its minute bounds. The somewhat archaic and unmodern aspect of it all, a kind of Renaissance suggestion, is also very characteristic of Rossetti.

In every direction he tried the paths of escape, and under his feet there sprung up ever exotic flowers of heavy and not quite wholesome fragrance.

Rossetti's best pupil, Edward Burne-Jones, shared the same nostalgia. In his hands the great legends of Greece and of the Middle Ages assume a pensive and wistful form. Characteristic is the charming picture of the Wedding Train of Psyche, in the Minneapolis Museum. These slender, languid girls, with deep wondering eyes, and trembling full lips, all nerves and ardors and sensibilities—are merely the more innocent younger sisters of the fateful beauties of Rossetti. With a great sensitiveness, a delightful linear sense, and at times a remarkable color, Burne-Jones succeeded amazingly in his task of creating a dreamland. Nor do I think that the echoes from the work of Mantegna and Botticelli are inharmonious. These merely emphasize the entirely alien and unmodern quality of the invention. Burne-Jones lived happily in that timeless country which is fairy land. It is a realm to which one might gladly escape from much that is rasping in our own civilization. Yet among the gifts the fairies have brought mankind, and they are many, great art is not one. This we should not forget in our gratitude for the small but lovely music that refreshes us when the horns of elfland blow faintly.

A certain element of cool intelligence made Burne-Jones not merely the most exquisite but also the most prolific master of his stamp. In tapestry, stained

BURNE-JONES: CIRCE

ALBERT RYDER: DEATH ON THE RACE TRACK

glass, mosaic, wood-cut illustration he was as felic-
itous as in painting. The very opposite of all this is
the most notable dreamer we have produced in
America, the late Albert Ryder. His work comes
only to a handful of jewellike little pictures, often
painted with bad pigments and already perishing,
yet the vision is keen and authentic. He goes back
joyously to legend, in the Rhine Maidens, the Ship
of the Flying Dutchman, or Constance drifting in a
Frail Boat in a great sea; or more often he simply
sees reality in dream fashion, or again he invents his
poesies. Such is the case with the strange little
allegory of death which is his most famous picture.
What the symbolism is you may readily divine.
Death in a dead world, perhaps. The track is dark,
the racers are gone, the last contestant still urges his
lean horse along the rail. Death can bring rest but
cannot rest. Literary considerations some of you
will scornfully object. Yet I cannot see why if it is
good to impress a poetical idea gradually through the
ear it should be evil to impress it swiftly through the
eye. And I think you will not deny the appeal this
little composition makes to the eye. You will not
readily forget it.

I can no more than mention certain other notable
dreamers, Thys Maris, our own Elihu Vedder, in his admirable designs for the quatrains of Omar Khayyám,
Arthur B. Davies still young enough to accept the
handicap of the new eccentric formulas—these are
some of the more notable. In France the recluse

Gustave Moreau carried the visionary mood to a kind of fanaticism. Especially his imagination worked about the blood-stained and lust-invested theme of Salome. One sees him in a more wistful and moderate vein in the picture of a Nymph, who fondles the severed head of the singer Orpheus. Quite evident is the affinity of the mood with that of Rossetti and Burne-Jones: it has a narcotic suggestion.

The dreamers, generally speaking, form the tender class of Romanticists. There is also a tough class which finds its outlet and escape in energy. Carry spontaneity to the verge of fury, forget your limitations in vehement self-assertion—such is their programme. There was much of this conscious athleticism in the founders of Romanticism, Géricault and Delacroix, but in them it was restrained by traditional considerations. The cult of vehemence seems to me first fully expressed in the work of the great painter-caricaturist, Honoré Daumier, everything considered the most powerful figure of the middle of the 19th century. Until he was silenced, he was a savage caricaturist of the tricky lawyers, and politicians of the Orleanist régime. For much of this work he employed the new medium of lithography. The coarse lines came and went, sharply indicating boss or hollow, cruelly telling of complacence, hypocrisy, or greed. The stroke seemed smashed or ground into the paper, yet with most telling accuracy. There is a marked economy of method; a single crumpled line tells the whole story of the poise and weight of a

DAUMIER: THE RIOT

DAUMIER: DON QUIXOTE

torso. In his later years he painted a few pictures, in what was a rich monochrome, carrying into the new work the style of the old illustrations. The Metropolitan Museum owns a capital example of the method in a splendid little picture, Don Quixote Halted at the View of a Dead Horse. It is an intense sort of sketching, which however suggests no incompleteness. The centrality and concentration of the vision are extraordinary. The very billowing lines with which the landscape is set in place are so many symbols for force. Even the pathos of the woeful knight errant is exposed in terms of power. In quieter subjects like The Reading, there is a sort of commutation of overt energy into psychological concentration. I do not need to insist on the intentness, and vivid sense of human relationship which make this little work a masterpiece. Technically it is wholly remarkable for the way in which the brusque and summary workmanship, so many blots and stabs, is bent not merely to the finest structural accuracy but also to issues of sympathy and tenderness. Since the drawings of Michelangelo and Rembrandt this accent had been missing to art. The epic side of Daumier's genius is admirably expressed in The Mob, one of the many great modern paintings in the Phillips' Memorial at Washington. Smaller men grasped eagerly at the style, Millet intelligently assimilated it, and in a kind of perversion it has become the basis of recent Post-Impressionism. The judgment of Daumier was as remarkable as his energy. Such has rarely been the case with the many who have sought escape in vehemence.

A more conventional type of vehemence is seen in the gory executions of the short-lived Henri Regnault, and in scores of minor romantics, down to such capable American practitioners as Estelle Rice and Eugene Higgins. Obviously the easiest way to be superior is to be boisterous and emphatic. Value, in the Romantic code, is wholly in feeling. Hence feel tremendously, and make your feeling sensational enough to compel notice. "I fling my barbaric yawp over the roofs of the world" wrote Walt Whitman, and this has been the golden rule of many a modern writer from Maxim Gorky in Russia to the late Jack London in America. This art of punch, to borrow an expressive colloquialism, is best represented by certain new Spanish painters, of whom Ignacio Zuloaga is the most accomplished. The truculence of Ribera and Goya is their precedent. A drastic emphasis is the note of Zuloaga's art, an excellent example of which is the group, Pilgrims.

In art this truculent manner has taken deepest hold in Germany. The forerunner of the movement was a German Swiss, Arnold Böcklin, an irascible, vivacious genius, equally ready for a drinking bout among the Italian peasants, who were his preferred neighbors, or for audacious and always unsuccessful experiments in aviation. His imagination peopled the garden of his Italian villa with a strange fauna—centaurs, satyrs, fauns, white nymphs rose before his

BÖCKLIN: THE ELYSIAN FIELDS

FRANZ STUCK: FIGHT BETWEEN A CENTAUR AND AN
AMAZON

vision. We have such an arcadia in the picture
Elysian Fields from the German National Museum,
Berlin. It is not a good picture, but it is very good
Böcklin. A kind of rawness and overinsistence
about everything, which would be greatly increased
if you saw the original colors, is the defect. It is as
coarsely felt as it is strong. More successful are
Böcklin's pictures of the gambols of strange sea
monsters of which the best known is the Sea Idyl at
Munich. It has power and gusto and a kind of
veracity. Yet how little any real lover of the sea
will admit the citizenship of these burly tritons and
nereids. Biologically these creatures simply do not
belong, they have shaken off their tourist clothes and
forsaken some tawdry Gambrinus-halle on the cliff.
One cannot deny them a portentous kind of vitality,
but I doubt if any sensitive person will or can enjoy it
for long. Böcklin's great but uneven talent is perhaps
at its best in such solemn and stately panoramas of
cliff and sea as the Island of the Dead.

Among the major prophets of the turbulent mood
are two recent painters, Franz Stuck and Louis
Corinth. Stuck is a specialist in the nightmarish and
semi-obscene, has made a fortune and fame out of
these wares. He is a kind of inverted Watts, a diab-
olist in symbolism. Lust and cruelty and madness
are the themes that fascinate him, and his colors are
the iridescence of putrefaction. With these subjects
and methods he produces striking results. I still
feel bruised and soiled from a rash venture into the

Stuck gallery at Venice, some years ago. Take one of his more decent inventions, the Furies Pursuing a Homicide. It is powerful and horrible enough, yet it seems to me to be terribly overstated, with an accent which is the ignoble emphasis of madness, not that of controlled power. And I feel this all the more because I am sure that the madness is merely assumed and calculated, the device of a cold and shrewd talent to get its hearing from an apathetic and jaded public. Compare it with the formally similar compositions, Blake's Two Spirits, or better with Prud'hon's famous picture of a Murderer chased by Furies.

Sensational coarseness is certainly the trouble with Louis Corinth, when in his picture of Ulysses Wrestling with the Beggar before the Suitors, he makes his æsthetic appeal to the best educated public in the world. Corinth's formula is a simpler one than Stuck's. Strip the nonsense from legend. Reveal the human beast as he is. Make of Ulysses just a bestial old tramp, of the suitors merely wine-soaked degenerates. Reduce everything to its lowest and most energetic terms. Corinth is famous, and justly, for his formula exactly expresses that so-called scientific conception of life which has abolished scruple and tenderness in favor of a ruthless dynamic efficiency. It would be very interesting to show how certain monstrous ideals which prevailed in German art before the war, prepared the way for still more monstrous deeds, but my theme is simply Romanticism, and if I have put sharply the distinction and the

LOUIS CORINTH: LAMENTATION

kinship between the Romanticism of reverie and
that of vehemence my task is fairly done. Both are
avenues of escape, albeit opposite outlets, from that
realm of delicate adjustment and compromise which
is both normal human life and art.

One may also escape from the world of mind and
standards into the flux of mere facts. The cult of
hard fact, is nearly allied to the cult of energy. It is,
I think, Ferdinand Brunetière who first showed that
a crass realism is merely the proletarian form of
Romanticism, implying rejection of all tradition, an
unmediated acceptance of all natural appearances.
What is, is good, and sole matter for art. We trust
our senses; we know nothing else.

"In a tavern where one is well at ease," wrote one
of the earliest Romantics, François Villon, one may
find all needed satisfactions. Such rejection of the
complications of society and of those funded social
attainments which are culture is as much an escape
from authority, as any form of primitivism or mere
dreaming. Thus realism is simply Romanticism in
its shirt sleeves, and Gustave Courbet who shouted
"I'll paint a goddess when you show me one," and
who longed to express not merely the look but the
stench of a corpse, truly represents the plebification
of the Romantic spirit.

If you had attended the World Exposition of 1863
at Paris you might have marked outside the gate a
pavillion bearing the legend "Realism," *Le Réalisme*.
This was Gustave Courbet's protest against all the

art you would have seen within;—as well against the
emotional glamour of Delacroix as against the classic
perfection of Ingres.   Courbet was a blunt, aggressive
man, and intensely vain, something of an anarchist
at heart, loving to shock all comfortable folk.   In his
lifelong pose as a gruff workman he was accused of
insincerity, but the fact that he cheerfully risked his
life in the red delirium of the Paris Commune seems
to prove his intellectual integrity.   For the rest he
was a bold and facile painter, devoted to the actual
crumbling texture of the earth and to the balance and
force of the rude men and women he loved to paint.
For most of his life he chose to pass as a vulgarian.
His subjects were Roadmakers painfully reducing
boulders to fragments; Peasant Funerals; Nude
women lolling awkwardly on a couch; sometimes
marines or landscapes.   Everything he touched he
expressed with emphasis and with regard to its actual
textures, and most vigorous insistence on mass.   All
feeling or interpretation he seems to deny himself:
here is a thing seen as it looked to me is his motto.
His friend Zola's definition of art Courbet would
gladly have accepted, "a bit of creation seen through a
temperament," and this implies the rejection of the
fanciful, the imaginative, the so-called ideal.   We will
not venture beyond our actual observation—this is
the law that applies equally to the painting of Courbet and to the fiction of Zola.   How fine the observation is you may see in his most famous picture A
Peasant Funeral at Ornans.

COURBET: THE WINNOWERS

COURBET: THE STUDIO, A REAL ALLEGORY

The just quarrel with Courbet seems to me to
be not with his choice of themes, but that he really
has very little temperament and imagination. He
feels little in his subjects and tells little about them
except that they exist. It is disconcerting too, in
a professed realist to find always the salon machine
and the artificial, murky colors of the studio. There
seems an element of charlatanism in his notion of
realistic allegory, exemplified in his great picture of
the 1855 exhibition, the Studio. The great canvas
represents the Artist at work on a landscape in the
center of his dusky studio. A nude model symbolizing
nature looks over his shoulder. In the gloom are
seen dimly many portraits of contemporaries representing so many ideas—commerce, work, religion,
social philosophy, music, poetry, prose, the theater,
free love, etc. The vast interior is well held together.
Perhaps no other contemporary painter could have
handled the problem so well. But the "real allegory"
as Courbet called it, has the sore drawback of not
explaining itself, the unity of tone is badly broken by
the bright spot of the landscape and the whole effect
is ambiguous. It is merely "very curious" as Delacroix observed with his usual precision. It requires a
literary and biographical commentary, which if given
would be of slight interest or importance. We have
to do with a rash adventure of a half trained mind in
the realm of ideas.

Even the energy which this and the earlier pictures
leave in abundance wanes in Courbet's old age into

something like an empty swagger. Still he is generally a true and powerful artist as far as he goes. He had the merit of standing by his own limitations, and to see one of his works after viewing a Meissonier, a Bouguereau, a Cabanel, or a Jules Breton is like coming out of a suffocating room into the open air.

Personally I have no quarrel with him except for his label. Realism is precisely the most misleading term I know, since no artist will admit the irreality of his work. It applies equally to the microscopic precision of the Pre-Raphaelites and to the breadth of Courbet. Materialism would probably be the right word for Courbet as he devoted himself rather to things, than ideas, giving with signal force the mass, consistence, texture, and almost the odor of whatever attracted his eye. All in all, a narrow potent man, a true force in the democratization of the art of painting. Rather a great craftsman than a great artist, for he lacked both taste and discipline and was a pitifully small mind, he made of mere existence a kind of beauty. He sought with utmost cunning the tones and textures that most powerfully suggest mass. This gives a new resource to landscape—in which branch Courbet is unqualifiedly a great master—and the idea worked fruitfully in artists as different as Whistler and Cézanne.

Something of the objective rectitude of Courbet recurs in the work of the great German painter-illustrator Adolf Menzel. His most considerable work is in illustration, drastic and truthful reconstructions of the world of Frederick the Great. In

A. MENZEL: THE ARTIST AND RELATIVES

the same vein he did a few brilliant little oil paintings. But his most important work is a handful of studies of modern life in which a scrutiny at once searching and imperturbable allies him to the early Impressionism of Manet. He has the distinction of being about the only German painter of the latter half of the nineteenth century who deserves consideration in a general survey. He was skillful in the notation of light, and generally holds an honorable if ambiguous position somewhere between the Realists, the Impressionists and the academic fine painters.

We shall see in another chapter that the academic work of the century largely escapes the romantic impulse, generally remaining at a mediocre level. Of the great Romantic tendencies, the cult of dreams, the cult of nature (including all forms of primitivism, realism, and impressionism), and the cult of energy are the most important. Nearly all the important work of the past century is comprised in one of these broad classifications. Plainly all these tendencies imply some exaggeration of individualism, and a maladjustment between the artist and society. Modern democracy has broken up the traditional standards of taste, in favor of unlimited liberty of the individual. With the older standards of taste, went the bond between the artist and his public, the like-mindedness which made the work of art both an individual and a social product. When the artist becomes an alien, he becomes as naturally a social dissenter. He must live from his own moral resources,

or at best from the support of a small group. He has
little like-mindedness with his nation or with society
at large. Evidently in such conditions we must
expect almost as many types of art as there are
artists. And indeed the tableau of nineteenth century
art is so confusing and miscellaneous that I have
attempted only the very broadest classifications.
Some more hardy critic must guide you through the
ramifications of the modern Romantic maze, where
perhaps you will find in the exciting richness and
variety of the route partial compensations for the absence of that simplicity, centrality, and assured power
which were the marks of the great art of older days.

If I have seemed to overemphasize the perils of the
programme of liberty and individualism, I have done
so not to exhibit the defects of the modern artist, but
rather that you may perceive with sympathy, the
magnitude of his task. He either travels at his peril
the various delightful roads of escape, or he must
heroically build up out of his own resources and without social aid of any adequate sort, a world of his own.
It was fortunate that the first consciously free artist,
Eugène Delacroix, did build up such a world. He
proved how great the artist could be in isolation. A
wiser age than Delacroix's and our own will see that
in such conditions it can hardly get the greatest
artists, while it hardly deserves the few great artists
that it does get. It may be well to admire the artist as
isolated superman; it is still better to challenge the social conditions that impose such isolation upon him.

OFFICIAL ART IN
THE NINETEENTH CENTURY

OFFICIAL ART IN
THE NINETEENTH CENTURY

(1815–1900)

THROUGHOUT the last century academies have largely regulated both the teaching of art and the honors and rewards of the artist. When Napoleon perfected the organization of the Institute of France, he inaugurated a great system of art patronage. The Institute offered its membership as the chief honor accessible to the artist. It conducted the École des Beaux-Arts, and the École de Rome and the Salon. Its members were state officials. Through their influence with the Minister of Fine Arts, they controlled, besides the medals, prizes, and scholarships in their own hand, the purchase of pictures for public museums and the award of commissions for mural decoration. In such distribution of patronage the Institute naturally preferred its docile pupils of the École des Beaux-Arts, and its pensioners at the École de Rome. These prizes and diplomas gave to the commercialized society of the reigns of Louis Philippe, and Louis Napoleon precisely the guarantee and trademark it required. Thus French official art tended to lose its traditional austerity and insensibly took the color of the new wealth of Imperial and Republican Paris, and whatever art did not conform

to the general taste of wealthy Paris had to shift
for itself. The Rousseaus, Millets, Manets, Puvises
are examples. However the particular form that all
the individualistic and more important movements
assumed, was largely determined by academic standards. What one revolts against, makes a difference.
Hence we must study academic art if only as a means
of understanding the freer tendencies.

The basis of modern academic art is the pseudo-
classicism of the Empire as expressed in the practice
and precepts of David, and modified by Ingres. The
chief canons are:

That drawing is to be preferred to color.

That drawing means defining the bounding line
or contour of an object.

That the analytical study of the antique and of
the nude model is the chief basis for instruction in
painting.

That skill in painting is best embodied in historical narrative, preferably classical, or in the representative of the nude.

This is the singularly restricted programme that the
academies set for themselves until about 1850. And
the programme tended still further to narrow itself
down. About the time that the legend of the First
Empire was merged in the will-o'-the-wisp brilliance
of the second, about the time that the Greco-Egyptian
chairs, clocks, and candlesticks were being discarded
in favor of plush more abundant, the old ideal of a
great historical style was quietly abandoned, and the

INGRES: ROGER AND ANGELICA

Louvre

INGRES: ODALISQUE

Louvre

Institute instead became the promoter of fine genre painting and clever portraiture.

Historical painting being quietly deposed, the staple of official painting became what Henry James used to call the "conscientious nude." With appalling monotony, ten thousand times ten thousand, she, for it was always she, appeared and reappeared on Salon walls. When her nudity had been approved by a medal, she was transferred to a public museum. There was even a certain sale for her, to enliven the chimney-pieces of new-rich palaces in Europe and the veneered and mirrored spaces, above the bottles, behind American bars. But in general the conscientious nude was merely a means of gaining scholarships and medals, whereby the artist should win fame enough to grow rich out of portrait painting. The typical French academician was a man who had done medalled nudes enough to prove that he could paint expensive portraits, and then expensive portraits enough to prove that he should have a wall to decorate.

If I have dwelt at length upon this academic vicious circle of the conscientious nude and the commercial portrait, it is because it is the best introduction to an extraordinary genius, Jean-Baptiste Dominique Ingres. Ingres thought of himself as a Greek born out of due time. He was a Greek in about the same sense that his master David was a Roman. The public and social ambition which was so strong in David was weak in Ingres. At most he was willing to fight for his own narrow conception of art. What he cared for passionately was the loveliness of woman's form as interpreted by his own magnificent line. Like David he was helpless without the model, but like his own adored Raphael he transformed the model into something of impersonal beauty. His greatness is chiefly in his studies of nude women. Take from him the Source, the Odalisque, the Angelica, and the composite of all these studies, the two pictures of the gleaming, relaxed bodies in the Turkish Bath, and you immediately dwarf him. To express the beauty he adored so passionately, he invented a line as searching as an all-comprehending caress. It swings grandly with the whole balance of the torso, it halts to record the subtlest tension or relaxation, it makes mere contour tense and thrilling like a vibrating musical string. That is the quality that counts at its height in his pencil sketches, as in that consummate notation for the Odalisque. It was his fear to efface this beautiful first intention in elaboration, and I think in the painting of the Odalisque there is some attenuation of the effect of the drawing through a rather small and tasteless arrangement of the hangings. But how little such defects count after all in comparison with a beauty which under its intense seductiveness retains an athletic candor. It was drawing of this kind which Ingres declared to be the probity of art. It was the probity of his art. To the probity of mass and motion which Rembrandt and Rubens had sought, and in his own day Géricault and Daumier, he was quite blind.

Naturally the power and accuracy of Ingres' line

INGRES: HIS OWN PORTRAIT

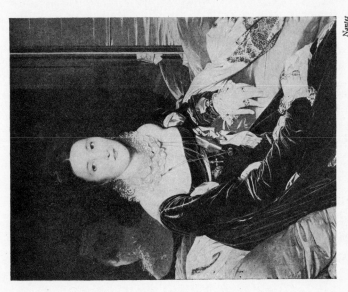

INGRES: MME. SENONES

made him an admirable portraitist.   From his eighteenth year he was a master in the pencil portrait.   For
some years at Rome he maintained himself by these
wonderful little sketches.   They are among the consummate masterpieces of that art which is mostly
research.   In his late years Ingres grudged the fame of
these tense and lovely memoranda, and hesitated to
show them in the general exhibition of 1855.   His
best oil portraits, like the Mme. Rivière of the Louvre,
are extraordinarily handsome.   Of course Ingres occasionally proved himself in the historic style.   The
vow of Louis XIII before the Virgin, in the Cathedral
of Montauban, is derived from Raphael.   It was
exhibited in the Salon of 1824, when Delacroix's
Massacre at Scio set Paris by the ears.   It certainly
exemplifies an excess of that calm which Ingres regarded as the goal of great art.

With all his concentration and apparent simplicity,
Ingres is a baffling figure.   His own statement that
he was a Greek may cover the extraordinary fineness
of his vision of line.   His cult of calm makes him the
fulfiller of all pseudo-classic doctrine from Poussin
down.   But he is very unacademic in his indifference
to the historical style, in his admiration for primitive
painting, in his bold rejection of studio recipes for
modeling through exaggerated shadow.   On the
other hand his conception of color as inferior to contour is purely academic, going back to the early
debates under Charles Le Brun's dictatorship.   In his
positive aversion from Rubens, who seemed to him to

display "raw flesh in the accessories of a butcher's shop," Ingres strikes the note with which Pseudo-Classicism came into the art of painting.

Yet in his resolute refusal to embellish nature, in his devout curiosity, he was a manner of realist—we know he always regarded himself as such—and has powerfully influenced such Impressionists as Degas, Renoir, and Zorn.   In his fastidious indulgence of personal tastes and dislikes—in a certain anti-social temper—he is really not so far from those Romantics whom he loathed.   One may guess that his example greatly strengthened the essentially Romantic dogma of art for art's sake.   Moreover the Romantic rift between man and artist found confirmation in his case.   It is hard to reconcile the small-minded pedant so truthfully and unsparingly set down by Théophile Silvestre with the godlike creator of the Nymph of the Spring and the Odalisque.   But perhaps we over-dignify Ingres' genius in retrospect.   His mind, to put it bluntly, was a marvelous harem, or perhaps we should prefer the more seemly Greek equivalent, gynecæum.   The proprietor designates with the pride of minute knowledge the points of his favorites. The exhibition is memorable because it is on a high and objective plane.   He unveils the beauties he believes in.   Such was Ingres, a smouldering voluptuary balanced by a stern conscience.   Himself suspicious of academic ideals, narrowly personal in his preferences, his example and his fame fixed the dogmas of the official art of the century.

From him derives the cult of linear drawing at the expense of color; the conscientious nude as show-piece and sufficient ideal.   Again his anti-intellectualism has left its deep stamp on the art schools of the century.   "Learn to draw stupidly" he enjoined upon his pupils, and many of them obeyed the precept.   His completely airless world is easily convertible into that of Bouguereau, Bonnat, and Meissonier.   His authority possibly saved the classical tradition in the art schools.   How much this was a service is very questionable.   Where Ingres had the force to make a robust and delicate adjustment with Hellenism, scores have failed.   Against his greatness we must set the littleness of the Gérômes, Bouguereaus, Leightons, Albert Moores, Tademas.   Thus, distinguished as was his accomplishment, the balance of evidence is strongly against his method.   The sharp descent from him to the modern academic Avernus was easily made over the sleek talent of Paul Delaroche.

Delaroche's appeal to the public was made in those pathetic incidents from history, engravings of which still adorn old-fashioned drawing rooms.   What need to recall the Little Princes clutching each other in their cell in London Tower, Queen Elizabeth wrung with anguish as she signs the death warrant of Mary Queen of Scots, the Duke of Guise assassinated and dying on his bed curtain, with a needed overturned chair to explain that there has been a fight—these things are still of recent memory.   They still speak to us in such later imitators as Brozik and Munkácsy.

DELAROCHE: EXECUTION OF LADY JANE GRAY

Luxembourg

GÉROME: THE COCK FIGHT

Delaroche, you will see, was slyly trespassing on the ground of his dreaded contemporary, Delacroix. Only when Delacroix served his history hot and raw and concentrated, Delaroche served his diluted, cooled, as it were safely pickled in facile domestic tears. He was a fair portraitist, and a narrowly intelligent teacher. He had the shrewdness to depart both from the publicism of David and from the isolated æstheticism of Ingres, in favor of an anecdotal and sentimental art eminently suited to the *nouveaux riches* of the Orleanist régime. Incidentally he confirmed in England and Germany an already strong predilection for the painting of anecdotal platitudes.

Ingres lived on till 1867, somewhat outmoded but always a potent influence, and the followers who at once broadened the scope and attenuated the quality of his art did so reverently, in his name. Among these, the most typically academic figure is Léon Gérôme who by his direct teaching as well as by his own painting dominated for nearly a half century the École des Beaux-Arts. Gérôme freshened up the classical tradition by blending it with the new *genre* style. But his anecdotes and dramas were archælogical or exotic. Into the minute work of reconstruction of classical antiquity he put a scholar's conscience. He carried into a life time the habits he acquired in competition in the École—always the classical theme, usually the nude, if not, at least historic costume. He is most ingratiating in such early works as The Cock Fight, in the Luxembourg.

Here the comparison with Ingres is inevitable. The
thing is less remote and stylistic, but it has also
warmth, charm and youth. Later he settled down to
those small pictures with elaborate settings—scenes
in the Roman Amphitheatre, the inevitable nudities
of the classic bath. He lavished his skill upon marbles
and textiles. While his eye was microscopic and his
hand cramped, his pertinacity and wit were unfailing.
He painted many bad pictures, from the modern
point of view, but no stupid ones. Such a painting as
L'Eminence Grise in the Boston Art Museum, illustrates his grasp of character, the more elaborate phase
of his art is represented in New York in the interior
of the Mosque of Cordova in the Metropolitan
Museum.

Where these laborious and very accomplished pictures fall short is in color. There is no organizing
of the tone, merely a minute record of the colors in
the subject. He sees one thing at a time; so did
Ingres, but Gérôme sees too many things. It would
be easy to regard Gérôme merely as a vulgarizer of
the classical tradition; that would be to do injustice
to his positive merits. Without the centrality and
simplicity of his master Ingres, he passed on much
of the nerve and stern conscience of the creator of the
Odalisque. There was a passion for linear beauty in
the man which is too often frittered away in the
elaboration of his painting, but it reappears in his
American pupils—in the early designs of George
de Forest Brush, the Leda, the Indian and the Lily; in

Kenyon Cox's drawings for the "Blessed Damosel."
The fact that these eager young men from across the
sea recovered the trace of Ingres in the atelier of
Gérôme is the proof that he had merits never fully
realized in his art.

He is the leader of all painters who have tried to
domesticate themselves in Hellas. In England Sir
Frederick Leighton brought more taste to the task,
and less skill. He had the same passion for linear
draughtsmanship, but his touch was debilitating. To
paint was merely one of the many accomplishments
that his rich and various nature required. There is
something amateurish about even the more charming
Leightons, the Greek girls tossing the ball on the
strand, the Pheidias-like group of the Summer Moon.
Such things represent beautiful thought, but are
devitalized in execution. The blight of culture is
upon them; they breathe nothing of the saving
robustness of the born artist.

To Laurence Alma-Tadema the reproach of amateurism, which lies rather heavily against Leighton
and Albert Moore, does not apply. There never
was a more dogged industry, nor a more duly stand-
ardized product. His art is the same domestication
of Hellas that we have noted in Gérôme. Hellas is a
young British person with flaming hair, draped in
cheesecloth for a chilly garden fête conducted amid
splendid marbles under the mournful gray light of the
Mediterranean sun. I have no mind to speak ill of
this harmless manufacture by a very amiable person.

And the pictures represent at least a nice British attitude towards the glory that was Greece, a pathetic desire to escape from mere clothes and wallpaper to drapery and outdoor marble. This mild nostalgia is about all that is in the pictures, the rest is languid drawing, physiognomy and drama substituting vision, and the multiplicity of colors producing a singularly dull and colorless ensemble.

As we return to France, we shall find even in academic petrifaction a greater measure of life. A Meissonier is less negligible even now than a Tadema. Meissonier, with Gérôme, dominates the art of Louis Napoleon. His tiny, elaborately polished, cabinet pictures were the delight of amateurs and auctioneers. Taking his inspiration from the little Dutchmen, he had an academic desire to eliminate the vulgarity from his models. Hence a familiar art, dealing exclusively with elegant masquerade. The model—refreshingly it is a he—as a smoker of the seventeenth century, costume Louis XIII, as a reader of the eighteenth, costume Louis XV—a whole puppet-world of gentlemanly figures doing nothing. Their dilettantism is hit off with a certain wit, the details of the interiors are painted with a dexterity that is amazing if wholly without charm. The scale of everything is small both to the eye and to the mind.

Now almost every good picture has its share of monumentality whatever the scale. A little Fantin nude is in its fashion monumental, so is a Vermeer of Delft, so is some tiny fantasy by Albert Ryder. I

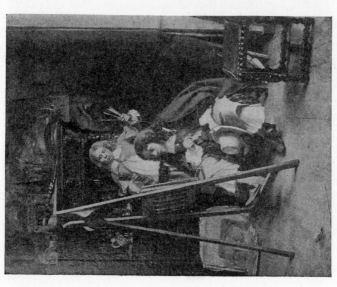

ED. DETAILLE: CAVALRYMAN

Metropolitan Museum

MEISSONIER: THE BROTHERS VANDER–
VELDE

suppose this monumentality of the little implies a
certain simplicity and dignity in the artist's attitude
towards the theme. He has cared enough to disen-
gage it from accidents, has seen widely its implications as a whole and complete thing. It is this
centrality of vision that was denied to such considerable cumulative talents as Gérôme and Meissonier. When Meissonier turned from his antiqua-
rianism to the Napoleonic epos, he slightly enlarged
his scale but not his style. He sees everything at
once in equal definition in an airless world. When
he paints a charge as in the very famous and costly
Friedland, 1809, he studies everything to the last
button, down to the crop of grain which he actually
bought that he might observe it trampled in place.
Yet the painfully studied picture remains a pretentious
and labored bit of still life, a frozen metallic thing.
Whether it was Manet or Degas, who remarked,
"It's all steel except the breastplates" does not so
much matter—the *mot* is attributed now to one now
to the other—but the truth of Meissonier's short-
comings is in the words.

The great success of his Napoleonic series gave the
incentive to such military painters as Aimée Morot,
Edouard Detaille and Alphonse de Neuville who
made the pictorial record of the unfortunate war of
1870. These were all relatively better painters than
Meissonier. Morot had a real energy, De Neuville a
notable gift for reconstructing episode. And these
military painters had the luck or the tact to work on

BONNAT: CARDINAL LAVIGERIE

Luxembourg

BOUGUEREAU: THE SHELL

the scale that befits narrative.   Thus, while failing to
reach the heroic level of a Gros, they never sink to the
wearisome average of a Horace Vernet.   They witnessed the last war that was conducted with spectacular pomp and in processional order, and they made
good use of a fleeting opportunity.

With the military painters of the '70s, academic
painting relatively emerges into the street.   Indeed
war and travel—preferably in the Orient—have been
the accredited evasion by which a member of the
Institute may relax the pursuit of decorum without
derogation of dignity.   In war and in the East much
is permitted.   Even the Institute felt that.   So many a
painter has followed Gérôme into the East and Meissonier into war.   But such compromises with the
average taste are after all, academically considered, so
many divagations from the centrality of the classic
tradition which is that of David and Ingres.

Your real exponent of the faded tradition of Ingres,
is Bouguereau.   He has the same faith in the female
model, but has lost the power of real observation and
contemplation.   So he multiplied vague, pink effigies
of nymphs, occasionally draped them, when they
become saints and madonnas, painted on the great
scale that dominates an exhibition, and has had his
reward.   I suppose every generation develops its
own ideal of that feminine form divine which even
with current fashions and the moving picture we see
imperfectly.   And I am convinced that the nude of
Bouguereau was prearranged to meet the ideals of a

New York stock broker of the black walnut generation.   It was the artificiality and insipidity of the
ideal that made it quickly obsolete.

The linear tradition of the Institute has been carried
into our own days by Léon Bonnat.   Everybody
knows that precise and rigid portraiture which has
first and last embraced all that is great in official
France of our times, and much that is prominent for
one reason or another in America.   The defects of a
Bonnat portrait, and the merits withal, are so patent
that complete analysis is unnecessary.   The technic,
adapted from the Spaniard Ribera, is one of corruga-
tion.   Small strokes are multiplied.   It has been justly
called an engraver's technic, for while in most hands
small strokes would soften the effect, in Bonnat's
they increase the hardness.   This academic precision
is attained at the cost of color and naturally in disregard of atmosphere.   Disagreeable as is the work as
painting, it has a kind of stark impressiveness, an
accentuated truthfulness of character.   A celebrity
probably would actually look like a Bonnat if con-
gealed in cold storage before the sitting.

Since Bonnat in his early Italian and oriental subjects is a colorful and fluent painter, his later style,
which is uniform in the official portraits and in the
melodramatic stories of St. Denis, in the Pantheon,
was deliberately elected.   And the case is strange indeed, for as an amateur and collector Bonnat was a
man of inerrant and catholic taste, while as a teacher
he always enjoined upon his pupils the synthetic eye.

I cannot explain the paradox. Possibly we have to do simply with a telescopic peculiarity of vision; perhaps Bonnat's official position as maintainer of the tradition of the École des Beaux-Arts produced a sort of fanaticism for linear design, which was otherwise alien to his temperament. In any case we find in him a sort of mummified embodiment of all the academic maxims. With him the scholastic tradition perished, for no reconstitution of a classical style is conceivable which so wholly ignores both facts of color in nature and charm of color in the conventions of the painter's art.

We have completed our review of academic ultra-orthodoxy, and now it is necessary to turn back a matter of sixty years and study certain more liberal phases of official painting. Long before Ingres was gone, gay Paris of the '50s and '60s began to find him a bit spare and unsatisfactory. Meanwhile a gorgeous and colorful new painting in Gros, Géricault, Delacroix, and Courbet, was offering a formidable competition to the art of the Institute. It must have sent a shudder over the École des Beaux-Arts when the young Empress Eugénie ordered some wall decorations from that gaily irresponsible colorist and incorrigible Romantic, Monticelli. The Institute prudently looked into the matter, and, adopting a classic conservative expedient, decided to steal the clothes of the Whigs. Paul Delaroche had gone pretty far, in a dull way, in assimilating the Romantic themes and handling. It was, however, a far more sturdy and workmanlike talent, Thomas Couture, who effected the reform, putting the official art of France on a modern and practical basis. Couture felt strongly the lack of painter-like quality in David and even in Ingres. He loved succinct and colorful brush-work, and sought it in the suspected Romantics, in Hals, and in Velasquez. He substituted for the gospel of the thrilling contour that of the exquisitely painted bit—*le morceau bien peint*. A good picture in his eyes was one that contained many well painted bits. Nothing else could reasonably be required of it.

This narrowly technical ideal implied a complete de-intellectualization. Subject-matter, emotions,—these were futile save as so many excuses for the pro-duction of well painted bits. Couture himself took his themes quite casually, now in the patriotic vein, now classical, often merely sentimental, after Ary Scheffer's fashion. It was the first time that an academic tradition had renounced mind. And it is odd indeed that the Institute began to deplore and suppress what brains remained to itself, only a little before the Impressionists grasped the notion that it is better to paint without taking thought. The motive in the two cases sunders sharply these two apparently similar choices. Couture bade the artist deintel-lectualize himself in order not to check the instinctive cleverness of the hand, truth being only incidentally in question; whereas Manet, quite as Ingres had recommended, chose to let his eye work unhampered by the mind, in order that he might see the more truly. Couture then initiated the parodox that the ostensibly cleverest painting of the century should be produced by the dullest individuals, the thing being mostly a question of muscular coördination and dexterity, like juggling knives or swallowing swords.

To substitute this superficial dilettantism for the older strenuous intellectualistic ideals of the Institute was a revolution. Couture characteristically effected it without opposition by first putting himself on record as completely orthodox. In the great picture, The Romans of the Decadence, painted in 1847, he established himself beyond cavil as a classicist, and nothing he did thereafter could forfeit this reputation. In the lovely curves and conventional masks of the women the picture is straight out of Ingres, the festooning lines of the composition are adroitly assimilated from Raphael, the muting of the color is again like Ingres. In a rather obvious way (the graven images of the ancestors reproachfully over-looking the revel) the picture even points a public and moral lesson after the fashion of David. Finally in the measured lassitude of the wantons and the gentleness of their intoxicated companions, the thing is in that unswerving tradition of decorum which had been preached from Poussin's time. To mention Poussin is to perceive in this admirably clever and tactful work of Couture's more than a shade of weakness and banality. This weakness, however, is in the conception, in a sentimental shading of the

COUTURE: DECADENCE OF THE ROMANS   *Louvre*

A. CABANEL: VENUS ANADYOMENE   *Luxembourg*

theme, and not in execution, which, as always with Couture, is resolute and consistent.

All the modern talk of structural planes, the dogma of the square touch, the cult of the *morceau bien fait*, derive from Couture. What counts in this art is to multiply brilliantly painted surfaces. A shop counter laden with rich stuffs, and metals and glass and porcelain becomes the most paintable thing imaginable. The critics begin about 1860 to lavish such words as velvety, nacreous, satiny; and when they condemn a picture it is likely to be for lack of textures. The academic painter no longer sees with the linear sparseness of the classical dictionary, but with the all-comprehending technical expertness of a man milliner.

Couture in his pictures, in his teaching and in his books, turns over and over the problem of fine painting, seeking to solve it by recipes. Directly or indirectly most of that painting to which journalism inevitably affixes the adjective brilliant has proceeded from him. So numerous are the apostles of brilliancy that I can name but the most eminent. Alexander Cabanel, a pupil of Ingres, sought to add to the line of his master, preciousness of intervening surface. His sea-born Venus lolling in the curl of a breaker may represent the compromise. It is of undeniable litheness of contour and pearliness of texture, yet to me it has always been one of the most repellant pictures in a museum that abounds with such. The man sees a cosmic and transcendent moment with the eyes of the maker of candy-box covers. He imposes

the eternal model upon us in the spirit of a beauty
doctor. He soon dwindled into a fashionable portrait painter, becoming in a tasteless way a quite
marvelous copyist of frills, satins and complexions.
As a teacher he had great vogue in the '70s when his
influence was potent and harmful.

One of the most amiable figures of the brilliant
school was Carolus-Duran. He too went off from his
promising beginnings, under the burden of teaching
and portraiture, but at his most superficial he could
not divest himself of charm. A kind of warmth in his
temperament drove him naturally to such models as
Titian. This set a restraint to brilliancy. To make a
picture brilliant you need not shine it, nor yet stick
bits of glass in it. Carolus saw the vulgarity of using
cleverness as a club wherewith to stun the public.
He cared enough for his sitters not to be sparkling at
their expense, he had the taste to consult such reticent
magicians of the brush as Velasquez. He possibly did
not fully realize himself, but he seems to me the high
type of academic portraitist of our day. Among his
American scholars were Kenyon Cox, Carroll Beckwith, Irving Wiles, John Sargent. The common bond
between them is a sort of probity. Indeed Carolus's
merit was to renovate and modernize Ingres' maxim,
"drawing is the probity of art," for drawing meant to
Carolus both contour and a rich and sensitive model-
ling in color. He cared for the hair's breadth in tone
and texture, just as Ingres had cared for the hair's
breadth in line. Carolus, like his beloved old masters,

CAROLUS DURAN: LADY IN BLACK

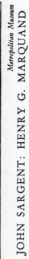

Metropolitan Museum

JOHN SARGENT: HENRY G. MARQUAND

worked out his refinements in the equable light of the studio, disregarding the baffling irradiations of out-of-doors, but his example of sensitiveness made it easy for his pupils to pass over to the problems of atmosphere. I think of John Sargent, who after unexampled success as an academic portrait painter of the brilliant school, turned over to an uncomprising Impressionism which he pursued with the zest of a beginner. The shift I am satisfied would have been if not impossible, at least far more difficult had Sargent been formed not under Carolus but under Cabanel.

For better or for worse, these two masters have set their stamp on the official portraiture of the world. To recount their followers would add nothing of general interest. Benjamin Constant, alike accomplished as portraitist and Orientalist may represent the succession in France, John Sargent in England and America. Sargent tempts to delay, but he is so various, and at times so fine. His decorations will be considered in their place. His portraiture is the acme of the neo-academic mode, swift, authoritative, unfailingly brilliant. As portraitist perhaps he is most engaging in the unaffected work of thirty years ago under Carolus' leading. Since then he has sacrificed charm to snap. His snap however is often consummately accurate. Its brittleness may be regarded as the necessary defect of its quality. A certain despitefulness, what the Italians call *sprezzatura*, is perhaps the distinguishing characteristic of the art. He rarely looks quite admiringly at anybody but a child, and

Metropolitan Museum

CHARLES BARGUE: THE SMOKER

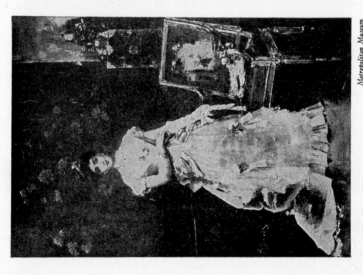

Metropolitan Museum

ALFRED STEVENS: PREPARING FOR THE
BALL

the finest portraits often have a tinge of caricature. His art is all nerve and intelligence, but it is only mind deep; there is little heart in it. Still it is much to have made of fashionable portraiture a fine adventure, to have tempered the rather empty cult of the *morceau* with perceptiveness and wit, and then to have thrown it all over for fresh adventure in the face of nature. Sargent, despite his final episode as a landscapist, must stand simply as the consummate international expression of the school of the well painted bit.

On the whole a more ingratiating aspect of the cult of the well painted bit, is offered by the little masters of the Second Empire, and their offshoots. In a sense the Belgian, Alfred Stevens, was simply a modish painter. All the moods of the sweetly spoiled Parisienne attracted him,—prinking in her boudoir, playing at motherhood, exchanging visits, enduring a most consolable widowhood. He loved the woman in her, and he loved the accessories, the silken and satin stuffs she wore, the very bottles and jars on her dressing table, the discreet sheen of light over her ormoulu furniture, and Japanese ornaments, the play of half lights over her walls. This was his sole theme, and he painted these things with a sincerity and exquisiteness that had not been applied to such subjects since the little Dutch masters. Merely as historical record these pictures are important. They make, half the history of the Second Empire vivid. The Stevens woman explains that era of speculative expansion that ended in the *débacle* of 1870. It was that she might wear these silks and satins and grace these richly appointed interiors. The n v avenues were cut starlike through old Paris that she might drive in them, the hopeless war was fought to win her praise. And all this is set down by Alfred Stevens without a shade of satire. He believed that a well maintained woman is the noblest work of man, and he had the reward of this conviction in an art, discreet, self-contained, and exquisite.

That profusion of fine workmanship which the feministe Alfred Stevens laid at the feet of the Parisienne the young Spaniard, Mario Fortuny, devoted to the gorgeous East. His painting is all staccato, it rattles with color or rather with glitter, his touch is as minute as that of Meissonier, but swift and witty. He is the arch-magician of the well-painted bit, and he knows it. He multiplies difficulties, heaps up problems, in order to master them. He seeks the East because in its mosaic of glints and hues it challenges every nerve in his fine hand and every color in his palette. The attitude is always of a joyously clever person, he has no deep insight into anything and does not desire it. What he wants is to show his hand. He is as pleased with the sophisticated complication of a Paris studio where the model is being chosen, as he is with the barbaric complexity of his Levantine scenes. In a sense these Eastern pictures represent a process of gilding the rose. They represent its effect upon an alien and excited eye; they indue it with European nerves. It is less a veritable image,

Metropolitan Museum

FORTUNY: CAMELS REPOSING, TANGIERS

Luxembourg

BASTIEN–LEPAGE: HAYMAKERS

than what has been called a "travelogue." What
counts is the clearness, wit and brilliancy of the
narration. According to one's rating of visual wit
Fortuny will take a pretty high or a pretty low place.
It is enough to say that of his sort the century produced no superior to him, while his lack of imagination and poetry was common to his times.

We must pass in a word the Orientalists who follow
in Fortuny's traces, producing little sparkling pictures
of the East. Zamaçois, Madrazo may represent the
succession. Charles Bargue pursued with greater
suppleness and finesse the miniature vein of Meissonier. We cannot ignore painters from whom the
mode has reacted violently. For these were the men
who in '60s and '70s passed for the finest painters,
and represented what seemed an ultra æsthetic ideal.
Their certainly accessible preciousness was hinted at
with bated breath by a score of salesmen in as many
plush-lined commercial sanctuaries of art. These
pictures were bought for a rise by impenitent mil-
lionaires. Perhaps the truth of the matter has been
hit off smilingly by my friend Royal Cortissoz, the
accomplished critic of the New York *Tribune*. He
calls these the best bad pictures in the world.

About 1870 official painting moved moderately
in a parallel direction with Impressionism in the
person of the gifted and short-lived Bastien-Lepage.
He studied out-door illumination, caught the general
blondness of such effects, but halted such research at
the point where clear definition of form was im-

perilled.   This reasonable compromise is represented
in such excellent canvases as The Mowers and the
Joan of Arc.   This endeavor to achieve high luminosity without sacrificing linear quality was shared by
other artists of ability such as Roll in France, Zorn in
Sweden, Carl Larsson in Norway.   On the whole
this cautious *plein-airsme* has gone the way of all
half measures.

   We have followed the course of official painting in
France to about the year 1880, when Impressionism
was already prevalent, and the founding of the new
Salon by the Société des Artistes Français broke
down the Academic monopoly.   It is time to attempt
an appraisal and a review, but first we must glance
away from France to other countries that boasted an
official art.   The other continental countries offer us
little specific.   They all had their part in pseudo-
classicism.   Italy and Spain produced brilliant painters of the Fortuny type, England alone claims our
attention.

   England, you will recall, never broke violently
with the eighteenth century tradition.   To the middle
of the nineteenth century you will find a hint of Van
Dyck and Rubens in the portraiture of Sir Thomas
Lawrence in England and Gordon in Scotland.
Raeburn with his quite marvelous justness of vision
and his intuition of Velasquez is of course the really
salient portraitist, but despite his astonishing antici-
pations of the painting of the end of the nineteenth
century, it seems better to reckon him to the old

school. With Chardin and Hogarth he is among its most modern figures.

The main tendency of the art of the Royal Academy was portraiture, the manner of which steadily degenerated into book-of-beauty sleekness, and anecdotes. David Wilkie, active in the first third of the century, hit off the humors of life with rare wit and charm. He had drawn shrewdly from Hogarth and the little Dutch Masters. The Philadelphian, Charles R. Leslie, carried the anecdotal manner successfully to the middle of the century. Both men willingly assumed the illustrator's rôle, drawing their subjects from Shakespeare, Sterne, Boswell. They were followed by duller men, who pipe in mouth and Tam O'Shanter on head followed the nice little bit and human interest into all the groves, gardens, and inglenooks of Great Britain. Landseer indued the dog with pathos and the stag with tragedy. Painting became the conscientious notation of whatever appealed to the home-loving Briton. Preferably there was some mixture of pets and children, radiant childhood and pathetic old age, to which the title pointed with the emphasis of jest and epigram. These pictures were done by men who had plumbed and outlined and then shaded the cast, had repeated the process on what they modestly called the "Muddle," had thoughtfully trained their eyes away from all real seeing. Instead they had good hearts, and led exemplary lives, and honestly sold the public what the public wanted, and gave the public what the public deserved. The few men of vision and imagination, Watts, Alfred Stevens, stand apart from the Academy. Similarly the Pre-Raphaelites represent a primitivistic phase of revolt. Meanwhile the Royal Academy kept its lucrative monopoly of human interest. For that reason, Mrs. Pennell writes in her amusing book "Nights," the word "human" was a term of extreme vituperation with a certain irritable critic poet, W. E. Henley, and his young men of the "Scots Observer."

The Academy held on as an influence nearly to the end of the century not because of any ideas it had, but because it had learned to live without ideas of any kind. It still survives. In this absence of doctrine lies the inferiority of the British type of academism. Whistler did much to sneer it out of court. Gradually better influences prevailed in instruction. The tense and delicate talent of Alphonse Legros imposed a Gallic sincerity at the Slade School. The more flexible talents like W. Q. Orchardson brought to the old human interest themes a finer pictorial insight and an elegance of touch based on intelligent study of the French cult of the *morceau*. John Sargent found his best subjects and his most congenial sojourn in London. Such partial adherence to Continental modes was largely forced upon the Royal Academy by the independent exhibitions of which Whistler's International Society of Painters and Engravers is the type. Fundamentally the average academician had no policy except to keep his full share of exhibition space and to sell his pictures. And the importance of the Academy has dwindled to next to nothing, as new walls have been made available by societies and dealers, and the French painters from Corot to Cézanne have become salable in England.

In America again it is hardly fair to speak of the existence of an Academic movement nor yet of an official style. When the National Academy was founded, all portraitists and landscape painters of any prominence were as a matter of course asked to join. Their number increased while the exhibition space, even in the glorified moment of the now vanished Venetian Palace on Fourth Avenue, was very restricted. The Academicians did a good business which they were reluctant to impair for anything so vague as the good of American art. In William Mount and Eastman Johnson the Academy produced *genre* painters comparable in excellence to Wilkie and Leslie. On the whole its merits were retrospective and colonial. Fine eclectics like Wyatt Eaton, and William Hunt, disciples of Millet, hardly existed for the Academy. The gracious and versatile La Farge stood apart from it. Then came the Centennial of the Declaration of Independence and the World Exhibition at Philadelphia in 1876, and a fair show of contemporary art. It caused a great rubbing of eyes.

What was revealed to America was on the whole the sleek and competent splendors of the painters of the Institute. Gérôme lorded it with Meissonier, Fortuny, and Bargue. Alongside of these masters were soon shown the works of their American pupils,

Shirlaw, Brush, Cox, Beckwith, Duveneck, Chase, Eakins. The evident competence of these young men was a reproach to the average dullness of the Academicians. It appeared that these good painters were excluded from the market and the exhibition hall. The evident unfairness of the procedure led to the formation of the Society of American Artists in 1877. It merely demanded the freedom of the city for a more intelligent academism, was by no means a theoretical revolt, but merely a justifiable business adventure. So it was an entirely logical step when in a matter of twenty-five years the National Academy, now somewhat liberalized, and the Society were reunited. We may note that only in France do the artistic revolutions concern themselves with any more central issue than the right to exhibit. It is a somewhat sad commentary on the lack of initiative in public taste that the right to exhibit may be also the artist's right to live. The American public will usually no more buy an unexhibited art than it will eat an unadvertised breakfast food.

What the infusion of the practice of the Paris schools into American art did was to produce a glorious moment, the promise of which has been only partially fulfilled. Yet much was done. The professional standard was raised to the European level. To men like Shirlaw, Duveneck, Chase, Cox, Blashfield, Beckwith, Eakins, we owe a great debt for their activities as teachers. In Abbot Thayer academic training matured into rich idealistic expression; in

George de Forest Brush we have a strenuous and
deeply studied portraiture in the tradition of Ingres;
in Eakins we have an intensity of research both in
narrative and in portraiture which results in a highly
intellectualized beauty.   Yet, on the whole, the pregnant influences in our Modern American painting
have been less that of the Institute of France than
those of the Romantic and Impressionistic schools.

The course of official art through the century may
be very briefly reviewed; to appraise it is a far more
difficult matter.   Everywhere we find the generous
ideal of a national and historical school, clearly
announced by David, being abandoned in favor of a
pure æstheticism like that of Ingres, or facile anecdotage, notably in England and Germany—or surface cleverness, of which the high type is Fortuny.
The academies gradually cease to uphold the old
classic, or pseudo-classic theories, and become pur-
veyors to the blunted taste of a mercantile and industrial middle class, finally yielding to the new scientific
naturalism.   No longer the custodians of doctrines,
the academies become simply the dispensers of exhibition wall space.   Such is the record of official art
without exception.   The best art critic that America
has yet produced, W. C. Brownell, in his admirable
book on French art makes a guarded apology for
the Institute and similar bodies—they maintain a
professional standard in slack and random times.

I differ very reluctantly from an associate for
whose opinion I have the highest respect.   The view

seems to me sound only to the end of the Napoleonic school. I hope not to be accused of frivolity when I say that academies thereafter have been useful in just about the sense that pins have saved many babies' lives—by not being swallowed. By giving the more personal artists something to reject, by thus inspiring courageous reactions—the academies may have been of service. Certainly we must understand the academic movement to understand the art of modern times. But when I think how tardy, grudging and inadequate has been the official recognition of such artists as Watts, Whistler, Millet, Rousseau, Manet, Renoir, Degas, Monet: When I see in America that our Academy has been of no use to men alike of the drastic raciness of George Luks or of the delicious fantasticism of Arthur B. Davies—When I consider these things, I cannot see but that as custodians of taste all the academies have gone progressively into bankruptcy.

I could imagine a profitable return to first principles. When in 1648 the French Academy first devoted itself to promotion of the fine arts, there was no idea that it was to be either a teaching or an exhibiting body. It was simply a group of artists of prominence who met regularly for discussion. The aim was to help each other, through the creation of sound professional opinion, and incidentally to foster such opinions among the cultured public. Such a voluntary high court was to stand against excessive individualism in the artist. Originally the French Academy had the advantage of being a disinterested body. It controlled no exhibition space, conducted no schools, awarded no scholarships, no medals, or ribbons. It was influential not from its vested interests, but from the importance of its membership and the merit of their opinions. It was a rather tolerant body, as it appears in the minutes of its early conferences. I do not know whether a return to first principles be possible. Sometimes in more hopeful moods, I see the newly founded academies of England and the United States playing so beneficent a rôle.

But if there ever is to be a reintegration of art in the world the first step I am satisfied will be to end all collective methods of teaching, cease indulging false notions of democracy, make it not easy but rather difficult to study art, close the art schools, give back teaching to the individual artist, substitute apprenticeship in a studio for matriculation in a school. I can imagine no real instruction in any art where the student does not constantly witness creative processes and to some extent share in them. Nor is this ideal of personal instruction merely theoretical. Nearly every great artist of the century has followed about the course I have indicated. If he has blundered into an official art school, he has quickly got out. He has attached himself intimately to some master whose work he admires, or has retrospectively established such a bond with the old masters. He has gained his public through the slow process of getting like-minded people to come to him, not by the short cuts of exhibitionism. What the Constables, Rousseaus, and Millets, and Homer Martins had to do in travail and solitude, I hope the great masters of the future may do in joyous companionship. And whenever people once more really want good painting, there will be plenty of it—thanks not to Academies or official patronage, but to a widely diffused and insatiable need of beauty.

LANDSCAPE PAINTING BEFORE
IMPRESSIONISM

LANDSCAPE PAINTING BEFORE IMPRESSIONISM

(1800–1870)

LANDSCAPE, as an inevitable expression of the Romantic spirit, is the characteristic art of the nineteenth century. Its pursuit called the artist away from society, and encouraged an unconditioned individualism. It corresponded to elevated and solitary states of soul. The mystic Wordsworth had made the case plain even before the 18th century ran out.

> "One impulse from a vernal wood
>   May teach you more of man,
> Of moral evil and of good,
>   Than all the sages can."

So, by one of those substitutions of *genres* which were first indicated by the late Ferdinand Brunetière, landscape painting largely usurped the function of the old historic style, enlisting the most elevated talents and evoking all the deeper emotions. There was of course a fallacy in the idea that man, essentially a social creature, can best fulfill himself in solitary communion with nature. Such a notion shows how far the art of painting was losing social significance.

Possibly it may seem strange to regard Constable, Corot, Rousseau, Turner as of less universal appeal than say Hogarth, Boucher, Fragonard, David. Our souls are so attuned to the mystical view of landscape, so thoroughly debilitated from three generations of Romantic teaching, that we readily identify our own state of mind with the normal feeling of the race. It needs only a little reflection to perceive that alike in the trenchant moralizing of Hogarth, in the calculated frivolity of Boucher and Fragonard, and in the frigid sublimity of David, the art of the eighteenth century made a cosmopolitan appeal, was approved through more strata of society than have ever been reached by the isolated poetry of the landscape painting of the nineteenth century.

Landscape as we know it in Constable and in the so-called Barbizon painters grows in the first instance out of an intense cult of nature, but it is also conditioned by artistic precedents.

What counted for the amateurs of the 18th century was the sinister picturesqueness of Salvator Rosa's storm-tossed, bandit-infested woodlands, the bucolic freshness of Rubens's grove-fringed meadows and hay fields, the grave serenity of Claude Lorrain's carefully balanced scenes undershot with the silver of dawn or the molten gold of sunset, or those solemn pastorals in which Nicholas Poussin expressed his noble melancholy. Other influences were the somewhat savage grandeur of Ruysdael's dashing waterfalls and gnarled oaks, the amber cheerfulness of Hobbema's farm and mill scenes, the richer saturation of the sun drenched pastures of Albert Cuyp. Such were the precedents, the Dutch counting more in England; Claude and the Italians more in France, with the universally admired Rubens serving as a potent bond across the Channel.

With the partial exception of Rubens, who now and then indulged a predilection for rainbows, coming storms and the like, all these landscape painters of the 17th century dealt with the mental and permanent aspects of nature. They made no attempt to copy exact local color, or exceptional effects, but gladly filled their foregrounds with those regulation brown trees which gave contrast and remoteness to their carefully graded distances. They chose appearances that are permanent, in the sense that they last for hours and are repeated many days in the year. Thus they sought rather to express repeated, verified, and approved feelings about nature, than to record a single visual experience. This is the tacit assumption which underlies all the best modern landscape before Impressionism. It is not just a thing seen, but a thing felt, sifted, and interpreted. Sheer reality, close resemblance, is not expected of it, it merely must shape its conventions so as not to offend the spectator's sense of the fitting or possible.

In the Fêtes Galantes of Antoine Watteau, in the backgrounds of Gainsborough's portraits and in his rustic landscapes alike, we find the feathery manner of Rubens invested with a certain languor. The masculine candor of the Fleming has given way to a feminine sensitiveness and a wistful charm. The

shadowy groves and promenades in which Fragonard's lovers comport themselves with more or less
indiscretion again echo Rubens. Even the setting of
George Morland's cottagers and smugglers is Rubens
almost unalloyed. Thus his sanely decorative conventions were carried well into the nineteenth century. Gainsborough's landscapes were wholly neglected in his lifetime. He did little more than to apply
to the charming scenes of his native Wiltshire the
genial, rural formulas established by Rubens. The
new note is merely a tendency to waive panoramic
effect in favor of more restricted scenes conceived with
greater intimacy. The mood is well represented in
the famous picture the Market Cart.

Neglected too were the landscapes of Gainsborough's contemporary, Richard Wilson. Trained
as a portrait painter, he turned over to landscape in
the early 1740's. His style was formed at Rome
where he picked up from Panini and Zuccarelli the
fluency of the current Italian landscape manner. But
the guiding influence was Claude. From him Wilson
drew the carefully balanced somewhat panoramic and
highly simplified arrangements which modern criticism
has slowly learned to value. Technically he advanced
beyond Claude by avoiding the cruder contrasts of
light and dark and seeking a blonde, bluish tonality
which presages the early manner of Corot. His
views of the Campagna and prospects of the lovely
lakes of the Alban Mountains remain among the most
tranquil joys of the art of painting. He made the

poorest of livings and died at 69, in 1782, in something like poverty.

It was a new educational fashion that made it possible to get a living out of landscape painting. To draw, or as it was more elegantly termed to limn in water color, became a necessary part of a polite schooling. So about the year 1750 there arose a painstaking topographical sort of portraiture of place, generally laid in carefully in sepia or India ink sparsely touched with green or blue. Soon there appeared engraved, often tinted, albums of famous sites, country seats and the like. Between teaching drawing and serving the print sellers and publishers, there was now a living for a landscapist. The fashion made possible the beginnings of Thomas Girtin and J. W. M. Turner. It stimulated the love of pictured landscape generally so that Crome and Constable made their modest livings where Wilson had never really gained a living wage.

In the robust and sympathetic figures of John Crome of Norwich, English landscape painting first comes to its own. Born in 1769, he was trained as a coach painter, and developed as an artist under the leading of a fine and patient enthusiasm for nature. He was the first man to put on canvas the succulent picturesqueness of British scenery. He loved the gnarled oaks casting shadow from dense foliage over the bright, smooth grass. He loved the rounded moorlands where windmills stand stately against the sunset, he found self-expression in solemn wood interiors,

CONSTABLE: WILLOWS, SKETCH

JOHN CROME: LANDSCAPE WITH
FIGURES

he coped with the magic of moonlight. With this reverence for nature he shared a deep and intelligent admiration for the great Dutch landscape painters. He copied Rembrandt's Mill, studied Hobbema, Ruysdael, and Van der Neer, above all considered intently the colorful charm of Cuyp. Indeed his style may be considered as a sort of blend between the plastic monochrome of Ruysdael and Cuyp's atmospheric iridescence. He went as far in the transcription of true local color as the ruling tradition permitted, naturally clinging to the sacred "brown tree." He died in a fruitful middle age in 1821, and left behind him like-minded disciples who worthily continued the Norwich school for still a generation. They produced one man of genius in the various and enigmatic John Sell Cotman. Especially in the etchings of his "Liber Studiorum," in his water colors and black and white sketches he shows a rare power of design. An uneven artist, at his best he seems greater than the men who put him in the shade, Callcott, Linnell, David Cox, Copley Fielding, Turner.

For so gradual an approach to our real theme, modern landscape painting, I should perhaps apologize. We have barely grazed it in casual mention of the English water-colorists. Yet I think there is something both fascinating and essentially British in this slow inevitable approach, so respectful of nature's privacy, so graced by the decencies of tradition. We reach modern landscape itself in the work of John Constable.

Constable seems less an interpreter of nature than a part of it. His quiet, patient force seems almost impersonal. Nothing fretted or retarded him. He waited years for his bride, who was of higher social station, counseling her not to indulge a harmful sensibility. He was untroubled by the indifference of the public and by the success of rivals. Within three or four miles from his father's windmill at East Bergholt, Suffolk, he found a sufficient world. Pictures greeted him up and down the slow winding Stour with its dense oaks and locks and water mills. Nobody before him had looked so fixedly at the sky, questioning its subtlest iridescences and divining the swirling bosses and caverns which make up its celestial architecture. With nature, indeed, Constable took the permissible liberties of an avowed lover. Where his predecessors and contemporaries met her on parade, he caught her most informal and casual moods. To the horror of everybody he painted into the sun, and, hardly less amazing, he declined to see foliage as brown or olive where nature showed jewel-like greens.

In this quest he was aided by intelligent study of earlier landscape. The beautiful balance of Claude and Wilson were ever present with him, helping to restrain and chasten his somewhat panoramic and discursive ideals. In his earlier years the sparkle of Hobbema and the torsion of Ruysdael are more or less directly imitated. Even Rubens with his continuous rhythmic line is drawn upon. The poise and centrality of the man are shown in the fact that with

him the study of the old masters was simply a new
approach to nature. He brought to each survey of
nature the precious freshness of a first time; here
he was a true precursor of Impressionism. Where
he differs from the Impressionists is that their first
time is brief, casual, and unexpected, whereas his
first time is arranged and prolonged. This capacity
both to see with the innocent eye and yet to bring
to observation the happiest expectations drawn from
study of older art, is his superiority. His specific
contribution to technic was the unifying of the
painted surface through enrichment of divided tone,
and the acceptance, as against the dogma of the
brown tree, of truth of local color.

Eugène Delacroix hit half the truth when he scrib-
bled a note on Constable's precious greens. "The
superiority of the green of his meadows depends on
its being composed of a multitude of different greens.
The lack of life and intensity in the foliage of most
landscapes, is that it is generally made of uniform
tint." Such was the deduction of the great Romantic
colorist from the Hay Wain of Constable and the
other canvases which were exhibited in the Salon
of 1824. But Constable did much more than add to
landscape the vibrant greens and blues of foliage and
sky. He conceived a principle of unity which depended less on balance of masses than upon consistency of handling. The idea was not new, but such
unity in Rubens, Gainsborough, Wilson, or Guardi
was unserious, resting on somewhat flimsy decorative

CONSTABLE: GLEBE FARM

CONSTABLE: RIVER MEADOW, SKETCH

formulas. Such unity as Goyen and Jan van der Cappelle, and Cuyp in his first manner had attained— and Whistler was to revive—was negative rather than positive, implying a reduction of the variety of nature to uniform tones of russet and silver. Constable's unity is serious and positive. His bold touch at once follows the variety of tree trunk, boulder, cloud and herbage, and keeps withal a consistency which is always vigorous and always harmonious. Indeed this firm and highly emotionalized touch is what holds together pictures which otherwise are a bit scattering and panoramic. It is the handwriting in which we may read a patient, wise, reverent and powerful spirit. He creates when other landscape painters are merely charting or measuring. And he has the discretion to remain in the potential stage, seldom being too explicit and always requiring something of his spectator's intelligence.

His achievement is so concrete, generous, and valuable that his influence can hardly be overestimated. Modern landscape in a true sense dates from his exhibition in the Salon of 1824. His style progressively broadened. The assertion of form is less emphatic, the sky and the enveloping atmosphere become his main concern. The atmospheric quiver and broken color of his latest works like the Cenotaph and Salisbury Cathedral anticipate both the themes and the procedures of later Impressionism.

The ungracious thought intrudes: Having gone so far in the direction of naturalistic color, and in the notation of light would not a first class intelligence have gone further? Already in their heavy contrasts of light and dark the landscapes of Constable look almost as old fashioned as those of Ruysdael. Yet on reflection these compromises seem highly intelligent. For the sake of shimmer he will not wholly sacrifice richness of color; to attain atmospheric envelope he will not too much efface the enveloped form. Mr. MacColl somewhere has an excellent epigram that "for the artist to paint like nature may be to ignore the nature of paint." It is a saying to remember when the naturalistic methods of the recent schools are being considered.

Whenever I think John Constable may have been just a shade too reasonable and calm, I look to his tiny oil sketches, for example that remarkable group in the South Kensington Museum, and there I seem to see the liberated man. In these swift notes there is the sap and vitality which the greater paintings sometimes just a little lack. Miles of heaving moorland under low hanging clouds come out of a few strokes of green and grey and blue. The ripple of the tide gnawing at sparkling cliffs is conveyed in a magical short hand. Stranger yet, there are marvellous indications of crowds, for example the Yokels of East Bergholt hanging Napoleon in effigy, on the anniversary of Waterloo Day. The panel would be an amazing anticipation of recent Impressionism did it not equally recall certain earlier sketches of Goya. Such evocations, almost the swiftest known to the history of art, and, significantly, evocations through color alone, show that Constable in his larger work put himself under a certain restraint.

I love to think that he died too soon to read the first volume of Ruskin's "Modern Painters." It would have taxed even his equanimity, for it proved how little England had learned from her only great landscape painter. By a paradox, which might not have pleased him, we must seek the succession of the most British of masters, not in England but in France.

If Constable represents the body and dynamic of modern landscape painting, Corot represents its soul and radiance. The opaline mist of dawn, half revealing half concealing the swing of rustling saplings is his theme. Paint vanishes into an evanescence compounded of dew-veiled clouds and the growth of things. It is an Ariel art—precise, delicate, elusive, at which he arrived almost unaided. Born in 1796, at Paris, the son of a shopkeeper, after a desultory schooling he was, himself, destined to be a ribbon clerk. Persuasive as always, he wheedled a small allowance out of his father, and began to study painting, passing successively under three singularly unfit teachers. Doubtless he saw and probably he admired the Constables in the historic Salon of 1824. But the very positive and material trend of the Englishman could hardly have influenced Corot. When his benign talent at last announces itself it is free from Teutonic heaviness and melancholy, an intensely

COROT: MONTMARTRE

COROT: MORNING

Gallic and Latin product in the proper succession of Poussin and of Claude.

At thirty, in 1826, Corot went to Rome, being so miseducated that he could not make the slightest sketch. Soon he mended that, developing that lovely system of calligraphic snares and nooses by which, without troubling about smaller details, he caught the movement and aërial balance of a scene. Soon came those solid, blonde little pictures of Roman sites and ruins: The Lake of Nemi, the Villa d'Este, the domes glimmering over Trajan's Forum, the Coliseum. He chose his subjects much as a British sketcher in water color would have done, merely subordinating the topographical detail to unity of effect, and giving the portraiture of place a somewhat generalized aspect and luminosity. For nearly ten years, either in Italy or in reminiscence of her charms, he worked like a more material Wilson or better like a Panini turned descriptive poet. From 1827 the Salon accepted Corot's works, but hung them obscurely. In 1847 the award of the Cross of Honor fell as a surprise. The aged father remarked: "We should give a little more money to Camille." Camille himself soon put behind him the manner for which he had received the prize. This involved a restudy of the mysteries of light in nature and a certain abstraction from ordinary affairs. It was probably in the year of revolution 1848, that hearing shots in front of his lodging and re-marking a barricade as he issued forth, he observed, "It seems that one is not content with the government."

The new style which marks his fifties rests upon the most consummate blend of observation with arbitrary ideals of beauty which modern times have witnessed. The transition is marked by such great canvases as the St. Sebastian of the Walter's Gallery, Baltimore, the Dante at Boston, and the evening piece, The Sleep of Diana, in the Metropolitan Museum. The browns still dominate. The more fully irradiated, the silvery style is represented by the famous Dance of Nymphs in the Louvre, or by any one of a hundred of the Souvenirs d'Italie or of the series composed on motives from Ville d'Avray.

In the early Corots we speak of the beauty and balances of the surfaces, using words that would apply to Vermeer of Delft or Guardi. In the later Corots there is only one surface—a gray that shimmers off warmly into rose, or coldly into blues and olives, a mysterious effulgence that seems less painted than powdered with the dust of black pearls. Gradually the eye goes back through iridescent veils of mists to creamy masses that are clouds. Across these swing strongly but faintly the lithe form of silvery trees that resume in themselves the rathe elegance of olives, poplars, and willows. The graceful stems are glimpsed rather than seen from sparse velvety darks in the bends and from silvery glints where the smaller branches thrust. About these firm and lovely forms is a crisp powdering of leaves which ripple in the morning breeze. Below there will be a bit of lake with perhaps a balancing boat, and on some

COROT: LANDSCAPE

COROT: HIS OWN PORTRAIT

further bank an ivory villa.   There may be a patch of
cool shadow under the greater trees.   If so it is often
enlivened by the tossing arms and legs of rollicking
nymphs who greet the dawn with dancing, as they
mimic the supple lines of the universal growth.

The whole vision is set far away and partly veiled
by films of mist.   To see, it requires a little patience
and good will.   As Corot himself once said "To get
into my painting, one must at least have the patience
to let the mist rise: one goes in rather slowly, and once
there he ought to be pleased since my friends are
never untrue to me."   How charming the words
"my friends" said impartially of tree and verdure, air
and water, animals and nymphs.   One must go back
to St. Francis's Hymn to the Sun for a like informal-
ity.   The best painting of Corot represents merely
vivid memory of ardent and delicate transactions
with these out-door friends.   He made thousands of
sketches, and hardly needed them, for he had nature
as it were domesticated in his bachelor studio.   One
might say he cuddled nature in his studio and that she
bloomed with new fairness, developed new pallors
and flushes under his caress.   He has virtually avowed
the relation in one of those too few boyish outbursts.

"After my excursions I invite nature to come and
spend some days with me; then my madness begins;
brush in hand I hunt hazel nuts in the thickets of my
studio; I hear the birds sing, the trees tremble with
the wind, there I see the brooks run and the rivers
with their thousand reflections of the sky and of every-

thing which lives on the banks; the sun sets and rises *chez moi.*"

It is odd indeed that this joyous and open-hearted art should have made its way slowly.   As late as 1879 the leading American artists were interviewed by the critic George Sheldon on the sore topic of Corot, and most of them declared that he was a reprehensibly slovenly and cryptic artist.   And America was at that moment only a little behind France while far more advanced than England in the appreciation of modern art.   Chief obstacles to the enjoyment of Corot were his evasion of certain established conventions of landscape and the baffling delicacy of his idiom. Nothing was more settled in landscape than that the spectator should enter through a regular proscenium. There should be a building, or a big foreground tree, or a group of figures to tell him where he was and give him his bearings.   Corot's habit is well preserved in an anecdote related by George Moore.   The young Irishman sketching near Paris had the luck to find the master painting down a pleasant glade.   After admiring the work, he ventured to remark, "Master, what you are doing is lovely, but I cannot find your composition in the landscape before us."   Corot said 'My foreground is a long way ahead.'   And sure enough, nearly two hundred yards away, his picture rose out of the dimness of the dell."

Corot not merely scrapped the proscenium but set his rural stage with means too refined for his day.   He seems to have been the first painter to interest himself systematically in the values—the amount of light and dark in colors. His pictures were schematized in four values, of which four, the sky was the brightest. The picture was built up from light to dark. What is baffling to an eye coarsened by the routine pictorial tradition, is the little difference between Corot's lightest and darkest values. It was mystifying to see so much achieved with means so tenuous.

Suppose we put the matter, following Corot's own mathematics, this way: there are, let us say, ten points between the extreme light and dark of the painter's palette. Corot got his effects between six and nine, never going very dark and never attaining the highest light. Claude goes much darker than Corot and attains as much light; he paints in eight points, between two and nine, has double the scale of Corot. Constable avoiding the heaviest darks, paints in perhaps in six points, between four and nine. Subsequent painters still further shortened and heightened the scale of values. We may say that Monet gets his characteristic effects in a scale of two—nine and ten, with infinite subdivisions. He goes to the maximum in brightness and entirely evades the darks. Whistler, on the contrary ordinarily evaded both the lights and darks, shrinking fastidiously from every extreme. He paints on a short scale in the center of the palette, say five and six. Most artists who have sought concentration and expression through minimum indications have learned much from Corot.

In his vigorous old age he amused himself with

figure pieces blocked out simply in creamy masses, cool, firm, and admirably placed. As Meier-Graefe, with some exaggeration, has pointed out, the best of these challenge comparison with Vermeer of Delft at one end and with Bonnard and Cézanne at the other. They are the logical transposition to the figure of his procedures in landscape—mass expressed not by artificial light and shade but entirely in brightness by just observation of its absorbence and irradiation of what Leonardo da Vinci termed the "universal light." Camille Corot died in 1875, being seventy-nine years old, full of honors and friendships. He was conscious that his bonds were with the past, with Claude and with Poussin. He disapproved the brusque silhouette of Manet, he felt disagreeably the coarseness of Monet's early manner. For a long life he had observed the rites of the Catholic Church with childlike faith, and he died in the hope of a Heaven in which landscape painting was still to be his occupation and delight.

Corot has the lucid, singing quality of a melody by Mozart, he seems a beautiful legacy from the age of Enlightenment; his younger contemporary Théodore Rousseau has the choking eloquence of Beethoven. Rousseau is wholly of our times, at his rare best, our greatest master in landscape. Like Corot he was born at Paris. The year was 1812, but his first keen impressions were gained in the rugged scenery of the Franche-Comté, where he supervised numerous small sawmills. At fourteen he gave himself to painting. He

TH. ROUSSEAU: VILLAGE OF BECQUIGNY

TH. ROUSSEAU: EDGE OF THE WOODS

passed relatively unscathed through a succession of incompetent masters, but had the good sense to decline to compete for the Prix de Rome, and like most radical youngsters of the time, fortified himself by study of the Dutch masters. Though a rather solitary spirit, he passed an occasional evening at the Cheval Blanc, where Delacroix lorded it over the new Romantics.

But Rousseau's special problems had to be faced in struggle and in solitude. He had set himself the most appalling of tasks, to combine a minute structural accuracy with richness of color, and sense of atmospheric envelopment. Rousseau declined all the usual compromises and evasions, seeking the fusion of the most refractory and incompatible elements. Often he fell short of the desired harmony. Struggle and spartan self-discipline were native to the man. Where Corot loved such nymph-like trees as the willow and the young poplar, Rousseau hardly looked beyond the gnarled oak, contorted with the effort to grow amid storm and cold. Under his brush these giant trees became heroic. A picture usually begins with a microscopically careful anatomy of such a tree. Too often it ends there. From this as a center he felt out for the composition, following, I am persuaded, precisely the path of Ruysdael before him. The initial motive was worked out in the open air. Then followed in the studio an equally minute process of enrichment, dotting and dragging, and glazing of finely broken color until the whole surface should become precious. This embroidery is partly in the interest of exact truth of local color, partly in that of atmospheric unity. Naturally the balance is not always equal. In his mature years he endeavored to break away from his myopic methods and in such masterpieces as the Hoar Frost, at Baltimore, and the roseate Edge of the Wood, in the Louvre he wholly succeeded. He was helped in this broadening process through the advice of his young friend and pupil, Jules Dupré, who in 1834 had the joy of seeing the great Constable work in England.

In that year Rousseau got a third class medal at the Salon, and then for the twelve greatest years of his art he was refused. There was perhaps a little consolation in the nickname *le grand refusé*. The year of the barricades, 1848, found him pacing the streets of Paris as a civic guard, when Corot, you will recall was wondering why the discontent. The same year saw a fairly liberal reorganization of the Salon, and his first State commission. He celebrated the event by moving to Barbizon. His period of poverty was now past, but he had the chagrin of seeing his rather superficial pupils, Dupré and Diaz, promoted from grade to grade, while he was ignored.

During his own struggle he had been of royal generosity to his poorer comrades, especially to Millet. On one occasion when Millet needed both money and encouragement, Rousseau, impersonating a rich American, bought a canvas at what was then a great price. Upon this compassionate and endearing phase of the man it is necessary to insist. It is the key to that stoic tenderness which makes his art. The stern joy of his endeavor breathes in his own words, "Were I allowed to have a wish, it would be that I were a millionaire, with nothing to do but to labor upon the creation of a unique work, to devote myself to it, to suffer and enjoy it, until I should be content with it, and after years of proof, I could sign it and say, There stops my strength and there has my heart ceased to beat."

At fifty-five Rousseau had worn himself out without attaining that unique work. What remains of him is often travestied by a darkening and decay which will affect the greater part of his paintings. But the little residue of pictures that have come near his wish and are painted to stand, is one of the most precious pages in the art of landscape. I think particularly of the crystalline coolness and justness of that view of the boulder-strewn Gorge of Apremont, in the old Vanderbilt collection, a picture instinct with the most literal truth of substance and texture and steely afterglow of the dying year, and yet invested with a restrained tragedy as if the unending struggle of frail green things against time and weather, were the true theme, and victory won through cramping and distortion. It is a picture like this which made the honest and lovable Corot declare himself a mere twittering lark, alongside of the eagle. It is the fullest expression of the Northern and half-mystical aspect of French genius, as Corot is of its Latin serenity. In the two masters the blithe serenity of Claude and the austere nobility of Poussin come to a modern and richer embodiment.

Upon such direct pupils of Rousseau as Diaz and Jules Dupré, it is not necessary to linger. Both caught the superficial richness of their master, both were admirable manipulators of paint. Their relative lack of depth had its reward in quick recognition, and their breasts were laden with decorations and medals at a time when Rousseau was still in the grip of poverty. The half Spaniard, Diaz, was trained in china painting and never wholly outgrew it. His little landscapes, reminiscences of the Barbizon oaks and glades are brilliant to a degree, a very fine performance apropos of the pleasantness of lingering out-of-doors. They lack alike seriousness of mood and structure; but they are gorgeous little cascades of paint. Dupré, on the contrary, has mood in excess. He too is a rich and dextrous painter, having sat at the feet of Constable, but his pathos is overt and operatic, adapted to untrained sentiments as his effects of ominous coming storms are calculated to impress lazy eyes. Millet's greatness lies in figure painting, but I should not fail to mention that splendid handful of landscapes, in which with a massiveness and richness not inferior to that of his friend Rousseau he achieves a more lucid simplicity. Unlike Rousseau he loves the note of habitation, the ivy-grown churches and wind-beaten granges of his native Normandy. Other French painters who more or

J. F. MILLET: LANDSCAPE, SKETCH

H. D. MARTIN: WESTCHESTER HILLS

Daniel Guggenheim, N. Y.

less grew out of the *milieu*, which is roughly and rather erroneously designated as the Barbizon school are Charles Daubigny, the short-lived Chintreuil, and the veteran Harpignies who carried the tradition well into the twentieth century, quickening it by cautious applications of the Impressionist innovations. Cazin, too, draws strongly from Barbizon, though he develops along lines of restrained tonality akin to Whistler's.

Holland and America have made the most intelligent assimilation of what we may call the standard landscape style. Jacob and Wilhelm Maris and Anton Mauve present landscape with the same intimacy and thoughtfulness, and Jacob Maris in his views of towns attains a rich and satisfying style of his own for which it is difficult to find exact precedents.

By a tempermental coincidence the earlier landscapes of Homer Martin are singularly akin to the gentler mood of Rousseau, similar too in richness of elaboration and beauty of surface. Later, Martin moved along with such transitional artists as Boudin and Whistler, and yet such late masterpieces as the broadly handled prospect of the Adirondacks or the Deserted Manor are again very like the rare unfinished Rousseaus. Alexander H. Wyant consulted with intelligent enthusiasm Rousseau, Diaz, and Corot. The result is possibly too eclectic to be completely satisfying. George Inness made the same studies, but his personal concentration, as mystic and sunworshipper, was sufficient to carry him through. I think the touch of the French school was very light on him till after he had painted the admirably solid Italian landscapes in the early '70s. If so he must count as a self-trained man, getting little from France but the counsel of breadth in vision and in handling. A reckless improvisor and repainter, he seldom achieves any sort of gravity or balance, often loses himself in reckless scintillation, but he has unfailing zest and great skill in reducing to its pictorial elements our somewhat refractory and confusing scenery. I doubt if he would seem quite a great painter outside of America, but he was refreshingly his own man, and possibly the only full blooded Romantic among our landscapists.

Let us turn to France again and consider the case of Courbet. The exhibitionism which is so marked in his figure pieces is much abated in the little landscapes and marines which he did chiefly for his own pleasure. He loved craggy ravines of the Franche-Comté where the deer feed, quarries jutting out over bristling groves, the surf crashing on the shingle. His insistence was on the substance and mass of things. Nobody in our time unless it be the cattle and landscape painter, Constant Troyon, has made the earth look more crumbly and absorbent. As a matter of fact Courbet did not take his landscapes too seriously. He knocked off his gorges and quarries in the studio, seeking chiefly sense of mass with surface richness. Corot taught him the theory of values, but he only half learned the lesson. Some of his best landscapes, like the superb Lake and

COURBET: ROCKS OF ORNANS *Phillips Memorial, Washington, D. C.*

WINSLOW HOMER: NORTHEASTER *Metropolitan Museum*

Falling Snow once in Mr. Kelekian's collection, seem happy accidents, yet in the emphatic assertion of rock and snow and torrent no painter of the century save Winslow Homer equaled him. For the sake of such emphasis of mass and material, Courbet willingly sacrificed variety and charm of color. Indeed his schemes often recall the more conventional painters of the seventeenth century. The color tends to reduce itself to an olive monochrome which at its best is very rich and at its worst merely treacly. In his emphasis upon mass and somewhat brutal simplification of planes he was the precursor of Cézanne and of more recent devotees of volume.

For a summer the swaggering apostle of realism and a very clever young American, James McNeil Whistler, painted together in Brittany. The youngster emulated the solidity of the elder, in one or two marines and in the quite marvelous painting of Westminster Bridge. I think too the influence of Courbet persists through the '60s in the objective rectitude of the Thames etchings. These are Courbet-like in their emphasis of substance, and absence of charm, but the selection is finer and Whistler's own. Already Whistler was studying the magisterial combination of silhouette and enveloping air in Velasquez. For ten years he was chiefly a figure and portrait painter, and his interest in landscape dwindled. Then, in the late '70s and '80s, he astounded London with the famous arrangements, symphonies and nocturnes. The skeleton of the style he drew from

the prints after the Japanese landscapist Hiroshige.
His is the asymetrical balance of diagonal forms, the
plotting of the planes in bold and simple arabesque,
the reduction of color to a dominant with its tones
and tints. The soaking up of objects till they become
mere gracious accidents in a luminous mist, is I
believe derived from Turner's later pictures, and
so will be considered more fully in the chapter on
Impressionism. There could be no more instructive
contrast than a marvelous glimpse of rockets de-
tonating over blue breakers by Turner and say the
Falling Rocket, Cremorne Gardens, or any of the
Thames or Venetian Nocturnes. What appears in
the confrontation is the wholeheartedness and
naïveté of Turner's glamor, as compared with the
anxiously exquisite preciosity of Whistler. He had
such an excess of taste that it nearly effaced the man
in him, and he gave the most unnecessary attention
to tasteless people.

He was so portentous an apparition in late
Victorian London, that his dandyism passed for
greatness with the emancipated Briton. This was a
transvaluation of the real values, for Whistler's
fastidiously reticent art, a thing of whispers and
raised eyelids, is charming, just that, and nothing
more. He gains unfairly from the ambience of the
Royal Academy; as you will certainly overrate an
orchid in a cabbage patch. His lucidity and satire
were useful, in riddling a galvanized official art, but
he had no better æsthetic than the faith that art will

TURNER: MORTLAKE, EARLY MORNING

TURNER: THE WRECK

"happen" by a kind of spontaneous generation of the artist, who is doomed to anti-sociality whether in revolt or in resignation.   Indeed Whistler so typically represents the Romantic cult of the Ivory Tower that it would have been proper enough to treat him as a belated Romantic.   His influence has on the whole tended still further to isolate and effeminate the art of our day.   A delightful mannerist in many phases, in none more so than in the nocturnes, he had little to communicate but his manner, and that when unquickened by his petulant fastidious spirit is merely a kind of satiny veneer.

His authentic ancestor, though he would never have admitted any kind of kinship with the friend of John Ruskin, is Turner.   And Turner is so baffling a theme for criticism that I would gladly omit him, and yet one might as well talk of the cosmos while ignoring the sky.   Turner was the animal shrewdness of Caliban plus the intangibility of Ariel, arbitrarily deposited in the body of an average sensual cockney. His power was so great, his fecundity so extraordinary that, had he had taste, he might have done anything. As it is, the best outlines for the "Liber Studiorum" show the finest apprehension of structure, and the best of the thousands of water-color sheets show not merely a most delicate dexterity but a rare clarity and spaciousness of vision.   Yet the paintings too often reveal at their height all the worst phases of the nineteenth century vice of exhibitionism, with the less tolerable extravagances of English Romanticism.

He was always outpainting somebody, periodically Claude, sometimes Wilson or Gainsborough, again Cuyp, and always Turner. And to outpaint meant simply to put more astounding things into a landscape and to key the color up. Essentially the compositions are fantastic, the product of a feverish competitive mind full of glints of genuine observation of nature, of envied merits of greater painters (generally badly discerned) of shreds of anecdote, personal experience or classical lore. It is one of the major ironies of literature that a most serious person and a most accomplished thinker like John Ruskin could have written five volumes tending to exalt this willfully fantastic and spectacular art for its sober and exemplary realism.

Protean stage manager as Turner usually is, he has intermittently his sincere side. No painter has been more intoxicated by the play of sunlight, rain, mist, and cloud. Probably no painter ever observed these irradiations and swirlings more intensely. He catches the very drive of fine rain in such a remarkable evocation as the locomotive plunging through a shower on a viaduct. Such knowledge lends glamour to the stately funeral progress of the Fighting Téméraire and verisimilitude to the otherwise operatic views of Venice, or to the welter of the Whale Ship.

He is immensely various. You have him anticipating the mood of Whistler's nocturnes in the blue and black of one of his best pictures, The Burial of Wilkie. Premonitory of the luminism of Monet is such a late picture as the Wreck, but the contrasts are more forced and melodramatic and there is a note of power and imagination such as no Impressionist willingly indulges. His undaunted curiosity allies him to the Impressionists, and it is certain that he powerfully influenced Pissarro and Monet. His pearly iridescences hastened the withering of the brown tree. A glance at some of those richly sober landscapes of his early time, like the admirable Saltash in the Metropolitan museum, which anticipates and combines certain perfections of early Corot and Courbet, will remind us how much he renounced. He endeavored to combine the extreme right and the extreme left of Romanticism, willful self expression with naturalism, and the result, however glorified by lights that never were, could only be a kind of splendid and pathetic failure.

So universal a genius as Delacroix inevitably left his mark on landscape. In the backgrounds of his figure pieces he falls back on the decorative methods of Rubens and the Venetians. In his rare outdoor sketches, however, he shows a sensitiveness to the prismatic effects of nature and a delicately strong balance of color that presage the scientific luminism of the next generation. There is a remarkable view of the Channel—fishing smacks scattered over a vast gently moving sea. One might guess it to be some lovely and exceptionally sane phase of Turner, in the 1830's, or, again, a more than commonly exquisite notation of Edouard Manet's in the 1870's. It is, however, dated in the '50s, before such harbingers of luminism as Jongkind and Boudin had announced themselves, and is one of the surprises and delights that Delacroix unfailingly affords.

Painting like this and like Turner's which concerns itself chiefly with facts of light constitutes the radical wing of modern landscape art. Corot, fastidiously choosing in nature the moments that afford a tranquillizing illumination, compromises between the new naturalistic luminism and the old dogma of Belle-nature. But all these early luminists agree in shifting the emphasis from form, mass, texture and pattern—in short from the traditional beauties common to Rubens, Poussin and the Dutch, to sheer light and coruscating color. Rousseau is, on the contrary, the great conservative. He loves light like the rest, but declines to sacrifice to luminosity one whit of substance and texture. He merely enriches the manner of Ruysdael, accepting the conventional color contrasts that are not in nature but are natural to paint. Late Turner and Rousseau are to the nineteenth century what Claude and Ruysdael were to the seventeenth, the champions respectively of irradiation and structural draughtsmanship. It has been our misfortune that our numerous prophets of coruscation have rarely consulted their great ancestor Claude. It would have saved them many gropings. Constable, like our own Inness, veered between the two aims. He mediates between the substantiality of Rousseau and the irresponsible splendor of Turner. His best adjustment is nearest substantiality. He is a moderate type of radical, as Corot is a progressive type of conservative. Such are the main tendencies in landscape painting before the dawn of Impressionism.

I have intentionally kept out of the general survey our perplexingly great marine painter, Winslow Homer. Just an inadequate word on him in passing. Winslow Homer falls out of all critical categories, and would want a chapter to himself. The simplest and perhaps the sanest view of him would be that he is our Courbet. He smashes through to what he perceives as reality. He scorns prettiness and adores force and substance. His beauties, in the old-fashioned sense of texture and tone, seem quite accidental. The Chardinesque loveliness of the great picture Eight Bells is almost unique in his work. Before Cézanne, he loved to see nature as raw planes thrusting and grinding against each other, and he settled at Prout's Neck where nature gave the daily spectacle of the gnawing and gnashing of the sea against the frayed edges of the land. Like Cézanne, of whom I suppose he never heard, he hated nonsense and casual acquaintance with his kind. He had the same gift of plucking a central theme, emphasizing it to the limit and keeping it in focus. His art is mostly bones, and will always be a shade unsatisfactory to epicureans who require succulence. But it is direct, virile and masterly, possibly the most distinctive and original thing America has produced in painting. Indeed our marine painting whether in

Woodbury, or Carlsen or Paul Dougherty has perhaps maintained a higher level of inventiveness than our landscape painting generally. In his lack of relation to the past Winslow Homer belongs to our times and to Impressionism. He may well serve as the foil to the artists we have been considering, and as the introduction to those whom we have yet to consider.

The link between Constable, Corot, Rousseau, Harpignies, Wilhelm Maris, Wyant and Homer Martin, is that their naturalism is qualified by a personal poetry and tempered by a respectful traditionalism. Their art is a delicate compromise between the thing that is seen and memories of similar seeings. In all this work there is a background of authority and funded notions of the beautiful. The art is an adjustment between competing claims, the artist indulges no impulse without considering also its opposite. Thus, despite the isolated estate of many of the landscape painters, their art has social quality, partaking of the general complexity of living; hence the work is rather classic in temper and the common classification of the landscape painters with the Romantic School is in part erroneous. There is rarely what Millet called a "rebel" artist among them, the tragedy and poetry in their lives are humbly interpreted as part and parcel of the tragedy and poetry of the race. This is the habitual note in the blithe Corot as in the saddened Rousseau; it is the attitude of the mystic, George Inness. In the smaller spirits the danger of the attitude is that it readily leads to a feeble eclecticism or to sentimentality. It is the rush away from that pitfall, which has dictated all landscape art from Impressionism on. Hence the real Romantics in landscape, the scorners of compromise, are still ahead of us. And while we shall possibly find them more exciting, we shall hardly find them better company than those chastened great spirits whom, without forgetting, I hope, we now leave behind.

IMPRESSIONISM

IMPRESSIONISM

(1870–1910)

EXALTATION of the individual was the war cry of the Romantic movement. It implied, however, that everything about the individual (head, heart, and hand, for example), was artistic value. Certain eager spirits found this view far too inclusive. Where Romanticism had merely split up the artist into creative spirit and common citizen, artist and bourgeois—these uncompromising analysts required more drastic subdivisions. They continued the task of eliminating the non-æsthetic, and thus carried the cult of impulse to one of its logical extremes. Artistic value, they felt, does not grow out of continuous states of the artist, much less out of his entire æsthetic experience. It consists in brief, intense states of vision. Make of yourself simply an eye; take in passively the fleeting loveliness of an instant; transfer it to canvas before the vision fades—that is the programme of the Impressionist painter. This cult of the instant implies a severe criticism of all academic art. Since the only reality is the momentary sure observation—the retinal image, they loved to call it—the only picture is the record of this observation. The mind and the memory must be kept out of the transaction. Memory blends various observations, mixes up the

183

several pictures, falsifies. Hence away with memory.
Thus arose the cult of the innocent eye. Every time
of seeing was to be a first time, instinct with pristine
ecstasy. There were to be no rules, no methods, no
schools, merely flashes of intensest vision interpreted
by the swiftly obedient hand.

   Evidently Impressionism is merely a realistic phase
of Romanticism. As a matter of fact, it develops
along lines increasingly scientific, contrives the most
ingenious expedients for imprisoning in dull paint the
very coruscation of noon-day sun, the subtler mystery
of moonlight, or the complexities of artificial illumination. We see nothing but degrees of light. Let us
paint only what we see, and ignore what we merely
know, or merely think we know. Certainly this is an
honest and uncompromising programme, and Impressionism has faithfully kept the wholesomeness of its
naturalistic origins. In the doctrine of the innocence
of the eye, Impressionism has gained, or recovered, a
beautiful and valuable experience. It is not surprising
that the Luminist painters—the term is more descriptive of their endeavor than Impressionism—exaggerated the value of their discovery. An innocent
eye is not necessarily the most important qualification
of an artist. Many artists have been well served by a
sophisticated eye. It is important that his eye be
capable of innocence, not that it remain permanently
infantile. Moreover, light, entrancing as is its appeal,
is not the whole of nature, while certain intensities or
ephemeralities of illumination may not be pictorially

available. To paint nature too resolutely may be to
disregard the nature of paint, Mr. MacColl has
wittily said. In short, the Luminist programme may
not be completely practicable; indeed, exactly and
scientifically, it is not.

There is a fundamental fallacy in the notion of
passive vision and the so-called retinal image. Mind
comes more or less into every act of seeing, so why
not admit it generously? What the Luminist calls
the mixing of several pictures, the academic painter
calls the mental enrichment of one picture. And the
academic painter may well be right. In short Luminism may be rather a stage in artistic experience than a
goal. Such it was in the great precursors Rembrandt,
Vermeer, Velasquez. Their names would suggest caution in limiting the effects of art to those of a fine
casualness; caution too in making specific illumination
the most important feature of the work of art.

But enough of analysis. Let us rather return to
the human ardors of the beginnings of the Impressionistic movement. Edouard Manet is not the first
man who saw nature swiftly and in the true terms of
light, but he is in every sense the father of modern
Luminism. Born in 1832, the son of a prosperous
magistrate, his parents sent him to sea in order to
put painting out of his head. He came back bronzed
from South America, only more determined to be a
painter, and wrung from the family their consent to
enter Couture's atelier.

Couture's compromise between academic classicism and the new naturalism was distasteful to the most uncompromising of pupils. Equally distasteful to Couture were the vagaries of a disciple who scorned the grand style, and ostentatiously studied such unacademic masters as Hals, Velasquez and Rembrandt. Couture dealt faithfully with the rash youth. "Go on, my boy," he said, "you'll never be anything more than the Daumier of your time." Manet was not to be deterred by this dire warning. He made so much trouble in Couture's studio, rebelling against the heroic poses of the models, heretically preferring to draw from the clothed model, that in 1856 master and pupil parted.

At twenty-four, Manet was a free-lance in easy circumstances, living on an inheritance. He set himself resolutely to the problem of form. This he conceived in another sense than had the professed realist, Courbet. Form is, for the painter, not what he knows to be, but simply what he sees at a given moment. The eye creates its world not by minute observations, but by swift interpretations of the more significant indications of mass. Resolve form into its constructive planes, find a reasonable equivalent for these planes in paint, and your picture is done. The eye will infer the mass creatively from such indications with far more zest and conviction than any minute inventory can arouse. Thus the *tache*, the spot of paint exactly tinted and shaped and balanced with all the other planes of the composition, came to be Manet's formula. He had rediscovered from

Musée Des Arts Décoratifs, Paris

MANET: DÉJEUNER SUR L'HERBE

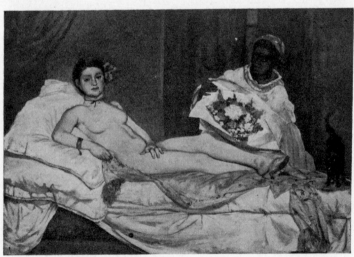

Louvre

MANET: OLYMPE

his study of Velasquez, Hals and Tintoretto the secret of synthetic painting, of really creating form in color as distinguished from merely charting form in line. The Guitar Player, exhibited in the Salon of 1861, is a strange blend of the technic of Hals with something of the tragic mood of Goya. The solidity and daring of the picture attracted the praise of Théophile Gautier. Manet seemed headed for prizes and popularity.

It was together with the rapidity, the hardness and casualness of his vision that finally repelled the public, and still does. The visible world evoked in him an unlimited curiosity but no more personal emotion. Personally a delightful and considerate man of the world, professionally he seemed to regard nothing but his own eye. His great picture of 1863, Déjeuner sur l'herbe, has never been forgiven. It was unpardonable to transfer to modern times a motive which we all approve in Giorgione, nude women and clothed men in reverie amid a beautiful nature. The poetry of the thing lulls and contents us in Giorgione's Pastoral Symphony. Manet has substituted for the full poetry of Giorgione a rather sullen pensiveness. For the rest, the splendid nude in the foreground is painted with an explicit incisiveness which any academician might envy. The reclining artists are brushed in with a square touch which Couture himself could not equal, the landscape setting is conventionally, and one would say inoffensively rural. The whole thing is restrained and experimental, a little dry, with nothing of the sheer richness of Manet in it, except the fine confusion of smock, corset and food in the left foreground.

Why the most intelligent and experimental of peoples should have been outraged by this most experimental and intelligent work is hard to see. It is simply a superlatively fine example of what the Parisian artist humorously calls a "Machine," a thing deliberately made for exhibition. Exhibited it was, but not in the Salon. The famous *Salon des refusés*, which harbored Cazin, Harpignies, Jongkind, Legros, Fantin, Pissarro and Whistler made of Manet's rejected pastoral its chief sensation.

In 1864 Manet exhibited in the Salon, Angels at the Tomb of Christ, and The Bull Fight, both rather striking pictures, which won little comment. In 1865 he once more flew into the face of the salon-visiting public with his notorious Olympe. If any one had predicted that in less than fifty years the unspeakable hussy would knock at the doors of the Louvre, and be admitted, such a prophet would have passed for a madman. Doubtless when Manet painted Olympe very white and shadowless against a white sheet he was thinking of the Nude Maya of Goya which he had recently seen and copied in Madrid. Where he sinned was in not imitating Goya to the extent of making Olympe alluring. Manet views his model with something of the fascinated contempt and curiosity which his friend Charles Baudelaire bestowed on womankind. In

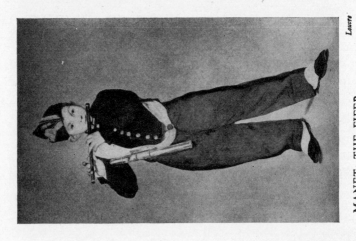

MANET: THE FIFER

MANET: THE BALCONY

fact the Paris of Napoleon III sniffed Baudelaire's
diabolism in the picture. Why the negro maid?
Why, O why, the black cat? Everybody thought
the worst, and even the eloquent and closely reasoned
championship of a stalwart young critic, Emile Zola,
did little to help matters. It was too clear that Manet
had offended unforgivably against certain artistic
fashions. Nudes were pink and pliant; Olympe
was white and hard. Nudes were rather graceful and
alluring; Olympe was somewhat awkward, stiff and
repellent. Nudes never had character, or were
any one, or existed in recognizable surroundings;
Olympe had unmistakable character of a dubious
sort, was distinctly some one, existed amid palpable
bed fittings, bouquets, handmaids and pets. These
considerations were naturally bothersome to devotees
of the generalized academic nude. What they might
after all have had eyes to see was the extraordinary
refinement and strength of a modeling which rested
on infinitesimal differences of bright color, and the
flower-like loveliness of the whites—all cream and
carnation and lilac in cautious iridescences. But
those things escaped the Paris that barely tolerated
Corot, while scorning Daumier, Rousseau and Millet.
Olympe definitely made of her master and creator an
artistic pariah. In retirement he painted the pictures
that all the world now knows—the Toreadors, the
Bon Bock, the Boy with the Sword, and that picture
which anticipates and includes much of Whistler—
the Girl with a Parrot.

Gradually, however, he was gaining support from the strongest young painters. In 1870 Fantin-Latour painted that Atelier aux Batignolles, with Manet at the easel, surrounded by Monet, Renoir and Bazille, with the critics Zola and Astruc. A little before that time, Manet's aim had changed. Indoor light no longer satisfied him. He moved out of doors. His style becomes feather-like in touch and blonde in tone. We have from the late '60s and '70s a few fresh and vibrant marines, with rarer attempts at full sunlight as that remarkable picture En Bateau which commemorates the youthful George Moore and one of those temporary passions of which he has made excellent literary capital. Meanwhile, as his health failed, Manet did fewer large works but solaced his eye and steadied his now trembling hand by doing the most remarkable still-lifes. In his last years his preoccupation turned to artificial light, and in that miracle of technic, the Bar of the Folies Bergères, he broke the road that has been so brilliantly followed by Degas, Zorn, Kroyer, Sargent and a host of others.

When he died at fifty-one, in 1883, a very sensitive gentleman, and a loyal friend, left the world. He had suffered in silence under twenty years of ridicule and abuse. Completely misunderstood, it availed nothing to explain himself as he did in the catalogue of his private exhibition in 1867. He wrote: "M. Manet has always recognized talent where he has met with it, and he has no pretensions either to overthrow an established mode of painting or to create a new one. He has simply tried to be himself and not another." His best biographer, Théodore Duret, sums up the case in the words, "The dissensions which arose between him and the public proceeded from a difference of vision. Manet did not see as others saw; he and they perceived the same images differently. Now, in the variance of opinion the painter was right.

"Manet was a painter born. He saw the world in a brilliance of light to which other eyes were blind; he transfixed on canvas the sensations which were flashed on his eyes. The process was an unconscious one, since what he saw depended simply upon his physical organism."

It would be impossible to put the fallacy of Impressionism or the limitations of Manet's art more tersely than M. Duret has done in these last words. There is no seeing which depends solely and simply on our physical organism. The mind and memory more or less enter in, or we see nothing. It would be truer to follow Manet's friend, George Moore, in regarding Manet as a supreme expression of the will to paint. "In him there is nothing but good painting." This is very near the whole truth. The acute vision and the masterful hand are all of Manet. He declined to think or feel much about the visible world; he chose his subject-matter almost casually. There is no humanity in his work and little charm, but there is abundant brace and surprise in it. All artists who overvalue the innocence of their eyes and hate too much what they call the nonsense of sentiment have inevitably drawn from him. There is much of him in Zorn and Kroyer, such talented Spaniards as Zuloaga and Angalada have profited by him. Whistler was not free from his influence, nor was John Sargent. Such robust young American talents as Glackens, Henri, and George Bellows have found their chief schooling in the study of Manet. His last open-air phase leads to that uncompromising Luminism with which we must now concern ourselves.

Because Manet was a pregnant spirit, living valiantly by the maxims of Impressionism, I have dwelt at length on his work. The word Impressionism and the complete development of the Luminist programme were reserved for certain young friends of his, Claude Monet and Camille Pissarro. These were the chief talents among the eager group that for four years before the disastrous year, 1870, gathered nightly about Manet at the Café Guerbois. Yet perhaps the future will be more concerned with other attendants, Paul Cézanne and Auguste Renoir. The critic Burty, a pioneer of the Japanese cult, was with Zola a frequenter of these discussions. The sedate and accomplished Fantin-Latour helped moderate the wrangling. Sardonic young Edouard Degas came occasionally and so did that very open-minded darling of contemporary fashion, Alfred Stevens. At the Café Guerbois, the talk was of planes, and tones and values, and of reverberation and division of colors. Wherever the debate drifted it in-

MANET: FISHING BOATS

JONGKIND: RIVER VIEW

evitably came back to the mystery and problem of light.

Constable, Jongkind, and Boudin had already used broken color freely, Monticelli most audaciously so, in his decorative gallantries—but all these precursors were tinged with tradition and with studio formulas. The young lions of the Café Guerbois accepted no compromise. They wanted to paint light, as it intrinsically is, a shadowless glare, a living incandescence, and not as a false contrast between extremes of light and dark which do not exist in nature. Manet had already essayed his out-of-door manner, and his example was potent in the group. He weaned Cézanne and Renoir from an early allegiance to Courbet, he aided Claude Monet both spiritually and materially. But Manet had never considered the problem of illumination as anything different from the problem of form. He merely brightened his palette and made the old planes more coruscating. Claude Monet, in a sense in which Rembrandt had half anticipated him, was to make the problem of light the sole problem of painting, form being incidental, unimportant, and pretty well left to take care of itself. As in later times he loved to insist, he painted not objects, but the veil of air that intervened between them and his eye. Thus although the term Impressionism arose in connection with Monet's work, following the excellent critic Gustave Geffroy I shall call him rather a Luminist.

It was the war that brought the new quest of incandescence to clarity. It scattered widely the friends of the Café Guerbois. For the master, Manet, it committed the inconsequence of relegating him to the military staff of the embattled academician, Meissonier; for Pissarro and Monet it meant a flight to London and the fructifying vision of Turner. In Turner's fantastic masterpieces in the National Gallery, the two young Luminists found very nearly the Ariel art of their dreams. Here were pictures in which solid objects swam in solution of translucent color asserting circumambient air. Certain expedients of Turner's developed art they immediately adopted; his white ground, his rejection of the traditional murky browns and blacks. Camille Pissarro, a prudent and intellectual Jew, declined to go the whole gorgeous way of dissolution with Turner. Pissarro's art remains exemplary of the saner applications of the Luministic hypothesis. The humanist in him refused to capitulate to the Impressionist. Claude Monet, on the contrary, returned to Paris with his peculiar vision highly accentuated, determined to see the world only as a swirling torrent of light, and art merely as the transcription of the eddies and forcelines of the perpetual flux. He abandoned the manner he had acquired from Manet. Color and light he saw with the intensity of one rapt between dream and waking. Having set himself an almost impossible aim, it remained to contrive possible means for its expression, and here the latent scientist in the man came out.

Ruskin had shown the dilemma of the artist who

would paint light. The brightest color on the painter's canvas is dull and dark compared to the lesser
brightnesses of nature. Thus the artist can only
transpose the effects of nature to a limited scale.
Suppose the difference of the blue-black mouth of a
cave and the disk of the noonday sun to be in nature
one hundred degrees of light. The painter at most
controls only five such degrees. His task is one of
clever transposition and inspired adjustment. He is
in a position of a musician who must render a piano-
forte sonata on some instrument of very limited
register, as the flute. It was with this inexorable
fact that young Monet dared to cope. In his solution
he was aided by the American student of optics,
Prof. Rood and by the French physicist, Chevreul.
They had both noted the superior luminosity of
broken color, the greater clarity of tones combined by
the eye over those mixed on the palette. From these
suggestions Monet evolved the procedure variously
called broken color, *pointillisme*, divisionism, etc. The
scheme is simple. Instead of making violet by mixing
up a blue and a red, put the blue and red in dots
or streaks side by side on the canvas and let the
eye, at the proper remove, mix them for itself. A
color will result which is not dead and painty, but
vibrant and full of light. The method admits of many
refinements. If the violet is to be warm, yellow
dots may be introduced into the web; if cold, white
dots. Such is the prismatic procedure, a sort of Morse
code for the transmission of light through paint.

MONET: ROAD TO VETHEUIL

MONET: HAYSTACKS

Monet applied it enthusiastically in the open air. Since every shift of light meant a new vision and a new picture, he drove out into the fields provided with a score of canvases, painting on each only as long as a particular effect of light lasted. Thus mere convenience, reinforced by the fact that only the light counted anyway, led to those first notorious and now famous series, the Haystacks, the Poplars, the Cathedrals, the Cliffs at Belle Isle, the Gardens, the Lily Pools, the Thames Bridges. The real theme is the splendor of sunlight, and we may accurately call this sort of luminism sunlight impressionism. The first view of these coruscating pictures enraged both the public and the critics. Here was a mere omelet, a crazy spilling of paint. When in 1874 Monet and a score of his friends ventured on a separate exhibition, the humorous *Charivari* threw the term of abuse, Impressionists, at the innovators. It meant creatures of foolish impulse, devoid of sense and reflection. In 1877 the Impressionists had the courage to exhibit as a body and to accept their bad name proudly. Already the critics were timidly rallying to their support, and far-sighted dealers like M. Durand-Ruel were providing the sinews of war. By the '80s Impressionism looked more menacing than ridiculous, by the '90s it was beginning to be fashionable. In 1877 Manet had proposed to aid Monet by buying ten pictures at 100 francs each. Less than twenty years later, Monet was heading the subscription to buy Manet's Olympia for the nation.

Meanwhile the doctrine of Luminism and modifications of the procedure of broken color had gone around the world. One can mention only a few of the Luminists who have excelled in landscape. Alfred Sisley, a less intransigeant figure than Monet, carried into France something of the winsomeness of his half-English character. He had learned much from late Constable. Guillaumin carried the cult of glare to its highest intensity. In Italy Segantini combined a scientific divisionism with a mysticism all his own. In England George Clausen was one of the first practitioners of the new technic. In Germany Max Lieberman. The American Theodore Robinson learned direct from Monet as early as the '90s. Childe Hassam has carried the method to a mature perfection. Aside from readily classifiable Impressionists, few of the more progressive modern painters have escaped the influence. They may or may not adopt the exact technic, but they accept the vision of light as king. Sensitiveness to effects of light, skill in rendering them, this has been the highest merit in painters who otherwise are diverse enough. Whether one thinks of Fjaested in Scandinavia, or Sorolla in Spain, or Mancini in Italy, or of our own Tarbell, Redfield, or Lawson we have to do always with phases of Luminism.

Thus Claude Monet has lived to see his conception of art become in its turn almost tyrannically academic. It is a turn which can little please the most open-minded and modest of masters. To estimate the gain

and loss from the universal lurch into Luminism is
difficult. We may perhaps take as our starting point
two opposite judgments. The brilliant German
critic, Meier-Graefe, bids us think eugenically of the
art of the future and so tie ourselves connubially to
the healthiest art of the present. "For such reasons,"
he writes, "this modern French is to be commended.
She is the youngest and healthiest, and we must not
reject her because she is but moderately endowed
with nobility of feeling and moral sense." Against
this hopeful view we may set the cheerless verdict of
George Moore: "The separation of the method of
expression from the idea to be expressed is the sure
sign of decadence. France is now all decadence. In
the Champ de Mars, as in the Salon, the man of the
hour is he who has invented the last trick in subject
or treatment . . . for many a year nothing will come
to us from France but the bleat of the scholiast."

The truth is likely to be somewhere between these
extreme opinions. On second thought Meier-Graefe
would probably admit that nobility of feeling and
moral sense are after all desirable in a mother; George
Moore possibly does not mean to imply that the cult
of the splendor of light is decadent. Both agree in
emphasizing the anti-intellectual quality of Impressionism. It is a defect which it shares with the
Romantic movement generally. Emphasis is set not
on the individual as a whole, including his social
relations, but upon a highly specialized faculty. The
visual experience upon which Impressionism rests

RENOIR: ARGENTEUIL

WHISTLER: CREMORNE GARDENS

is so intense and beautiful that we are likely to forget
how narrow it is, how life-denying. It is perhaps
ungracious to repeat that the isolated ecstatic moment
of vision is simply a psychological fallacy. Association will not be denied, and there is invariably more
or less overlapping from state to state. At best the
Impressionist minimized this overlapping, and that
was enough to produce a very bracing and novel
type of art.

The sacrifice of the form and mass of things implied
in the thoroughgoing luminism of Claude Monet
seems excessive. Light and air are fascinating, but
are they the only valuable experience in our visual
life? The deliquescence of form in the Monets of
the middle period attests not only a mind too much in
abeyance but also a vision overstimulated by mere
reverie. There is something hectic in the charm of
this work. Renoir's landscapes of the same time are
more achieved and considered, indeed representational
painting of landscape has nothing finer to show.
Monet was at once too scientific and too lyrical to
cope objectively with appearances.

Such reservations should not affect a conviction
that Impressionism has generally been a sound and
wholesome movement. It has austerely checked
individual vagary by reference to the actual data of
vision. It has attempted and relatively achieved a
fine naturalism. It has substituted for a decrepit
tradition a living quest. If it has been defective
precisely on the side of society and tradition, it has

C. PISSARRO: THE WILLOWS

SIGNAC: SEAPORT

been so consciously; it has had the uncommon grace
of knowing what it was about.

Concerning the technical procedures of the Luminists not much need be said. Candidly the rougher
stippling of Monet was simply an execrable way
of painting. Everything that is fine in texture and
handling, all the supererogatory graces of the painter's art, were sacrificed to effect at a particular range.
It was a heavy and unhandy way of painting. Often
it missed the more deep and precious qualities of
light and substituted a bleak chalkiness. Nothing
could be intrinsically uglier, for example, than the
treacly streakiness of the Rouen Cathedral series.
Moreover through the reckless use of ill understood
pigments and the creation of surfaces ideally contrived
to trap dust many of the Luminist pictures have already faded. With the disappearance of their delicate
transitions nothing much is left. These canvases age
badly, and I am often appalled at the virtual disappearance of pictures which thrilled me only thirty
years ago. In short, in much of the work the dogma
of the particular moment of vision and of the particular point of view of the spectator is pushed to an
extreme. Monet in his ripest work has been perfectly
conscious of the fact, for in the Lily-Pools and in the
Thames pictures he has adopted a method of great
suavity, admitting the painter-like manipulation of
the brush. Moreover most of his ablest followers, as
Twachtman in America, have departed from the strict
recipe of the dash and dot.

Alongside of Luminism, or in more ordinary phrase sunlight impressionism, there throve a twilight art of great refinement and charm. It also finds its precedents in the last phase of Turner, its most accomplished expressions in the art of Whistler, Cazin, Carrière, and Le Sidaner. In its later phase a conscious school of blur and twilight developed; calling itself Intimism. The relations of this penumbral art to Impressionism are not obvious. It avoids high colors and streaking of colors, all particular tricks of the brush, is not blaring but highly reticent. Moreover it is not wholly naturalistic, but very regardful of compositional pattern and style. It is somewhat traditional also, being influenced by Velasquez and Rembrandt.

Despite these differences, I think we do well to regard this crepuscular art as a form of Impressionism. Its basis is searching observation of actual effects of reduced light. This element of research and discovery is impressionistic. Impressionistic also it is to win the effect of specific illumination not by studio conventions, forcing the contrasts of light and dark, but by infinite subtleties comprised within a few tones. Thus I feel that the art which is most effectively represented by Whistler's nocturnes and arrangements and symphonies is a branch of Impressionism. It is, however, more mental and traditional than the Impressionism of Manet and Monet. The example of the Japanese landscapists counts for much, as does possibly that of the brown and gray

tonalists of Holland,—Van Goyen and Willem van der
Velde, and of the gray-and-blue tonalists of Venice,—
Antonio Canale and Francesco Guardi. But here
again the precedents are themselves most delicately
naturalistic.

Whistler very slowly developed this vein. His
earliest landscapes, the Normandy sea pieces, the
amazing Westminister Bridge, have the solidity and
frankness of Courbet. Whistler had worked with
him. The series of Japanese fantasies, the White
Girls, culminating in that loveliest of all his works,
The Little White Girl, and The Music Room, are
merely very intelligent expressions of the new academic theory of the *morceau bien peint*. They are
tours de force of arrangement and texture. Alfred
Stevens magnified is the thought that arises before
them. The great portraits, The Mother, the Carlyle,
Miss Alexander, Rosa Corder, Théodore Duret—
a few masterpieces amid many failures—mark an
advance. The leading influence is Velasquez in
his last phase. The ambience of gray air is what
counts,—envelopment. The form is an inference.
You get it by looking very hard at very slight indications. The art is one of fine and accurate suggestion. Here it parts company with Manet, who,
though working along similar lines, is always explicit.
This twilight intentness produced a few great portraits, and has been a demoralizing influence ever
since. There is no value in dim light unless you can
fill it full of thought, observation and sentiment.

With the nocturnes which were mostly painted in the '70s Whistler, without relinquishing that decorative intention which had ever been imperative with him, advances towards a kind of naturalism. It is unlike the naturalism, say, of a Pissarro or a Monet, in being painted not before nature but in the studio. Indeed the effect depends so much on memory and taste, on a sort of transfiguration of actual appearances— that one might feel the appeal is purely to reverie. But since Whistler would have stoutly denied this, and since he never fails to emphasize the actual truthfulness of these night pieces, we may well accept them at his own valuation.

His success in discovering in nature the intimations of certain preferred decorative arrangements of his own mind was remarkable. How lasting it will be is another question. It is a bit dangerous to let us into the secret of seeing in blue and gold or rose and gray. Nature, as he once predicted, may catch up with Whistler. In short these evanescent charms of twilight and moonlight may after all be fitter for direct observation than for mediated enjoyment through pictures. We must make up our minds before the nocturnes and symphonies perish. Many of them are painted in such bad material and technic, that they will hardly survive our century. It is no fault of the fastidious genius of Whistler that it has wrought havoc as an influence. In Whistler's name has thriven an art of fog and evasion, offering little but sentiment; and of that not much that was worth while. He did a rather small thing amazingly well, and in retrospect I fear his delightful art will diminish. It hung too much on his wit and personal legend. He had the magnificent background of Victorian London and the Royal Academy. His exotic brilliance too easily dominated such a scene.

The suspicion of amateurism which ever attaches to Whistler is entirely absent from other twilight impressionists—Cazin and Eugène Carrière. Cazin, a most versatile landscapist, is a kind of link between the Barbizon school and the Impressionists. He prefers attenuated color and the evening hour, but he interrogates these effects with a most searching interest. His reticence covers knowledge and strength.

Such is the case with Eugène Carrière. He paints his portraits and portrait groups in a penumbra that half veils the forms, but one divines the traits of a resolute and passionate draughtsmanship. He conceived the luminous mist which invests his creations quite mystically as a universal medium in which move the forces of love and sympathy. He never could be induced to paint any one whom he did not esteem. Thus he left an incomparably sensitive series of portraits, Verlaine, Rodin, his own family. The very intimate portrait of Alphonse Daudet and his little daughter represent the mood not in its most poignant but in its finest expression. The mysticism of Carrière should not make us ignore that fund of actual observation of twilight truths which after all links the work, if remotely, to Impressionism.

More recently Alfred le Sidaner and others have carried forward the style of Whistler and Carrière in the manner called Intimism. George Fuller in America developed the mode independently. Very talented American artists like the late Wilton Lockwood and John W. Alexander have brought the style to a fine personal expression. There is a small sweet charm about this type of work in general which often evokes the unkind thought that the mystery and reticence may suggest more sentiment than is really there.

We have lingered long enough in these twilight regions. The main business of Impressionism was after all simply to let in the light. It has done so triumphantly. It has compelled all manner of painters to consult the actual look of the thing, and to eschew habits and even graces of the studio that natural appearances do not warrant. The narrower procedure, that one must paint fleeting effects in the open air, or that one must stipple in prismatic colors, have not necessarily been followed. The artist merely has been compelled to see like an Impressionist, otherwise retaining full liberty of action. A genuine naturalism has replaced pretty much all the traditional formulas. By anticipation I have treated already the absorption of Impressionistic vision and methods by academically trained artists. Zorn and Sargent, water-colorist; Liebermann and Sorolla, Lucien Simon, Frieseke, Alden Weir, Charles Woodbury, Tarbell, Mary Cassatt—these are so many examples of painters who without departing from the older notions of the mental picture, have scrupulously renovated their art by closer reference to the look of things. Indeed this process has been so universal that outside of the necessarily conventional fields of decoration and portraiture, it has become difficult for any artificial beauty—and most of the beauty of art has hitherto been artificial—to hold up its head.

It is perhaps still too early to appraise Impressionism justly. Yet the lines of a decision may be indicated. Fundamentally we are weighing two kinds of enjoyment, of diverse æsthetic satisfactions. Let us ask ourselves what happens when a well trained person enjoys let us say a fine Ruysdael and a fine Monet. I have in mind that extraordinary masterpiece, the Jewish Cemetery, at Dresden. First one is aware of the whole thing, the ghostly light on crumbling monuments as a torrent rushes below and storm clouds press ominously over the dark canopy of great oaks. The sudden pathos of it grips one. Then the eye travels about in the picture, more or less investigating and verifying the first impression. It may delight in the crisp severity of the silhouette of the trees, in the tumble and drive of the clouds, in the heavy rush of the torrent, in the masterly indications of plant growth in the foreground. During such investigation the sense of the whole thing is somewhat in abeyance. But I think a good picture-seër always keeps some consciousness of the whole even in close study of the parts. Besides asking what one sees and in what order, there may be a similar recognition of what one feels. Goethe standing before this great picture was oppressed by a sense of that ruthlessness in eternally self-renewing nature, by which not merely man but even his most permanent memorials yield to the storms while frost and roots attack the most durable foundations. Did this vision—this nightmare, if you will—of an inconscient nature ever striving to efface man, help Goethe to see the picture or not? Doubtless every reader who has attended an art school will repudiate the process as a sentimentalism. It is a matter which we must discuss. Meanwhile after our excursion into the particulars of this landscape and into the recesses of our own emotions, we may come back once more to the general impression. We shall find it confirmed and enriched. I have been describing what happens in appreciation of all pictures painted by analytical methods.

An Impressionistic picture, say one of the Thames pictures of Monet, is seen in quite a different fashion. The whole thing grasps one, then without losing the central theme, without shifting the eye or change of focus the forms and spaces establish themselves more strongly till the maximum of effect is reached, when it is high time to look away. The art of vision is more intense and concentrated. The concern is simply with the thing seen, there is no analysis of it and next to no appeal to reinforcing memories. This is the way one sees a Velasquez, a Whistler, a Monet, a Mancini.

Comparing the two ways of seeing pictures, which

is best? Most moderns will choose the Impressionistic way, precisely for its unity and intensity. They will say that the old fashion of alternately looking to the whole and to the parts of any picture is to see so many pictures, hence no real picture at all. Your first interpretation of the whole composition, your survey of the parts, your revised apprehension of the whole, are so many different experiences, and all extra-pictorial. Similarly, the appeal to visual or emotional memories is again a contamination, a false substitution of other images for that which is actually under the eye. The impressions of art should be self-subsistent and self-contained the æsthetes of modern type will insist, like that of music. Has not Walter Pater once for all laid it down that all the arts aspire to the freedom of music? Such in effect is the Impressionist argument.

I do not think it is necessary to take sides. Evidently those satisfactions that depend on concentrated vision, *pure* seeing, are only to be attained impressionistically. And the magical beauties of painting are best evoked along these lines. To put mind and life in abeyance to the eye as Chardin did, as Cézanne did in his still-lifes, is to attain the keenest and purest pleasures of the eye. But this may not be the sole pleasure that painting properly affords. As it allies itself with emotions, ideas, memories, of all sorts, it requires an expression at once more highly organized and articulated and less synthetized than that of Impressionism. The art grows out of a com-

plex of vision and memory and must itself be complex.
It took time and analysis to paint John Sargent's
extraordinary decoration of the Sacrament, it will
take time and analysis to appreciate it.   It will not
bloom gradually on one's passive vision like a cathedral front by Claude Monet, for its appeal is both
visual and extra-visual, and the parallel experiences
of sight and emotion-memory must be adjusted into a
kind of composite visual poetry by the spectator, as
by the artist in the task of creation.

In fact the legitimacy of the old-fashioned way of
taking in a picture—which should be clearly distinguished from a mere casual ogling that is destructive
of all pictorial effect—this legitimacy is best vin-
dicated by recalling that the spectator does in epitome
and without halt what the artist did slowly and by
process of trial and error.   When I take in the serene
beauty of Puvis's staircase decorations in the Boston
Public Library, feel their large serenity, then, with the
general impression still in the corner of my eye, observe
the lovely and thoughtful detail, and the articulation
of the panels as a series, and then come back with
enhanced admiration to the whole, when I do this, am
I not actually repeating the creative process by which
Puvis himself, with a clear but incomplete vision of
the whole, studied the parts until he wrought them
into dignity and loveliness and right articulation,
until once more the whole, now fully enriched and
completed, stood forth in its destined beauty?

Indeed is not such a process of appreciation and

of creation really more akin to music than is the swifter æsthetic transaction of the Impressionist? We have the thin, precise, unelaborated presentation of the theme, followed by the subordinate themes and variations, and finally the resumption of all these incomplete satisfactions in the enriched restatement of the central theme. As you study any well conceived monumental painting, say Watts's Jurisprudence in Lincoln's Inn, London, or John La Farge's Transfiguration, your eye and mind trace in small precisely the curve that your ear and mind do in enjoying a Beethoven Sonata. Contrariwise, in Impressionistic vision, what you get is not a complex organization needing much time or aid of memory to sustain its effect, but something like the swelling and vanishing of a single rich chord. It is musical only to the extent that this is a musical experience, or only on condition of reducing music to a continuum of unorganized tones.

And the end of the matter seems to be that one should quarrel neither with the intensest use of the eye nor yet with the widest use of the mind in painting. No exclusive domination can in the nature of the case belong to either. There is no painting worthy of note without a fine and considerate act of vision, and there is no painting, notable or otherwise, from which the mind can wholly be excluded. There is a kind of painting in which the memory part of the mind is relatively in abeyance in favor of the present vivid moment. A wholesome and lovely art has

grown out of this preference. But the richer and more
complex impressions of art, particularly of monumental painting, require a fuller coöperation of the mind
and memory. In the past century the mind and the
memory were so often stupidly used, in routine
anecdote or banal symbolism, that mind and memory
have seemed to be the painter's lurking foes. There
could be no sorer error. No picture was ever harmed
by intelligence either in creator or spectator. Harm
comes from the stupid use of mind in painting, as
elsewhere. Imperfect attainment naturally comes
from the intelligence of persons who paint without
the painter's gift of eye and hand. Generally speaking what is disagreeable in a bad and pretentious
picture is not mind but the false pretension thereof.
Fromentin has admirably written:

"Any work of art which has been deeply felt by its
maker is also naturally well painted. And any work
of art in which the hand reveals itself in felicity or in
splendour is through that alone a work belonging to
the brain, or has its origin in it."

But the paths for the mind to follow are many.
Fromentin has again set the case in his delightful
book on the African desert. With a friend he saw a
market place with the sun high, and deserted except
for playing children. He asks, Where is the picture?
"Is it these children playing in the sunlight, or is it a
place in the sunlight in which children are playing?"
Here are sharply opposed the impressionistic and the
humanistic possibilities of the theme. The picture

can be a vision of Levantine glamor with childhood quite incidental, or it can be childhood with the Orient merely hinted at or even ignored. And if the playing children were taken out of the sunlight and expressed in red clay against the polished black of a Grecian urn, it might still be great design, fine painting, consummate art.

To end a discussion too much protracted, though still only fragmentary, the militant maxims and the psychology of Impressionism are mostly partial or false. Impressionism itself is rather a means than an end, a desirable stage in every artistic experience, a crowning stage only in the artist whose life is imperfectly intellectualized. Within its limitations, it has provided the keenest of transient ecstacies of the eye, it has shattered the stupider academic pretensions. It is become in its turn a beautiful convention, for a moment it bid fair to be an exclusive convention, and that would have been unfortunate indeed for the progress of painting. For if it is not a good convention to overcoddle the mind with tonics and stimulants, neither is it a good convention habitually to kick the mind downstairs. It is too simple a solution for what is a very complex and delicate problem. I may best warn you against too simple formulas, by quoting from my old mentor, John La Farge, a passage which finely shows what a composite is really the simplest act of artistic appreciation. It is a thing to bear in mind as you consider the alluringly unitary formulas of the new painting.

La Farge was discussing the effect, mind you, of a quite impressionistic sketch, a Turner marine. He writes in that admirable book "Considerations on Painting":

"The illusion suggested by the artist's work is directed by him, but mostly made by us; that we no longer see his mere piece of canvas, when he tells us that it is a hollow mirror of the world; that the marks he makes upon the piece of gray or white paper become to us memories of what we have seen or desired to see; and that, though I know that this is Naples yellow, that that is cobalt, that I can name each colour and each mixture of colour, in the five minute sketch that Turner puts on a bit of Whatman, I can at the same time that I see them all separately, the paper, the kind of color, the paint and brush-marks, see also the blue Mediterranean basking in the southern sun."

Such thoughts of a wise and searching spirit I commend to you at a moment when on every side one hears that art is very limited, fractional and specialized. Do not believe it. Art is just as broad and fine and complex as is the human spirit itself, of which art is merely one of the highest and most comprehensive expressions.

GREAT TRADITIONALISTS

GREAT TRADITIONALISTS

THE task of classification grows more difficult with the greatness of the thing classified. It is so with the painters of our times. We have seen that while many artists seem readily to fall under such categories as Academic, Romantic, Impressionistic, the boundaries are not rigid. Delacroix, for example, we must consider as Arch-Romantic primarily, but also as mural decorator, and as precursor of Impressionism. In such cases one can only try to discern the master tendency of the artist. In the case of several very great geniuses, and some who, without being so great, are geniuses all the same, the task of analysis is difficult in the extreme. This may mean merely that their geniuses are too broad to be readily held within our categories and too individual to be docketed in logical bundles. But precisely the depth and sweep of these great artists is a reason for getting our thinking in order as regards them and for carrying our feeling about them through first stages of fervidly confused adoration to something like clearness. For after all it is the homage that knows what it is about, and has considered alternatives, that counts.

As we have followed the course of the century you will have missed certain notable figures. The sensuous reverie of Prud'hon, an alien perfume amid the

223

arid sublimities of the Empire, could not be readily stamped as classic, romantic or what not. Similarly the art of the ill-fated sculptor-painter, Alfred Stevens, escapes contemporary classifications.

Nor can George Frederick Watts's art so subtly compounded of dream and waking mind, thriving paradoxically again amidst the thin poetry and thinner prose of Victorian painting, be readily set down under any general caption. And so the solemn and gracious idyllism of Millet has a note apart from that of his contemporaries. There is a similar isolation in the finest phase of Whistler. Are the portraits of his Mother and Miss Alexander impressionistic? There is an evident absurdity in such a designation. Again the austerely charming work of Whistler's friend Fantin-Latour—how classify it? It is a thing apart. He never let himself be caught in movements of any sort. Auguste Renoir superficially is an Impressionist, at least he mastered that kind of art, but there is no master of the century who so fully embodies all that was greatest in eighteenth century France and earlier in Rubens. Edouard Degas again controls all the resources of Luminism, but stands apart from it technically in virtue of his impeccable linear draughtsmanship; and spiritually apart also, in virtue of his clear and bitter observation of states of mind. Finally the quiet classicism of René Menard is not superficially to be rated as academic, it wants a finer analysis to detect under the formula the lucid force of the controlling emotion.

Now what to do with these exceptional artists has been my urgent problem. It might seem logical to accept the fact of isolation, and to give an essay each to the greater figures, omitting or merely glancing at the others. But the scope of this book forbids such a solution. Perforce I have had to look for some bond between geniuses quite disparate in accomplishment and in power. Could there be any genuine tie of heart and mind between these artists whom we have thrown together simply because they do not fit elsewhere? Yes, there seems to be a real bond in the resolute traditionalism of each and all of these men. From Prud'hon to Renoir we find that all these men consented to life in the present, and gladly linked it with the past.

The element of revolt and of deliberate self-assertion is as absent from the art of Millet as it is from that of Fantin. Whistler, habitually self-assertive, only enters this class exceptionally when dominated by affection, admiration and the fortifying vision of the past. Watts lived habitually in a mood of Olympian reflection, the outer eye on the marbles of the Parthenon, the inner eye on the idealisms of his time. About all these men there was the strongest sense that they were merely continuing something. That sense of a first time, all that we mean by the innocence of the eye, all that is implied in Impressionism and Romanticism was alien to them. Their eyes were brimming with memories of great painting and great visions of nature. That state of things they welcomed. Millet looks superficially like an innovator. But one of the beautiful things about his art is, that he never took the slightest credit for discovering the peasant, never descended to showmanship. What seemed wonderful to him was the immemorial existence and toil of the peasant, not himself as perceiving it. It is the simplicity of the man that sets him apart from those Romantic painters with whom he is often carelessly included. And for all the novelty of the art of Millet—a novelty which bothered and offended his generation—it is cast in a most traditional form. It would have been something quite other had there been in the past no Poussin, no Correggio, no Michelangelo, no Old Testament, no Virgil. It is this sense of fellowship with and aid from the great masters which constitutes much of the charm and power of Prud'hon, Millet, Watts, Fantin, Renoir, Degas. They entirely escape that mere contemporaneity which has been the bane of more recent painting.

Before considering the great traditionalists of the century very briefly, it is the part of candor to admit that the list might be extended. Delacroix is largely a traditionalist, so is La Farge; so, in a lesser sense was Ingres. Manet, in his early phase, has a distinct traditionalism. Even more Puvis de Chavannes. Indeed the mural painters generally are likely to lean heavily upon the past.

Further to define our theme, I must try to make the somewhat delicate discrimination between a traditionalist and an eclectic. There are scores of artists who immediately remind us of some predecessor. Burne-Jones is redolent of Mantegna and Botticelli. Gaston Latouche smacks quite unmistakably of Fragonard. Jacques Blanche is like an eighteenth century English portraitist come back to charm us. Why are they not traditionalists? It is largely a question of more or less complete assimilation. The artist who here and there picks up attractive traits and thus arrives at a magpie art is an eclectic. Sir Joshua is the high type of the class. It is also a question of fountain head. Your traditionalist resorts to great and permanent and more or less collective movements. Your eclectic is rather likely to resort to minor, individual and derivative sources. There is, properly speaking, no tradition of Botticelli, Mantegna, Fragonard: these are exquisite individual apparitions; there is no real tradition of Gainsborough and Sir Joshua, for they were themselves derivative artists. To be a traditionalist, is to assimilate a central tradition, to draw from some real fountain head. But more attractive matters than definitions invite us onward.

At the moment when French art broke sharply with the rococo tradition of Boucher and Fragonard, it seemed like the end of an era. For the rococo after all represented the inheritance, somewhat dissipated to be sure, of the Renaissance. At this critical moment, when a new pedantry menaced the artistic stores of civilization, there appeared a reincarnation

Louvre

PRUD'HON: PSYCHE CARRIED AWAY

of the Renaissance spirit in the person of Pierre
Prud'hon. Born in 1758, he sojourned in Italy for
seven years of his early manhood, returning to Paris
at the outbreak of the Revolution. At Rome he paid
little attention to the second-rate antique marbles
which were then the vogue, but looked at the. few
that were inspired by the noble sensuousness of
Praxiteles. Of the older Italian painters he studied
not Michelangelo and Raphael, but those painters
who had most definitely evoked the poetry of the
flesh, Titian and Correggio. The mystery, the com-
pelling fascination of womanhood becomes his sole
theme. In his nudes it is given with the most penetrating completeness. Take the great picture of
1808, Psyche carried Away. A delicate grandeur is
the note. The actual representation is in that traditional modulation of light and shade which Leonardo
da Vinci discovered and Correggio perfected. The
great relaxed figure has no look of nature. Prud'hon
has no care for the actual appearance, what he seeks
is the ivory perfections that are visible only in dreams.
There is absolutely no curiosity in the work—and
curiosity is the leading characteristic of the naturalistic nude—but a sensitive ardor and a contemplative sort of passion.

It is this capacity for a frankly sensual yet restrained and noble reverie that is the distinction of
Prud'hon. It allies him to the most permanent source
of poetry. It is his hymn of praise to the lovely
woman, Constance Mayer, who without demanding

a wife's name, shared his lot. Prud'hon brought to
his erotic life faith and idealism. His sensuousness
has a pagan openness and nobility, and withal a
refining melancholy.

Over and over again with an insistence that is
never monotonous Prud'hon sounds his single note.
It is as evident in his portraits as in the nudes. In the
portrait of the Empress Josephine in her solitary park
at Malmaison the theme of desire assumes an especial
wistfulness. He did the most admirable chalk drawings, completely devoid of cleverness, but magnificently composed and with an elegance enlarged to
monumentality. What a genius it required to cut
through the triviality of the *École galante*, to the
thing it travestied—passion, to endue passion with
contemplative grace and nobility, and recover for
modern use the delicate adjustment which Antonio
Correggio had made between monumentality and a
pagan wantonness. It is perhaps more than a coincidence that the leading of Correggio is also strong
in Prud'hon's quite different successor, Jean François
Millet.

The most significant work of the century in painting is that of a peasant. Jean François Millet did
nothing more than to magnify his earliest recollec-
tions of fruitful toil in his native Normandy, and his
daily vision of work in the pastures and fields border-
ing the forest of Fontainebleau. He loved, himself,
the task of spading, pruning, grafting; by preference
wore the peasant blouse and sabots. Unconsciously

he renewed the theme of the toil of the months that French sculptors had carved on cathedral portals, and French miniaturists had emblazoned in pictured calendars: but where the mediæval craftsman had seen the episodes of an amusing idyl, Millet saw the solemn acts of an immemorial epos.

Born of a peasant family in 1814, in the village of Gréville near Cherbourg, he came up amid the sights and sounds of a labor rendered in the spirit of love and piety. With the poverty of the family there went aspiration. The father conducted a village choir famous for its skill and spirit. An uncle in the priesthood initiated the boy into the solemn cadences of St. Jerome's magnificent Latin version of the Bible, and led him also to the sweeter cadences of the "Georgics" of Virgil. Now and then the idyllic monotony of this boyhood was shaken by the tragedy of the sea. The wrecks crashed high on the shingle, and under the tarpaulins lay water-soaked, mute forms. While most of his artist contemporaries drank the heady wine of revolt and individualism, young Millet learned resignation, that grief must be borne, and that sorrow and toil have their beauty.

At twenty-two, his vocation for painting was so pronounced, that the Commune of Cherbourg granted him a tiny stipend to continue his studies in Paris. There ensued twelve bitter years, leaving a lifelong disability in invalidism. Millet was preposterously misplaced in Paris, and he knew it. He drifted into Paul Delaroche's studio, where he was on the whole treated well. He early cut loose and picked up an uncertain living by doing little nudes, and imitations of the pastorals of Watteau. But as he staggered along, his mind built up standards. In the drawings of Michelangelo, at the Louvre, he sensed a draughtsmanship that blends and conveys the finer bodily and deeper mental meanings. He rejoiced in the tragic humanity of the work. The same generalized poetry he found less tragically in Poussin. Correggio, Titian and Giorgione told him of the nobler physical splendors. Among his contemporaries only Delacroix, whom he knew slightly, seemed to him capable of great feeling.

Imagine the discord between this cult of nobility, and the necessary pot-boiling. Millet brought a young bride to Paris, where hardship soon killed her. With the improvidence of the birds of the air, he remarried and founded on nothing a family of patriarchal scale. One day before a shop window he heard himself described as a painter of nudities. The phrase rankled. He would no longer compromise. The new wife valiantly backed up the adventure, and in 1849 the little family returned to its own peasant life in the three room cottage, with beaten earth floors, at Barbizon.

The little nudes which Millet so brusquely repudiated are in their way notable works of art. These little pictures are massive, potent, highly condensed. The endeavor is for the dynamic line of Michelangelo, with a sober beauty of light and shade doubtless

Boston Museum of Art

J. F. MILLET: THE SOWER

Lille

J. F. MILLET: THE BATHERS, DRAW-ING

inspired chiefly by Correggio. Why should he have been ashamed of these superb little masterpieces? Precisely because their mastery was external. They were perhaps deeply understood but not deeply felt. They were what he particularly detested in other artists—display pieces. His own art was to draw on every fiber, to claim his completest devotion. So while we do well to admire these admirable early studies, he also did well to repudiate them, in favor of the epic of toil.

Before leaving Paris for good, Millet, had dreamt of figures of mowers or the like which should seem as grand as the sibyls of Michelangelo, and in the Winnower he had painted such a figure. But the real herald of the new style is the Sower. Years before in Normandy he had sketched the essential gesture and composition which through successive versions he refined and emphasized into the great picture. The night when man cannot work is falling, and the Sower lengthens his pace and swings his hand with a fuller pride. Only the tired uneasily upright head tells of exhaustion. The powerful strewing hand seems sacramental; the land rises to a pale sky against which the oxen prepare the field for the morrow. The scale and the authority of the figure are like some Grecian metope. It has with the specific beauty of painting, the simplicity and dignity of sculpture. The appeal is heroic. One of an apostolic succession of toilers who have made possible the ever recurrent harvest, looms suddenly and unforgettably before us.

We assist at the immemorial act which marks man as man. Nothing human antecedes the Sower, and nothing can supersede him. It is to have made such an eternal symbol out of a mere observation—in his own words "to have given character to the type"— that marks the humanistic greatness of Millet, attuning his particular vision with all the most valuable perceptions and reverences of the race.

Oddly enough, only the superb dilettante Théophile Gautier grasped the great traditionalism in this new work. He hailed it as the masterpiece of the year. Smaller critics saw "a severe and threatening figure," a "Communist who is flinging handfuls of shot at the sky in open defiance of God and man." Witty spirits, caviling at the calculated simplicity of the forms, regretted that the artist's poverty was such that he could not afford folds in the garments of his creatures.

The power, the conciseness, the high yet controlled intellectualism of Millet, his brooding and tender spirit are so evident in this masterpiece, that a critic might well rest his case with it. There remain in the twenty-four years to come only modulations of the mood. In the superb Gleaners of 1852, the rhythm is less vehement and subtle, and the landscape counts for more. Again the work had been refined and intensified through many versions. The slow, fatiguing, determined progress of the gleaners seems part of the order of the world. These toilers for the scanty surplus of the harvest are the symbol of that

J. F. MILLET: THE GLEANERS

J. F. MILLET: THE HARVESTERS, CHARCOAL

heroically narrow margin by which man holds his place in the world. Millet himself refused other comment on the picture than that he thought it successfully distinguished between what was upright and flat. And this indeed suggests the sheer material probity of every work by his hand.

It was a similar answer that he gave to those who mocked at the stately action of the peasants in the picture Carrying Home the Calf. These wits noted that if the Ark of the Covenant had been in question, the dignity could not have been more exaggerated. Millet simply asked had these complainers ever really looked at any body of men carrying a heavy weight together? If so, they might note that it could not be done except processionally and in rhythm. It was characteristic of the proud humility of Millet that in controversy he fell back on the great commonplaces of balance and tension. He preferred not to insist on the poetry that was so dear to him, but rather to meet the critics on the side of ordinary truth.

For ten years at Barbizon his poverty was occasionally dire. Through limitations and mental and physical distress—he was a lifelong sufferer from devastating headaches—he fulfilled his purpose. Gradually by shy approaches he knit a firm friendship with his neighbor, Théodore Rousseau. Genial and worthy persons, Diaz, Corot, loved to come to the earth-paved hut. Eager young Americans, William Hunt and Wyatt Eaton, did him reverence, and spread his fame beyond the Atlantic. Placidly he fulfilled his

destiny, seeking wisdom and poise in the great con-
soling books, Theocritus, Dante, Shakespeare, Scott,
our own Emerson.

As life grew easier a noble idyllism came into the
work. It reaches its high point in such a picture as
the Goose Girl, an evocation as lovely as any attic
stele, with a homeliness for the like of which one must
go to the Odyssey, say the incident of the house-
wifely princess, Nausicaä. The thing has the dignity
of beautiful feeling. This is the essential of great
art. As Millet himself once wrote: "We can start
from any point to reach the sublime, and everything
is proper to be expressed, if only your aim is high
enough. Then what you love with the greatest
power and passion becomes the ideal of beauty which
you impose on others. Let each of us have his own.
A profound impression will always find out a way of
expression, and naturally seeks how to declare itself
in the most forcible manner."

The humanism of the man, his conviction that the
high values of art are first those of life itself, his sound
traditionalism are all in these words. I commend
them to people who believe artistic creation takes
place in some cavern of the emotional self from which
life is barred.

As example of the tenderness of the man we may
take any of the pictures of motherhood, or better the
admirable little idyl of the Shepherdess. The sweetness of the thing is oddly allied with grandeur. Rarely
there are lapses, as in the possibly too famous master-

piece, The Angelus, where the sheer sweetness and tenderness have little saving austerity.

Fundamentally Millet is not merely one of the greatest temperaments of our age, but also one of the clearest and most powerful composers. He approached the concise perfection of his masterpieces through long meditation. He made, however, few preliminary working studies, trusting the intensity of his observation and the strength and accuracy of his memory. He painted in the studio, seldom from other models than himself and his wife. His drawings are generally complete pictures, and the chalk drawings, lightly tinted with pastel or water color are, for many critics, more notable than his paintings. However that be, his mind always demanded order, and refused merely to play with details. I suppose this invalid actually created more compositions than any artist of whom we have record. Below the level of creation he declined to live, anything less than that higher air was unbreathable.

In his last years honors came to him, and a sufficient measure of prosperity. As a long due expiation, the French state gave him a wall in the Panthéon to be enriched by the legend of St. Genevieve. The compliment pleased him, but at sixty, his powers were spent. He could not have done the work with greater taste than Puvis actually lavished upon it, but he might well have invested the idyllic legend with greater robustness and actuality. He died in 1875, being sixty-one years old.

The teachableness of the man is one of his greatest qualities. He wasted no energy in futile revolt. He consented to obscurity and drew wisdom from hardship. He enlarged and ennobled his specific vision of toil by allying its expression with the Olympian art of the past—the divine suavity of the Pheidian marbles, the awesomeness of Michelangelo. The stab of actuality in his work he drew largely from his friend, the caricaturist Daumier. Thus thinking nothing common or unclean, he welded out of the homeliest and most various elements a true synthesis, a style as heroic in its degree as that of his adored Poussin. In the general artistic triviality of his age he towers gigantic, and the just measure of his praise has not yet been reached.

In England, you will recall, the style of Rubens, well diluted, persisted far into the 19th century. So it is not surprising that the greater intelligences, such as Alfred Stevens and George Frederick Watts, went behind Rubens to his own fountainhead in the Venetian Renaissance.

The great and neglected English sculptor, Alfred Stevens, who was born in 1817, and died in 1875, would, with favorable conditions have revived the splendors of the Renaissance in England both in sculpture and painting. As it was, his art-loving contemporaries kept him designing fire-dogs and similar minor objects for a living, and when finally they did assign him the tomb of Wellington for St. Paul's, they underpaid him in his last years and after

ALFRED STEVENS: MRS. COLLMANN

his death mutilated his design. Painting is merely
incidental and fragmentary in such a life, but enough
remains, with his drawings, to tell of the grandeur
of his style. Even in a little decorative figure like the
Amoret, we find without servile imitation, the fine
swing of a sibyl by Michelangelo. To have been a
great decorative painter he needed only opportunity.
Scores of powerful and most rhythmical sketches
from the nude tell the same tragic story of genius
unfulfilled. There are a few religious pictures, mere
episodes, and a handful of portraits of fine design and
extraordinary intensity of character. Alfred Stevens
seems the one Englishman of the century who was
fitted to cut through the modern specialization of the
arts, and revive the universality of the Renaissance.
His genius was to attach himself to that great time
without losing sight of nature or modern life. Even
in his partial and broken achievement he represents
the finest type of traditionalism.

Where Alfred Stevens made a sort of synthesis of
the Italian Renaissance, George Frederick Watts
tapped it at a single free-flowing source, the art of
Titian, and reinforced his own art by constant study
of the Parthenon marbles. Watts too may be regarded as a great mural painter who from the evil
chance of conditions fell short of his vocation. As a
youth he won a prize in one of those endless com-
petitions for the new Parliament Houses which
needlessly tried the souls of the early Victorian artists.
He even executed a fresco, Alfred building Ships

against the Danes, which is still hidden in some light-less corner of the vast pile at Westminster. In his serene years of growth and contemplation at Florence he painted some charming narratives for the Villa of Carreggi. In the seven years between 1852 and 1859 for the mere costs he made for the Hall of Lincoln's Inn the great fresco of Justice, represented by a stately group of legists after the analogy of Raphael's school of Athens. Of its type it has always seemed to me the best decoration of the times. He con-templated a vast cycle treating the rise of Civilization, and, had the mere expenses been met, would have given the labor. New Euston Station was to have been the setting for this epic of humanity. One may doubt if it could have been taken in while catching a train, but an art-loving nation, while wisely refusing a railway station for such a purpose, would have made some other more suitable provision.

Watts, disappointed in his main issue, settled down to creating those great allegories and symbols which have been very variously appreciated, and that ex-traordinary gallery of portraits, which, somewhat dubiously received by the critics, has won universal acclaim of laymen of taste. A grave and kindly spirit, he enjoyed the friendship of the best and greatest of his contemporaries. He made it a matter of admiration and duty to preserve the likenesses of these friends, eventually bequeathing the entire col-lection to the British nation.

In a few early portraits Watts is technically at his

best. In beautiful arrangement and combination of vigorous line with fine surfaces and rich color such a portrait as Lady Somers recalls the contemporary triumphs of Théodore Chassériau. A most winsome delicacy is on the contrary the characteristic of a few early portraits of children and young people. Such insight and candor are at their height in the double portrait of sisters. It immortalizes the youthful fascination of that woman of genius, Ellen Terry, who was for some few unhappy months the artist's wife.

What may be called the standard portraiture of Watts is of another type. We have simply heads, extraordinarily vivid and intent. There is no longer the painterlike fluency of the early portraits, but often a labored loading on of fine strokes. It is this apparently unhandy method which has troubled the critics. It seems to me, however, that such heads as the Browning have extraordinary vitality, impressive mass, and somberly rich color; and that the apparent unhandiness of the means by which such effects are obtained is none of our business. An artist who is pondering deeply what is behind the face of his sitter, as Watts did when he painted, say, his Burne-Jones, is not likely to be swiftly dexterous in execution. Rembrandt is not so in his most deeply felt portraits, as in that heroic and pathetic evocation of himself in old age which is in the Frick collection. So I think we shall do well to take or leave such portraits as Watt's likeness of himself irrespective of usual canons of handy painting, just as we have to take the adumbrations of Titian's old age for what they have of meaning and splendor, even though they lack the lucidity of his more painterlike years.

Thwarted in his hopes of being a mural painter, Watts gradually built up an ideal world in symbol and allegory. Its denizens were in part the Gods of Greece, but an even more personal mythology was that he evoked to embody his own finest thinking. Watts was characteristically of his age in identifying religion, while repudiating its straiter formulas, with all our higher aspirations. It was the mood of his friends, the poet Tennyson, of Matthew Arnold, of James Martineau. Thus with a peculiar warmth and conviction, Watts returned to the symbolical methods of the Middle Ages.

His subjects are those you will see in Gothic glass, or sculptured portal, Hope, Charity, Mammon. Where he was superior to his mediæval predecessors was in conviction and warmth. They took their symbols in a somewhat perfunctory way, he had won through to his symbols in very personal struggle. In so doing he had affected a beautiful synthesis in which the valuable residuum of mediæval, Christian idealism reclothed itself in the humanistic splendor of the Pheidian marbles and of Titian.

Whether the endeavor was or was not wholly successful our age is hardly competent to judge. The notion of painting has so narrowed down to fine craftsmanship, that precisely the qualities of high thought which would have made Watts seem unquestionably a great artist in the Middle Ages or in the Renaissance, make him a literary suspect to-day. I cannot suitably plead his cause at this time. Let me only suggest that when we think of his famous designs, the Diana and Endymion, the Orpheus and Eurydice, the Hope, the Love and Life, and the Love and Death, the Rider on the White Horse—we ask ourselves what are the analogies for this art? Does it in any way suggest the work of such bankrupt titans as Haydon in England, or Cornelius in Germany? Does it not rather require a parallel with admittedly great things—Titian, Delacroix? Such it seems to me is the case. Watts fell on evil times. Paradoxically, Victorian England, whose spiritual representative in the art of painting he was, had only the most fumbling appreciation of art. They neglected Watts's embodiment of Tennyson's greater vein, in such a picture as Love and Life, while they applauded Burne-Jones's transcripts from Tennyson's more trivial and decorative mediævalism.

The classic in Watts was manifested in his determination to count publicly. Where other artists disdainfully sought the ivory tower, he made communes and nations his beneficiaries. He believed his work was valuable enough to give away, and he actually gave away most of it. I hardly know of another instance in the history of art which shows us a great and most representative artist literally crying in the wilderness, and the measure of Watts' personal greatness is that he accepted that situation with

G. F. WATTS: TIME, DEATH AND JUDG-
MENT

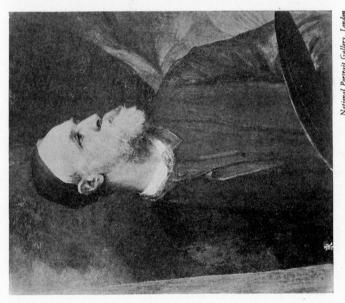

G. F. WATTS: HIS OWN PORTRAIT

equanimity and made of it a source of strength. He combined with the most modern thinking two central traditions, that of Greece and Venice, and seems to me one of the purest types of traditionalist and classic that the last century offers. He once wrote:

"If I could carry out my own feeling perfectly, my pictures would be solemn and monumental in character, noble and beautiful in form, and rich in color: but the subtle varieties of sunlight I should never aim at producing. I can see in nature what Turner saw, and can appreciate the excellence of his imitation, but my natural tendency is to see nature with such eyes as Giorgione and Titian had: I see only with their eyes, but do not work with their brains or hands, Alas!" The pathos of that alas is qualified by the fact that Watts's best works will after all assert to posterity a real affinity with the gracious and solemn poesies of his revered Venetians. He is the last great traditionalist that England has produced, for I cannot consider the very able and vastly over praised contemporary, Augustus John, as other than a very adroit eclectic. We complete our survey of the retrospective movements with four French Artists, Fantin-Latour, Auguste Renoir, Edouard Degas and René Ménard.

Fantin-Latour is hardly a great artist, yet I know few painters of our time who have achieved a more consistent and well rounded work. He combined much of the exquisiteness of the school of fine painting with a self-criticism that few of the fine painters

ever attained to. He studied with a then famous
master, Boisbaudran, who assiduously trained the
memory of his students. They were to grasp mentally
and retain the salient and necessary traits of an object
seen only in a moment of intense concentration. The
procedure, you will see, was the opposite both of that
of the Impressionists and of the academic fine painters,
being more mental. Corot and Millet had worked in
this sense, depending not on the presence of the subject-matter but upon memory of intense observations.
When Millet was chaffed for his habit of idling out-
of-doors, he used to reply tranquilly, "I'm working
all the same." Such was the background of Fantin's
art, though he also made sufficient and intelligent
use of the model. His work naturally divides itself
into the nudes and little pastorals, still-lifes, portraits
and portrait groups. The pastorals and compositions
of nudes are perhaps best known in America, through
his admirable lithographs, especially the musical series
devoted to the great composers. Here he renews in
miniature very much the mood of Prud'hon, the
inspiration in both cases being that of Correggio.

Without going over to the obscurities of the twilight impressionists, Fantin reduced his color to an
enriched monochrome of grays and browns. It is an
art of reticence. It is clear; there is no haphazard
about it. The letter to Fantin in which Whistler
envies his friend his fund of solid knowledge, is one
of the most instructive documents of modern art. To
be perfectly informed and lucid without losing his

sympathy was Fantin's gift. It is a classic trait, depending on delicate compromise and adjustment.

His extraordinary tenacity and memory made him a fine portraitist. There is one, At the Easel, which represents well the unaffected rightness of his arrangements, the fullness of character; and in the vase of flowers on the table, the delicacy of his painting of still-life. But Fantin's fame depends on those portrait groups in which he assembled likeminded men, who were his own friends, and preserved the very look of those conferences in which the leading ideas of modern painting and poetry were beaten out. These groups, Homage to Delacroix, Homage to Manet, that Table Corner where the Symbolist Poets listen to Verlaine, are of course famous. Posterity will find them indispensable and unique records.

This desire to preserve worthy things that would otherwise perish is of the very essence of the classic spirit. Fantin is perhaps the greatest conservator of the century. He chose harmonious, undistracting grays, so that the character should count. There is reference perhaps to those somber impressive groups of Hals's latest years, even more to the sobriety of Velasquez. What is remarkable, since the sitters were all contemporaries and the individual portraiture profound and truthful, is the collective character of these groups. Take the somewhat gallant alertness of the belated Romantics who gather about the portrait of Eugène Delacroix. About the conventional black coats there is a suspicion of cape and sword, and young Whistler who stands in the middle with head defiantly turned towards the world is the very type of a knight errant.

Then take the solid business-like group that gathers about Manet's easel in the most famous of these groups, An Atelier at Batignolles. What composure and poise! These are the searchers after the mysteries of light, inquirers into the refinements of optics, true brothers of the heroes of the study and laboratory. They deal quite literally in dry light.

Then consider the somewhat dreamy and disheveled group of symbolists gathered about the emaciated and battered figure of that poet whom desire, disease, and prison wasted, Paul Verlaine. Even the apparent casualness and disorder of the arrangement is itself a symbol. Mark the tousled head and weak inspired face of the half madman, Arthur Rimbaud, the depraved poet who discovered that the vowels were so many colors. How true, how free from satire, is the revelation of that sickness of spirit which produced few and exotic flowers of an art mostly poisonous.

What would we not give for such a visible symposium of the wits and thinkers of the Renaissance, say Pico della Mirandola, Poliziano, Marsilio Ficino, Sandro Botticelli, Lorenzo de'Medici assembled for a Platonic conference; Cardinal Bembo, Sansovino, the slippery journalist, Dolce, and the venal scourge of princes, Aretino, seated in Titian's studio! Such analogies tell us the worth of Fantin's austere and accurate work. In a manner he did by direct por-

traiture what Watts attempted to do in symbolism—
personified the ideas of his time, and did it more
successfully. Capable of an exquisite poetry, as his
nudes and fantasies attest, Fantin, when he would
leave a record, chose a firm and definitive prose. This
too is the evidence of his classicism, of a sane and
discriminating traditionalism.

The artist who has most successfully combined
the new impressionistic vision with a sound traditionalism, is Auguste Renoir. An immensely versatile talent, he escapes the tinge of eclecticism
attaching to artists like Degas, who have made a
similar endeavor. Born in 1841, Renoir was largely
self-trained. Like Diaz he began as a china painter.
In his thirties Renoir fell for a moment under the
influence of Courbet, but soon attached himself to
the group of luminists that followed Manet. He
accepted the luminist vision of light and color, but
applied it with reservations. He rejected the casualness of the Impressionists, drawing from Delacroix
the counsel of rhythm and from Ingres the cult of
beautiful and energetic line. He accepted cautiously
the practice of broken color, rejecting the coarse
stippling of Monet, and using instead infinitesimal
weavings of fine strokes. For sheer accuracy of registration a handful of his landscapes may seem the consummate fruit of the Impressionist movement. His
intentness, unlike Pissarro's was never dry; his natural
lyricism, unlike Monet's, was never incoherent.

Until his fortieth year his art seemed after all just a

FANTIN: A TABLE CORNER (THE SYMBOLISTS)

RENOIR: LA MOULIN DE LA GALETTE

variety of Luminism. Only he put a personal ardor
into his pictures, unlike the luminists, preferred figure
painting, essaying landscape only as an occasional
recreation. His famous picture at the Luxembourg,
the Dance at the Moulin de la Galette, is perhaps the
most entrancing bit of impressionistic figure painting
in art. It is not merely dappled with sun and shadow
with the loveliest truthfulness, but also instinct with
motion and warmth of life. Rowers at Breakfast
repeated the triumph. The same palpitating life is in
his portraits. Here he declined to regard smaller accidents of light, giving himself to emphatic assertion
of color, form and character. Such a group as the
Mme. Charpentier and her children, in the Metropolitan Museum is impeccable. There are few masterpieces that would not assume thinness and pallor if
hung beside it.

From the '80s Renoir steadily emancipated himself from a narrow Luminism. Preferring the new
blond color and the general effect of out-of-door light,
he ignored smaller accidents of illumination, controlling the light the better to express the form. His
pronounced sensuousness expressed itself in his preference for the nude. He made it his staple as Ingres
had before him. But the nude of Renoir in such a
picture as La Source, is a new creation. In the beautiful pattern and monumentality, it vaguely recalls
Rubens; in the agile and sensitive line there is reference
to Ingres; the shimmering, nacreous surface, the
frank carnality, suggests certain triumphs of Tiepolo

RENOIR: LA SOURCE

DEGAS: REHEARSAL OF THE BALLET

and Fragonard. It is Renoir's contribution to invest decorative monumentality with a very individual accent. The Source is almost as much a person as Manet's Olympe, but with what a difference in the direction of style! Such are the characteristics of the scores of nudes which he has created from the tiniest panels to the great interlace of sportive white bodies in the several versions of the Bathers. In his later years Renoir, perhaps accepting a physical disability, made his methods always intangible, light to evanescence, mere stain and blot. His surface creates form and life and emotion by the subtlest modulations. There is no surer test of a technically fine picture than this unity of surface. A bad picture has a confusing variety of surfaces, copying those of nature. A fine picture has one lovely surface, which here and there, by some magic of slight differentiation becomes this or that object, depth, or action. Such is the case with a Titian, a Delacroix, a Constable, a Corot, a good Whistler. Renoir had this magic in a superlative degree.

His career remained unfulfilled. Fitted as perhaps no modern painter to revive with a finer sincerity the decorative glories of Tiepolo, Renoir rarely had a wall to decorate. He spent his great powers in doing exquisite exhibition pictures and cabinet pieces. What should have thrilled an age, has entranced a favored few. His sanity and vitality counted heavily against him, and he struggled obscurely, while mere audacity and eccentricity were crowned. His partial

achievement is so great and vital that it cannot be
forgotten, but his career remains a parable of that
dissidence between artist and public which has
deprived our age of the richest fruits of art.

The eclecticism of Edouard Degas somewhat disguises his essential traditionalism. Without sacrificing
the athletic contour learned from Ingres, he adopted
from the Luminists a love of natural and artificial
coruscation, while from the Japanese he caught the
knack of finding odd and unexpected arrangements.
His subjects run in series—jockeys, washerwomen,
ballet dancers, bathers. The expression is grim.
Degas wants the true truth concerning the human
animal in fruitful or fruitless toil. One may say that
nobody has found more beautiful gestures in unlikely
persons and situations. To catch the grandeur in
the familiar, even ignoble act, was his genius. Again
a generalizing quality oddly akin to Millet's places
Degas's figures on the side of tradition and style.

In the solemn landscapes of René Ménard we find
the last important phase of traditionalism in France.
These pastorals, often representing an Arcadia amid
templed groves and hills, are in the grave tradition of
Nicholas Poussin, though of less significance. They
represent poetical reflection, mental reality. They
show as well the careful study of actual form, often
they achieve with suavity that abstract emphasis of
mass and space which Cézanne effects with calculated
brutality. Though this art gladly has recourse to the
nymphs and the half-gods of antiquity, it by no means

Fenway Court, Boston

DEGAS: PORTRAIT

WHISTLER: MISS ALEXAN–
DER

requires their aid. It is self-sufficing in the great
landscape, painted to decorate a bank at Toulouse,
which represents merely a vast sweep of lake and
mountains behind the plowman.

I have included in this chapter only the traditionalists who seem to me great, and who do not fit in
narrower classifications. Had I included the smaller
men of delightful quality, the case for traditionalism
as the artist's best attitude would have gained
strength. You will recall also that the innovating
artists are often finest in their traditional phases.
Are the fine Whistlers, the Mother, the Carlyle, the
Miss Alexander, with their intimations of Velasquez,
or the Japanese fantasies and nocturnes? Are the
memorable Manets, the Boy with the Sword, and the
Olympia, or the out-of-door studies, and that glitter-
ing miracle the Bar of the Folies Bergères? Let
me remind you too that all the great landscapists
before Impressionism, Constable, Corot, Rousseau,
are deeply rooted in the past, and that almost without exception the great decorators, Ingres, Delacroix,
Chassériau, Baudry, La Farge, Puvis, have felt themselves descendents of great ancestors in the Renaissance, while the greatest Academic painters from
Ingres down have been of the same temper. This
mere roll call will suggest how episodical and incomplete are those revolutionary movements comprised
in realism and impressionism. An immense amount of
good they have done in the way of general ventilation
and refreshment, but as regards artistic results their

case is still to be proved. It may well serve also as a corrective to the individualistic theories now over-running the field of art to perceive that the great pictures of a hundred years past have been done by men who grounded themselves deeply in older art. Reverence for the great masters may be as important for the artist, even more so, than reverence for his own innocent eye.

If art be largely a mental product, then the artist may no more spin his masterpiece spiderlike out of his own inside, than the layman can become great without accepting and using the ethos of a particular family, nation, and race. Something must first be put into the inside, and that something is very largely the approved and tested experience of a past still living because its finer part was never subject to the common hazard of mortality.

MURAL PAINTING

MURAL PAINTING

UNTIL recent times modern mural painting has preserved a traditional character. That it should do so was inevitable. When we picture the walls of a public building,—a capitol, town hall, church, or palace, or, in our days, an opera house, hotel or business building, the appeal of the decoration is not to the elect but to all sorts and conditions of men. It must be quickly and surely apprehended, its scope is collective. Hence the decorator quite sensibly is prone to use the most familiar conventions and symbols, or, if he adopts history or narrative, to seek the most generally understood themes. And this is as it should be.

The eighteenth century, despite its official dogma of the grand style, is a declining age for the wall painter. In the main we have simply boudoir decoration as the characteristic art—hovering cupids, vivacious mythologies of the Boucher type, or artificial pastorals in the vein of Watteau. Indeed the larger style of Rubens and the Venetians lived on chiefly in tapestries. In this way it kept a measure of life even through the chill days of the Empire. Rubens once more then, is the real starting point. Two of his important decorative series, the ceiling at Whitehall, London, and the stories of Henry IV and

Marie de Médicis in the Luxembourg were continuously seen just where their effect could be greatest.

Rubens as decorator is often called scornfully a baroque master. The animation and swirl of his design, the full pictorial realization of the forms, the ornate accessories, and gorgeous color go to justify such a classification. But, as a matter of fact Rubens avoided the cheaper extravagances of the baroque and retained much of the discretion of his great exemplars, Titian and Paolo Veronese. Whether in ceiling or wall, he avoids excessive foreshortenings and tricks of illusion. Where the real baroque masters set their figures floating away from the wall, he keeps his behind the picture plane. A classicist in his fashion and an eager collector of ancient marbles, Rubens freely indulges symbolism and mythology, but his characteristic vein is a mixture of these classical modes with historic or even contemporary narrative. The more splendid canvasses of the Médicis series are of this sort, none finer than the scene where the affianced princess Marie moves gravely down the gang-plank to Marseilles while the nereids writhe below with unrestrained gratulation. It is a magnificent combination of pagan exuberance with the finest courtliness—a magnificent episode for an opera of Goldmark.

At first sight this very artificial blend of mythology with history smacks solely of the 17th century, being an Olympian sort of flattery of the great of the earth.

But the mode has proved singularly available ever
since. Realists scout it as cheap make-believe, but
possibly it corresponds to pretty deep sentiments of
human nature. Strong collective feeling seems to
require mythology of some sort. The case is precisely
that of the figure of impersonation in poetry. Take
the famous ode of William Collins:

> "How sleep the brave, who sink to rest,
> By all their country's wishes blest!
> When Spring, with dewy fingers cold
> Returns to deck their hallowed mould,
> She there shall dress a sweeter sod
> Than Fancy's feet have ever trod.
>
> By fairy hands their knell is rung;
> By forms unseen their dirge is sung;
> There Honour comes, a pilgrim grey,
> To bless the turf that wraps their clay;
> And Freedom shall a while repair
> To dwell a weeping hermit there."

Is this merely rhetoric, bad proof reading, surplusage
of capital letters; or is there in these admittedly quite
conventional personifications some real image, some
unmistakable enhancement of emotion? If the latter
be the case, then we may well hesitate to refuse the
painter of history and legend his mythologies and
symbols simply because he cannot find them in the
flesh at an employment bureau.

Returning to the mixed style of Rubens, it is plain
that by selection therefrom separate styles of pure
symbolism, mythology, and historical narrative may

be formed. And in fact most modern decoration would conform to one or the other of these categories.

While the decorative style of Rubens was the only one that lived on uninterruptedly, there was always the possibility of the revival of the simpler mode of Raphael. He was universally regarded as the greatest of painters, and his great designs for the Vatican and the Farnesina were familiar through engravings to all artists and amateurs. Where Rubens sought an active balance of thrusts and full color, Raphael chose a quieter balance with stronger emphasis on linear pattern and restricted color. He was a frescoist of course, while Rubens was a painter in oils, and, in principle, Raphael in his best estate never departs far from the gravity and simplicity of such early wall painters as Giotto. He is not at his best in the fresco of the Parnassus, but it illustrates his manner capitally in its serenity and monumental ease. He rarely indulged tricks of perspective—here Rubens is more ingenious and various—but treats all surfaces, ceilings included, as so many side walls.

Modern decorative painting in France, for I think we may for our purpose ignore Prud'hon's very clever revival of the baroque ceiling formulas, and Baron Gros' sad misadventure in the dome of the Panthéon—begins with a devout adorer of Raphael, and an equally devout adorer of Rubens, who naturally hated each other, Jean Dominique Ingres and Eugène Delacroix.

By his very limitations as a colorist, Ingres was well served as a wall painter. His pattern was clear, his conception simple, his line superb. These qualities are manifest in the Apotheosis of Napoleon which he did for a ceiling in the Hôtel de Ville. With many other precious things it perished in the fires of the Commune, but the sketch in the Louvre preserves the design. It is treated precisely like a wall medallion, and the fine ivory white figures are set against a uniform ground of blue, like a Wedgewood relief. The motive was taken from a well-known antique cameo of Augustus. An admirer of Ingres once remarked on its cameolike charm in the presence of Delacroix. The great Romantic simply answered, "I don't care for a cameo on the ceiling." All the same the decoration must have been, if in a frigid way, very fine.

But Ingres is more himself in The Apotheosis of Homer, which he finished in 1827 for a ceiling in the Louvre. Before an Ionic temple sits the blind poet. From behind, a winged genius lowers a laurel wreath towards the grand brow. At the foot of the throne the splendidly swung forms of two women symbolize the Iliad and Odyssey. The great poets of Greece and Rome approve the rite, and on a lower level are seen the heads and shoulders of great writers and artists of modern times. The composition is built up with severe symmetry and the carefully balanced curves dear to Raphael. Again the color based on a pervading creamy brown with the reds and blues reduced

INGRES: THE GOLDEN AGE

Louvre

INGRES: APOTHEOSIS OF HOMER

by the addition of white is that of a finely tinted but
not very strong fresco.

It is characteristic of Ingres' attitude that he makes
no concession to the fact that he is designing for a
ceiling. He makes his soberly balanced design as if
it were for a side wall. He appeals to universal
stylistic qualities which do not depend upon dodges
in perspective. Fundamentally the work is a nobly
calculated pattern, a flat thing of intricate balance and
limited color, meant at once unobtrusively to adorn
its surface and to tranquillize the eye of the spectator.

The sterner qualities of Ingres are perfectly embodied in the Homer. More than twenty-five years
later, in the famous design, The Golden Age, for
the Chateau of the Duc de Luynes at Dampièrre,
Ingres returned to decoration with a theme that
evoked his gentler idyllism. The thing is an interlace of graceful white bodies; in the center, executing a
solemn dance, at the sides and lower margins, reclining beside a flowing spring. They are knit in tender
and very gentle embraces, or modestly holding converse with the few draped figures of visiting Olym-
pians. The scene is where a quiet grove opens upon a
meadow. It is what all the greatest compositions of
Puvis de Chavannes were to be, an ideal conversation
piece, a set of symbols for an Elysium verified only
in dreams where our bodies assume those more
beautiful meanings which usually lie unembodied in
the mind. This higher academe, where unclothed
nymphs enact the life contemplative, white breasts

and limbs becoming moral axioms, while blameless
fauns in sunburned athleticism symbolize our noblest
active life—this Elysium is pretty nearly Ingres's
discovery. There is only a hint of it in such a work
as Raphael's Parnassus, while the warmer and more
individualized allegory of Correggio and the Venetians, and the more emphatic sublimities of Rubens
and the baroque painters are in quite another mood.
It is a very mental art, the appeal being not to nerves
but to inner beatitudes, where the sharp issues of
actual living are strangely transvalued. It is the
mood of Poussin raised to monumentality. It is an
art which implies not specific emotion but a realm
which Schopenhauer describes as devoid of self and
will. Hence these Golden Ages are not desired by
artists who love the sharp flavor of deed and passion.

Alongside the solemn ceremonials of Ingres, Delacroix spread on the best walls and ceilings of Paris a
painting vibrant with color and action, which revived
for modern times the audacities of Rubens and of his
Venetian predecessors. This violent yet marvelously
balanced orchestration of color and emotion, is the
specific gift of Delacroix. Almost from boyhood
Delacroix had painted on a great scale and had
sold his pictures to the State. It was inevitable that
he should receive commissions for mural painting.
In 1837 he finished the decoration of the Salon du
Roi in the Chamber of Deputies. The scheme called
for gigantic pilaster figures, with a series of spandrel
designs with the usual subjects, Justice, Commerce,

Industry. There was nothing that evoked the leonine rage of the master. Merely his fastidiousness expressed itself by the most ingenious and complicated massing and twisting of draped and nude forms in the awkward space of the spandrel. Again the work suggests the Venetians, and is unlike Ingres, in freely admitting cross lights, cast shadows, and reflections. It has, for all its decorative complexity, an out-door quality.

In 1837, before the Salon du Roi was quite finished, he was charged with the decoration of the two Parliamentary libraries of France, in the Chamber of Deputies and the Luxembourg. He was nearly ten years about the task, and freely employed assistants after the fashion of the Renaissance masters. It requires some pains to spell out those decorations, for they are badly lighted and partly obscured by profuse carving and gilding. They at least show Delacroix's faith that decorative effect permits all emphasis of color, action and emotion. The scheme for the Library of the Chamber called for a half-dome with Orpheus coming to civilize the Greeks and teach them the Arts of Peace. It is a conversation piece, very reticent yet full of ardor in reserve, lovely in color, and painted by Delacroix's own hand. It represents that full-blooded type of classicism which stems from Venice, and is embodied in modern times in Watts and Chassériau.

The side walls of this hall are devoted to historical examples of war and peace in great lunettes. None is

more powerful than that representing Attila raging
through Italy.   The Huns sweep across the plains
like a sinister wave of which the curling crest is the
head of Attila's war horse, in front, like an undertow
which must be overtaken and crushed by the next
wave, run and crawl and grovel the delicate forms of
Roman women with their children.   What a symbol
for destructive intelligence, what a vision!   What a
fact!   It is Delacroix's love of treating great ideas and
emotions in terms of what actually happens, that
makes him paradoxically the real fulfiller of the
academic ideal of historical painting.   Only his history is shot through with tears and blood, and
moderated by no smaller decorums.

In 1851 Delacroix, to complete the decoration of
the Salon d'Apollon in the Louvre, painted the
magnificent ceiling decoration, Apollo slaying the
Python.   The hall had been planned by Charles Le
Brun and contained his very ornate and heavy
paintings and sculptures.   Hence in the focal point,
where his ceiling was to be, Delacroix gave reins to
his vehemence.

The Chariot of the God hurtles through swirling
clouds where, lightly poised, sit the radiant forms
of the Olympian deities.   They witness the turning
moment of the great strife with that obscene world of
which the python is the type.   The God strains forward over the rim of his chariot as he lets fly the dart.
The monstrous snake writhes in a murk peopled with
dragonlike forms.   Light and mind have smitten

DELACROIX: CEILING OF APOLLO

DELACROIX: JACOB AND THE
ANGEL

darkness and vice. In sheer energy, in brilliancy of color, in incredible balance of excessive thrusts, so that the abstract pattern remains restful, this is the most remarkable decoration of its sort that modern times have produced. Its sort of course is Venetian—Tiepolo's ceilings, which Delacroix had seen in Spain, afford the closest precedents. The ceiling is opened up like a sky, but with no petty reckoning of perspective and point of view. The whole thing rests on a series of magnificent, humanistic compromises—balancings of thrust and equipose, of exuberance and measure; of a maximum of sheer imagination with a sort of historic credibility.

At the same time with the Apollo Delacroix was painting an elaborate series of decorations for the Hôtel de Ville. These were burnt in the awful months of the Commune, and are only partly represented by preliminary sketches. Only a little later the master undertook what was to be his last and perhaps greatest mural painting, the decoration of the Chapel of the Archangels, in the church of St. Sulpice.

Jacob wrestling with the Angel, occupies the left wall. The surge and strain of the two rather little bodies communicates itself to the great oaks and the distant hills. The thing is saturated with color and surging with action. But the more intense and rich expression of Delacroix's genius is the right wall, where is represented a scene already consecrated by the brush of Raphael—Heliodorus expelled from the Temple. The book of Maccabees tells how the Exarch Heliodorus, having plundered the treasury of the Temple at Jerusalem, was trodden down by a miraculous horse bearing a rider panoplied in gold, and was scourged by two angels, until bewildered and blinded he abandoned the profanation. In his conception Delacroix has adopted a far more energetic and complicated scheme than Raphael before him. The whirling oval composed of the divine horseman, prostrate Heliodorus, and the flying avengers, is balanced and locked in a kind of fret pattern formed by the columns and staircases. The flutter of the main group is carried up by the woman staggering in fright up the steps, and by the gestures of the High Priest and his attendants and by the snapping curtain. Without producing confusion, there is variety of light and dark, half veiling, half revealing distant rooms and colonades. Yet all this various richness, representing all the resources of the most advanced painting of the day, ministers to the grandiose simplicity of the scene. The less relevant element— the frightened crowd, is merely suggested as is the profanation itself merely by the splendid vases and flagons littering the steps.

In the picture Delacroix has consciously and successfully emulated the greatest work of the most vehement of the Venetian painters, Tintoretto's St. Mark delivering a Christian Slave. It too was a decoration. Delacroix indulges an even more audacious variety of color and inscenation, with a less

sensational and more realistic lighting. Here Tintoretto's great rival Paolo Veronese has been the
guide. The great design, finished in 1860, is Delacroix's artistic testament. It triumphantly expresses
everything for which he had striven. Three years of
invalidism remained to him, and then the end. He
had carried forward into modern days the torch
kindled by Titian and fanned by Rubens. No one
has been quite strong enough to bear it since, but the
most equal to the succession has been an American,
John La Farge.

I suppose the first question a knowing person will
ask about the Heliodorus is "Is it decoration? or
merely a fine picture out of place on a wall?" Certainly if the chastened manner of Ingres and Puvis is
decoration, the Heliodorus must be something else.
Is one decoration and the other not? or are both
decorative in different ways? Possibly decorative
effect does not depend either on calm or vehemence,
or flatness or depth, or sparseness or richness of color.
It depends rather on monumentality, equilibrated and
rhythmical pattern, which may be composed of the
most various ingredients. A flying angel is restless and
undecorative only if his thrust is uncompensated.
Note in this picture the function of the columns and
of the consoles under the balcony in steadying the
group and reducing it to compatibility. Perhaps both
Giotto and Tintoretto are great decorators, as are
Puvis and Delacroix. The thing depending on quite
other and more complicated issues than dosing all

Louvre

CHASSERIAU: YOUNG MOTHERS

Opéra, Paris

BAUDRY: PASTORAL MUSIC

colors with white, eschewing varnish, and tinting the wall flatly. To all these matters we must return.

Ingres and Delacroix set the extreme terms between which later decoration has balanced. While both rivals were still living, a talented young artist, Théodore Chassériau, arrived at a kind of superb compromise between the two styles. Chassériau was born at Santo Domingo, and, if his portraits are to be trusted, had, as so many colonial French families, his tinge of warmer negro blood. At fifteen he was working with Ingres, who soon was to take charge of the École de Rome, leaving his young pupil, at sixteen, an accomplished master. Chassériau excelled in the nude, combining with the severity of line which he had learned from Ingres, rich color, and an exotic strangeness of sentiment. The mood is deeply passionate but also quiet and restrained.

Soon he got church decorations. Then in 1844, being only twenty-five years old, he was commissioned to decorate the great staircase of the Cour des Comptes. In four years he spread on its walls frescoes of War and Peace. The building was burnt in the Commune and the crumbling masterpieces neglected for nearly thirty years. Then the ruin was destroyed to make place for a railway station. Fortunately certain reverent lovers of art saved what could be recovered of the damaged frescoes. With these fragments and the original sketches we may partially reconstruct the lost fresco of Peace.

A drawing shows the general plan. Peace, a god-

dess such as Ingres might have conceived, stands
before a great tree and presides over a scene, where
young mothers gather her olive branch, fathers till
the soil in the background, while artists ply their
crafts before a temple. The fragmentary group of
young mothers now in the Louvre, better conveys the
idyllic intimacy which persists through the classic
stateliness of the poses and composition. It is this
remove from action that takes Chassériau pretty
far from Delacroix, allies him to his old master, Ingres,
and makes him the precursor of Puvis de Chavannes.
Chassériau died in his thirty-eighth year, in 1857.
The public to-day hardly knows his name, but his
influence has been transmitted by artists as different
as Puvis, Gustave Moreau and Degas.

It is necessary to note only in passing the in its day
very famous decoration for the Hemicycle of the
École de Beaux-Arts, by Paul Delaroche. It represents the masters of the four arts grouped about
Apelles. The inspiration, so far as there is one, is
Raphaelesque. It strings out indefinitely towards
the flanks and presents a tedious surplus of plausible
portraiture. Its color is bricky and unpleasant, again
possibly a tribute to the worst manner of Raphael.
I cite it chiefly as a reminder how far a laborious and
competent painter had misunderstood the manner of
Ingres.

We may consider in passing a much more competent
successor of Ingres in Hippolyte Flandrin, whose
decorations on the walls of the solemn Romanesque

PUVIS DE CHAVANNES: DRAMATIC POETRY

church of St. Germain des Près, and at St. Vincent de
Paul, if a little cold, do not discredit their grandiose
settings.

You will have noted that most of the artists we
have so far considered have been only incidentally and
exceptionally mural decorators. The case is different
with Pierre Puvis de Chavannes. From the first he
conceived of his work as decoration, and the few
easel pictures he painted have mostly been permanently affixed to some wall. He not merely practiced mural painting, but he thought much about it
and created a theory. Its chief articles were simplicity
of tone, unity of pattern, and flatness of effect, above
all repose and quietude. Puvis naturally approached
these convictions by gradual stages. Born in 1824, of
a gentle and prosperous family, there was no element
of outer struggle in his life. He began rather late in
painting, passed rapidly through the ateliers of Henri
Scheffer, Delacroix and Couture, but soon quit the
schools and followed his own star. His early works
were regularly refused by the Salon, and in the year
of Courbet's famous exhibition of Realism, 1855,
Puvis too had his private show. The public which
had dubbed Courbet the raging madman, *le fou
furieux*, humorously called Puvis the "harmless
madman," *le fou tranquille*.

In 1861 he exhibited his great picture Concordia,
which received a second-class medal, was bought by
the State, and used as a decoration for the Museum
of Amiens. The general inspiration is plainly from

Ingres and even more definitely from Chassériau's
Peace, in the Cour des Comptes. The colors are pale
like the tints of faded tapestry, the gamut is reduced
to a general gray-blue neutral tone against which the
white bodies shimmer in a soft yet clear definition.
The motive, that of a pastoral golden age, is one to
which Puvis constantly recurred.

Puvis lived in an atmosphere of detachment and
high idealism. He had only two themes, the heroic
legends of Gaul, which he treated at Amiens, Marseilles, and Paris, and a kind of symbolism of civic and
intellectual qualities, a world of mind, peopled by the
lingering sweet figures of lightly draped maidens and
athletes, and of sages sunk in contemplation. It was
the world of Chassériau only less concrete and more
idyllic. Indeed this influence of Chassériau Puvis
received in the most personal of ways. The noble
lady, Princess Marie Cantacuzène, who was for years
his friend and counsellor, and eventually his wife, had
earlier been the friend and adviser of Chassériau.

Where Puvis advanced on Chassériau was in the
delicate naturalism of his settings. Take the last
of the decorations at Amiens, Ludus pro Patria,
which was finished in 1882. There is a homely sense
of a real scene in the grange and willow tree and
backwater. In fact it is a Picardy farm which Puvis
once glimpsed for a minute from a railroad train. It
is very abstract in omitting minor details of form,
lighting, and shadows, but marvelously true to the
great effect. A similar quality is the lovely panel,

Doux Pays, which he painted in the same year, 1881, for the home of his friend the painter Léon Bonnat. I suppose the delight of the work depends precisely upon the combination of a delicate naturalism in the setting, with a highly wrought stylism in the figures, every curve and upright, and thrust being woven into a beautiful balance quite after the fashion of Ingres or Raphael.

In 1889 was unveiled the famous decoration for the great hall of the Sorbonne. The Sorbonne personified by a Madonnalike figure sits enthroned in a solemn grove peopled by gracious figures impersonating the arts and sciences. What is remarkable about this long frieze-like design is its unity. It does not seem pieced out as does, for example the decoration of the hemicycle of the École des Beaux-Arts. This unity is obtained by the general flatness and by the careful adjustments of the curves and repeats of the figures. It is a pattern, and in all essentials what a Giotto would have done, had he had the vision of Greek antiquity and curiosity as regards atmosphere.

This procedure of flat pattern, quiet and ease, with color reduced to neutral tints and tones is Puvis' contribution to mural painting. He not merely fortified himself by reference to the best decorators, but he also formulated his own theory of what a wall painting should be. It is best suggested by an anecdote. Hearing that a young painter, having a mural commission, had said: "I don't bother about the wall," Puvis replied with almost untranslatable energy, "If he doesn't bother about the wall, the wall will spew him out."

Which is to say the mural decoration is not a round or restless thing that falls out of or breaks into the wall, but a quiet, flat, stable pattern, a part of the wall and sharing in its character and stability and repose. How well Puvis applied his theory any of the great ensembles, the decorations of the Hôtel de Ville, of the Boston Public Library, and of the Panthéon remain to show. It is an art of reticence and of finest selection, austere, nobly logical. The theory has found much favor with critics and artists, but oddly enough modern wall painting has on the whole pursued other ways.

With the fullest admiration for Puvis' achievement, I cannot accept his theory as a comprehensive dogma. He presupposes what the Italian fresco painters usually had, but the modern decorator very rarely, that the artist has a wall for entire treatment, controlling the whole decorative situation. Generally the Italian decorator undertook a smoothly plastered room every square inch of which was at his disposal. This was what Puvis wanted and what he sometimes got. In the Panthéon he had it approximately. His chagrin where he found carving or gilding or coffered ceilings already in place, as in the Hôtel de Ville, is pathetic. In short he was virtually trying to reintroduce a style based on fresco painting in buildings of another genius than ours. When there is in Puvis's

PUVIS DE CHAVANNES: DOUX PAYS

HENRI MARTIN: SUMMER HÔTEL DE VILLE

sense a wall, a great blank space entirely at the artist's
disposal, it seems to me his canons hold absolutely.
Where, on the contrary, there is architectural
decoration, moldings, gilding and the like, a more
colorful and pictorial style, such as that of Venice,
seems not merely proper but inevitable. The final
decorative effect is shared between the architect and
the painter; there is no wall, but a series of gorgeous
frames, ready made settings in which the decoration
must be so many jewels.

Still the rigorous idealism of Puvis has been most
salutary. It has forced the decorator to think, it has
emphasized the difference between mural decoration
and the mere picture. No artist of our time has had a
more single purpose. Puvis lived in contemplation
of the finest thinking of his age, ever seeking symbols
for the things of the mind, and significantly finding
those symbols in a Grecian golden age. Beside this
timeless country, which is his most personal creation,
he revived the legends of France, saintly or heroic.
His last picture, which immortalizes the form of his
life-long companion, was St. Genevieve in vigil over
Paris. It is a marvel of beautiful feeling, and in its
just and delicate indications of a city sleeping under
the moon, a marvel of beautiful seeing. In the dignity
of the pattern it was well fitted to be the artistic
testament of the greatest of modern decorators.

It may be interesting, as showing that there are
many ways of wall painting, to consider what is
really a completion of Puvis's stories, The Death of

Ecole de Pharmacie

BESNARD: THE LABORATORY

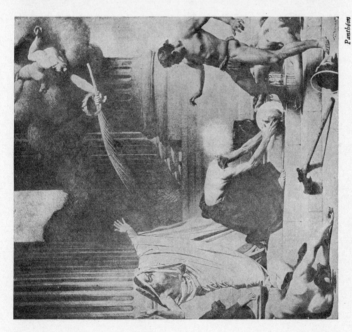

Panthéon

BONNAT: MARTYRDOM OF S. DENIS

St. Genevieve, by Jean Paul Laurens. In its sturdy
archæological realism it is an interesting contrast
to the Puvises. There we have legend, a tradition
that has acquired tenderness in passing through
reverent minds. Here we have not legend but the
resolute attempt to reconstruct a fact, as it might have
been. It is very able and honest. It vividly suggests
the actuality of a half barbaric France. Yet I think
the legendary mood more proper to decorations as
more collective and simple. Just a look at the very
shocking failure which Léon Bonnat made of the
Martyrdom of St. Denis, will remind us of the need of
Puvis's reform. The combination of a raw realism
with archæology has merely produced sensationalism
of the cheapest sort. The solemn walls of the Panthéon cry out against it.

Delacroix, we have seen, reconstituted wall painting on the basis of the Venetian manner. That has
become almost standard for our times. But Delacroix
in his titanism ever tends to strain the bounds of
decoration. As pure decorator in the Renaissance
tradition Paul Baudry is a more representative figure.
He was trained in that cult of fine painting which
grew up with the new Empire and he was asked to
decorate the most sumptuous building of that day,
the new Opera House at Paris.

The architectural setting is so elaborate that the
paintings barely hold their own. Yet they are among
the most accomplished products of the century.
Baudry goes back for inspiration to Paolo Veronese.

The key of color is kept high, blues relieved by rose predominating. There are no heavy shadows and there is some sense of out-of-door lighting. The balance is active, depending on sharply opposed and compensating thrusts. All these qualities as also the elegant geniality of the work are capitally illustrated in the ceiling panel devoted to comedy. Comedy is an unashamed but splendid hoyden tearing the heroic lion skin from a humorously appalled Hercules. Mere strength avails not against laughter, especially against the potent laughter of the female of the species.

Baudry's spandrel and lunette designs for the Foyer of the Opera are extraordinary examples of successful space filling. The blitheness of the mood is appropriate to the place, the combination of a thoughtful classicism with an unmistakably Parisian verve is delightful. On the side walls are ovals with smiling geniuses representing the music of the various countries. Undoubtedly Baudry has been inspired by those designs which Correggio set in the ceiling of the nuns' parlor in the convent St. Francesco at Parma. Baudry's ovals are the minor part of the whole decorative composition and recall not merely Correggio, but, by their Gallic spirit, the best eighteenth century decorations, as those of Boucher.

It was the merit of Paul Baudry to show, as a greater Paul had proved three hundred years ago in Venice, that the finest painting, and all the more intimate mysteries of handling are available for decoration. Indeed there may be just a shade of supererogation about these panels for the Opera, just as there is about Paolo Veronese's ceilings. One asks if poorer painting and less precious would not have done as well. Of the decorators who bear the stamp of the Second Empire Baudry is the greatest, and his influence has been great in all the higher ranges of what we may call, descriptively and not disrespectfully, commercial mural painting.

When Luminism became a leading motive in modern art, naturally its influence reached to decoration. At first blush one would say that nothing could be more anti-monumental and more undecorative than the patternless coruscation of Claude Monet. Yet he had made notable innovations in color which were bound to be widely tried. He has cherished, I am told, the ambition of decorating great spaces. In general, however, the lack of organization in plane of Luminist pictures is evident. And the twilight impressionists, as Carrière, are also ineffective as decorators, clarity being a requisite of all monumental design. Of course the bright key of color has forced its way into decoration, in Anquetin in France, in the earlier decorations of Robert Reid in America, for example. But the only successful attempt to introduce into wall painting the division of tone, and suppression of line seems to me that of the contemporary French artist Henri Martin. Martin began in the late '80s when symbolism was the latest note in French poetry. He belonged for a time to a mystical group of artists who called themselves the Rosicrucians, and his earliest successes were in mediæval subjects, as the Vision of Dante, expressed in a modification of the method of Claude Monet. Martin uses instead of dots a multiplicity of short strokes of frank color which the eye blends into a coruscation.

When the State gave him a great mural commission at Toulouse he shifted with startling suddenness and skill from mediævalism and the Red Cross mode, to a kind of realism in which Millet and Pissarro seemed to blend. The theme was work, the treatment contemporary. The great panel of the Mowers was a sensation in the Salon of 1893. For the first time in art a great space was filled with the inner glow of Monet, and it was done without sacrificing form or rhythm. The critics generally hailed it as a masterpiece. Others differed. I recall a delightful little old French lady, all black silk and ivory wrinkles, who sniffed, turned her back on it and audibly exclaimed, "How vulgar—" Comme c'est vulgaire! She was a survivor of the era of fine painting. All the same Henri Martin had made a successful transfer of the procedures of luminism to monumental design, and in that vein has added triumph to triumph.

Rather few have followed him though luminism of a fantastic and artificial sort is vivaciously represented in minor decoration by the poster artists, Willette and Chéret, as it was in the more festive phase of Besnard in France and Robert Reid in America, and Frank Brangwyn in England. I think the value of the prismatic method for decoration is still more or less questionable. Certainly Martin is the only man who has achieved monumentality along these lines.

The quest of light and reality was followed by a most various genius, Albert Besnard. He has adventured in every vein, expressing, like a new Fragonard, the greatest audacities of brush work, and in his Algerian and Indian subjects the most intense and delicate preoccupation with light. Much of his work like the ceiling for the Hôtel de Ville, and the decorations of the Opera Comique at Paris is fantastic, such decorations as those for the Petit Palais hark back to the *École Galante*. But his deepest mark on modern decoration is the series of wall paintings finished in the early '90s for the École de Pharmacie.

In these epoch-making designs he asserts the obvious but also audacious principle that the decoration of a building should grow out of its everyday use. In the case before him he felt it would be enough merely to magnify the theme of medicine, to follow the doctor to the bedside, the chemist to his laboratory, and to give the whole a background of the history of healing herbs and minerals. It would suffice, he felt, merely to see all this in a large way, and the results fully justified him. In the actual painting he adopted the new compromise with Impressionism, kept the whole key high and accurate without sacrificing line and pattern.

This notion of letting decoration grow out of daily use or out of intimate history has been frequently followed. In America, notably by a very accom-

plished mural painter, W. B. Van Ingen. He sticks
to what my students of a few years back used to
call the "brass tacks" of the matter. When he
decorates the Directors' room of the Edison Company, the panels represent the crucial experiments in
electricity from Benjamin Franklin's kite down. His
decoration for the Administrative building of the
Panama Canal, is an actual record of the main phases
of the excavation studied on the spot before the
water was let in.

What from its most successful example we may call
the decorative procedure of Besnard is you will see
entirely akin to literary realism. It has the same
merits and defects. It permits a certain exaltation of
common things, but keeps such exaltation pretty
well within the limits of prose. Indeed the greatest
men who have used this realistic mode have done so
rather exceptionally, and have declined to be bound
by the formula. Henri Martin becomes idyllic poet
in the decoration of the poet Rostand's house, and
Besnard often adventures freely in the realm of the
mythological and heroic.

The latest notable movement in French wall
painting is the search for naïve simplicity. It grows
out of Puvis and is somewhat influenced by Post-
Impressionism. The most distinguished representative of the class is Maurice Denis. He pushes the
simplicity of Puvis to conscious naïveté, with con-
sequent loss of dignity, he shrewdly observes all
the new discoveries in color, whether in the nat-

uralistic glow of Auguste Renoir or in the conventional schemes of the Post-Impressionists. An admirable example of his manner is in the house of the amateur M. Charles Stern of Paris. The subject is the prologue to Boccaccio's "Decameron." The bathing scene is strangely reminiscent of Puvis. A companion piece, the Evening Song is more original. I think we have to do with a romantic primitivism very charming and possibly not very important. One may be grateful for the strain of poetry in it, even if the idyl be as sophisticated as a pastoral by Verlaine.

France is the leading nation in decoration as elsewhere in the Arts. America in mural painting is a good second. Before sketching our own development, just a word is necessary on the mural painting of other European countries.

England had always in sight the splendid ceiling of Rubens in Whitehall. Through the eighteenth century traveling Italians like Sebastiano Ricci and Verrio spread on the walls and ceilings of country houses or palaces mythological designs which retained some flavor of the Renaissance. Even the realist Hogarth accepted this florid style in the big picture of the Pool of Siloam, which is virtually a decoration, for Bethlehem Hospital. Sir Joshua Reynolds, in the latter years of the eighteenth century, preached the grand style of Raphael and Michelangelo in his famous "Discourses" but the result was little at the time. Sir James Barry in his ambitious canvases representing the history of civilization, in the new home of the Royal Institution (1780), made a serious but unsuccessful attempt to live up to the austere doctrine of the "Discourses." Just before the century closed the delightful illustrator, Thomas Stothard, in 1783, decorated the grand staircase of Burleigh Hall with compositions depicting Temperance and Intemperance. There is vivacious mixture of the draped and nude figure, graceful symbolism, and rich color framed in rather incongruously heavy architectural backgrounds derived from Rubens. It was the last gasp of a lovely tradition.

But the first real interest in mural painting in England was parliamentary. When the new Parliament Houses were finished, in 1842, a Royal Commission undertook to make the event memorable for "promoting and encouraging the fine arts in the United Kingdom." There ensued about twenty well meaning but heartbreaking years. Instead of going directly to good artists, the Commissioners held competition after competition. Everybody was stirred up by false hopes and impelled to fruitless labor. The commissioners further complicated a bad matter, by resolving to revive the noble lost art of painting in fresco. It was a worthy ambition, but a thing that could never be done to order in a hurry. It resulted in futile study of ambiguous old treatises on the art, and in official consultation with Peter Cornelius, who at Munich was quite successfully perpetrating in the valued fresco medium about the worst art of the century.

The commissioners enlisted only two painters of decorative gift, the venerable William Dyce and young G. F. Watts. I have no need to dwell upon the merely competent work of Edward Cope, Armitage, Maclise, and Gilbert. It was produced under conditions of appalling difficulty; the plaster and the colors went wrong; the work had to be done over many times. At last it was unveiled in dusky Gothic halls with impossible cross lights, which were further complicated by stained glass windows, so that the finished frescoes have been from the first decoratively ineffective, and virtually invisible. The great adventure so earnestly believed in since Sir Joshua, ended in a fiasco. What might have happened had suitably lighted spaces been provided, the artist left free to choose his own materials, and men of the decorative strength of Watts and Alfred Stevens, or of the great native talent of Rossetti and Millais selected, is pleasant to dream of.

Before the Parliament Houses were provided with their invisible decorations, the Pre-Raphaelites made their endeavor to revive legend on the library walls of the Oxford Union. The year was 1856. Dante Gabriel Rossetti was the leading spirit, and he enlisted an extraordinary lot of young men—Arthur Hughes, Burne-Jones, William Morris, and Spencer Stanhope. From the first the work went badly. The stories of King Arthur were tinted in ordinary water color on the dry plaster, and the wall literally drank up the decorations as fast as they were finished. To-day

G. F. WATTS: JURISPRUDENCE

G. F. WATTS: CHAOS, THE TITANS, STUDY FOR MURAL
PAINTING

only a few blurs in the Gothic lunettes tell the story
of a generous but ill-considered endeavor.

Plainly the forte of the English is not monumental
painting. What they have done in mural painting
has been sporadic, and little of it notable. They have
given the control of such work to amateurs; they
have used not at all or grudgingly their greatest
decorative talents Blake and Watts, and they have
gladly given perfectly good walls to mere nobodies.
Fortunately we have some fragment of what might
have been the vast decorative achievement of Watts.
The great cycle of the history of civilization which
he contemplated he was never allowed to undertake,
but there are sketches and here and there a picture to
indicate its importance, such as the grand study for
the titans at the Tate. There are good frescoes
by Watts in the villa of Carreggi near Florence,
and in 1852 the benchers of Lincolns Inn, London,
accepted his offer to do for the costs a great fresco
representing the law. Watts wove the group of great
law makers and advocates together after the fashion
of Raphael, in carefully balanced uprights and curves,
achieving without loss of warmth a real dignity.
Somewhat obscured by the ornate architecture and
accessories of the great hall, it is one of the best
modern decorations in the serener tradition of the
Renaissance.

Only a little later Sir Frederick Leighton did for the
new South Kensington Museum two immense frescoes, the Arts of Peace and the Arts of War. The

tradition is still Raphael's, the work more competent than inspiring. The great medallion in St. Pauls, done in his last years and entitled "And the Sea Shall give up its Dead," makes no more favorable impression.

Of course the popular and characteristic decoration of Victorian England was that of the Pre-Raphaelites, especially William Morris and Burne-Jones. The style has certain excellences. It is lucid and regardful of pattern. For a private house one could not imagine a more charming decoration than a suite of fairy tales, the Enchanted Princess, the Story of Psyche, or the like, by Burne-Jones. But it is minor decoration after all, without monumentality, better fitted for stained glass and tapestry than otherwise. It has become, in various dilutions and infusions a standard mode for church decoration. But even there, it by no means corresponds to the heroic aspect of religion, and you can hardly imagine it in a civic hall worthily conveying the sterner legends of a nation.

About the most strikingly inventive painter that England has produced since Hogarth is Ford Madox Brown. In his early maturity he gave the fillip to Pre-Raphaelitism, in his extreme old age he became a pioneer of realistic decoration. In the late seventies he undertook the decoration of a room in the Manchester City Hall. Besides the inevitable historic subjects, the Romans Building the City Wall, etc., he painted what one may call the inner greatness of the city. It was an audacity to make a mural painting out of the astronomer Crabtree in his darkened room, demonstrating the Transit of Venus. Even if the panel is not notably decorative, as it is not, it shows freshness of mind and a new departure. Brown may well have influenced Besnard in the decorations of the École de Farmacie, and he unquestionably prepared the way for Frank Brangwyn's poems of work. Brown died regretting that he had not studied Rubens in his early years and learned to paint. If more British artists had come in time to so intelligent a conclusion, there would be more British art.

Frank Brangwyn is an enigmatic apparition. At bottom he is a romantic of the vehement type. He is a gorgeous colorist and conversant with all the procedures of Luminism. He dazzles rather than charms, and in his very able visions of toil in the mills and fields, such as he has done in London and San Francisco and Cleveland, I feel rather the immensely clever person than the great artist. At least he is a refreshing and valid impression amid the general tedium of recent English painting.

German art with its tendency to minute detail, individual characterization, and inwardness has rarely attained monumentality. Its greatest achievements are not in painting, but in the copper-plates and woodcuts of Dürer and Holbein. Yet the endeavor of Germany to achieve a monumental art worthy of her growing greatness, has been so earnest, that we cannot, because of its partial success, wholly neglect it.

Pathetically, the more serious the German mural

painter is, the worse paintings he perpetrates. This
was the case with the initiator of the monumental
style, Peter Cornelius. He was born in 1783, at
Düsseldorf, the son of the local gallery director. In
his eighteenth year he found himself at Rome closely
associated with the so-called Nazarenes—Overbeck,
Schadow, Veit. Like them he was a pious Catholic,
an admirer of the chaste and timid perfections of
the early Italian masters. Cornelius dreamt of a
revival of German art. All that was necessary was to
master the forgotten art of fresco and spread upon
the walls of Germany the Scripture narratives and
her own heroic legends. So Cornelius made himself the most competent practitioner in fresco of the
century.

In 1818 the dilettante Maecenas, Crown Prince
Ludwig of Bavaria, came to Rome and interested
himself in the Nazarenes. Cornelius was called back to
Bavaria with the directorship of the Academy at
Düsseldorf, and a splendid commission to decorate the
new sculpture museum at Munich. Upon the vaults,
lunettes and spandrels he spread the Grecian mythology and the story of Troy, with a mixture of sentimental insipidity and outrageous sensationalism which
won immediate and universal applause.

Honors and commissions were thenceforth show-
ered upon him. He painted the Loggia of the new
picture gallery at Munich, and covered the end wall
of the new Ludwig's Church with a Last Judgment,
the vaults being occupied by groups of Apostles and

Church Fathers. The decoration is heavy and rest-less. Again the endeavor to blend the sweetness of Raphael with the grandiosity of Michelangelo results in failure. It is, or at least until lately was, the largest single fresco in the world. The statistically minded will be glad to learn that it is just 700 square feet larger than Michelangelo's Last Judgment. Cornelius executed every square inch of it with his own hand. Cornelius's design is as feeble as it is pretentious. Nothing is strongly felt or firmly asserted. It is pieced together almost mechanically, and represents only a colossal painstaking.

In 1855 Cornelius told King Ludwig: "We have fought a good fight; we have left the Fatherland a better art than we found." This was true in a pathetic sense. They had found nothing and they had left not much but yet something.

In 1861 Cornelius was translated, one may say, to Berlin, where new honors were piled upon him. He did grandiose cartoons for the Royal Cemetery, and another Last Judgment for the new Protestant Cathedral. He was venerated as no artist of our times. I used to hear my old master Hermann Grimm compare his designs with the best of Dürer's. There could be no more striking instance of the eminently Teutonic habit of judging rather by intention than by accomplishment.

More significant than the mythologies and relig-iosities of Cornelius are those designs in which the Rhinelander, Alfred Rethel, and the Austrian, Moritz

SCHWIND: THE WILD HUNTSMAN

RETHEL: CARTOON FOR TOMB OF CHARLEMAGNE

Schwind, embodied the folk lore and the heroic legends of the German race.

Alfred Rethel was born in 1816 near Aix-la-Chapelle, within sight of the basilica which covers the tomb of Charlemagne. At thirteen he studied at Düsseldorf under the inspired Nazarene, Schadow, but he soon escaped and began the roving, uneasy career which wore him out prematurely. He developed as an austere and expressive illustrator of the Bible and of the great National Epic, the Niebelungenlied. In 1842 the city of Frankfurt-am-Main intrusted him with four of a series of Emperors for the historic hall called the Römer. Rethel went to Rome to learn the technic of fresco, and later accomplished his task with competence and dignity.

In 1847 he was charged with the decoration of the great Gothic Hall of the Rathhaus of Aix-la-Chapelle—the subjects being the deeds and posthumous legend of Charlemagne. He had to deal with refractory spaces, Gothic lunettes. For seven years he toiled under the most ungrateful conditions, the hall being open to the noise and comment of tourists and busybodies. Through defective technic the frescoes have almost perished, but the original designs tell us of their real monumentality. It would be hard to imagine anything more stately or justly proportioned than the picture of the Baptism of the Pagan Chieftain, Wittikind. Rethel has recovered much of authoritatively simple contour of Giotto, and fairly anticipates the grandeur of Puvis de Chavannes. Of

a Blakelike awesomeness is the scene where Kaiser
Otto III, having broken into the Tomb of Charlemagne, kneels before the grimly enthroned mummy
of his great predecessor. Creations of this power and
sincerity suggest in Rethel a genius for historic painting which is only half realized in these fading frescoes
in Charlemagne's ancient capital.

The world justly knows Rethel best as the creator
of the admirable wood-cut series the Dance of Death.
The work speaks the tragic despair that followed the
abortive Revolution of 1848. An ardent Democrat,
Rethel agonized when he saw what he believed
noblest and most promising in German idealism trodden down by Prussian *Junkerthum*. The tragedy of
it all bit deep into his spirit, and his mind perished
some years before 1859, when his body also died.
Under more favorable conditions he might have been
the greatest monumental painter of the century; as it
is, he is one of its greatest spirits.

Far the most captivating figure in modern German
painting is Moritz von Schwind. He was born of
noble family, at Vienna, in 1804. A friendly, whimsical man, an excellent violinist, he easily gathered
everywhere about him the choicest spirits. Years
of his boyhood were passed in the country in Bohemia
on a soil redolent of history and legend. When he
moved to Munich, to work with Cornelius, he began
that remarkable series of illustrations of German
hero and folk lore, which quickly endeared him to the
public. The swagger of Puss in Boots, the sweet-

ness of Cinderella, follow his pencil point. The
story of the Seven Ravens and of the fated water
nymph Melusine gain new life through him; and there
are entrancing little scenes from contemporary life
touched with a quaint mixture of wit and sentimentality. All his life long he turned off book illustrations, always of highly decorative character, and
mural decorations which often seem so many big book
illustrations.

Schwind's frescoes for the venerable Cathedral of
Speier have dignity, but do not fully enlist his tenderness. In 1854 he received the alluring commission to
decorate the historic castle of the Wartburg, with the
legend of St. Elizabeth, including the traditional scene
of the singer's tournament in Tannhaüser. Schwind
on these haunted walls charmingly revived this
legend and that of St. Elizabeth. The little panel in
which before the reverent eyes of St. Louis the
loaves in St. Elizabeth's apron turn to roses, is familiar
and sufficiently representative of the style. It recalls,
with a difference much in Schwind's favor, the nearly
contemporary work of the English Pre-Raphaelites.

In 1863 Schwind was called back to his native
Vienna to design lunettes for the foyer of the Opera
house. These were so many suggestions of favorite
operas. The quaintness and mystery of Weber's
"Freischutz" are admirably visualized in the scene of
the homekeeping women between the terror of the
wild huntsmen on one side, and the cheerful departure for the hunt on the other. The whole series is a

delightful example of what may be called intimate decoration.

Within the limits he set for himself, Schwind's art is perfect. It emulates not the great heroic designs of the Renaissance, but the best legendary panels in Pompeian houses, or the little stories with which the Italians adorned their *loggie*. The deeper imagination is not expected of such work. Its quality is to be tactful and appealing. A tender sort of fancy rather than a strenuous imagination is its mainspring. A delightful residue of homeliness is its distinction. Moritz von Schwind was so perfect an exemplar of all that was most amiable in Germany of the Romantic period, that I cannot believe he will be forgotten. He finished the winsome lunettes for the Vienna opera house in 1866 at the moment when the new *Real-Politik*, at Sadowa and Königratz was shooting German romanticism to pieces. So Rethel eighteen years earlier had toiled at the Charlemagne frescoes at Aix-la-Chapelle, through the hours when the political liberalism of Germany was bleeding to death on the barricades.

This kind of a fate has followed mural painting in Germany. The times have been adverse to it. The few stately or lovely examples I have been able to cull are so many flowers plucked in a desert.

To give an adequate idea of American mural painting, in the space allotted to me, is impossible. Yet the main tendencies may be indicated. What impresses me is less individual artists than the devel-

opment as a whole. In the thirty-three years since
the Columbian Exposition at Chicago, mural painting has come to be part and parcel of our life. In 1890
you could have counted the notable decorations in
America on the fingers of your two hands; to-day the
mere list would make a considerable book. This
means opportunity for the artist and best promise for
the future.

Our decorative origins were both humble and exotic. In old houses of Charleston and New Orleans
you will find in panels over the doors the survival of
the *École galante*. Italy appears in dilapidated estate
in the dome of our Capitol, in the allegorical frescoes
of Brumidi. Our earliest native product is in the
historical paintings of the Rotunda by Weir, Trumbull and others. As adornment, they are not ex-
hilirating, but at least on the topical side they set a
sound precedent which has been far more ably
followed by such contemporaries as C. Y. Turner,
Francis D. Millet, Violet Oakley, Edward Simmons
and Robert Reid. Art came into American mural
painting in the person of John La Farge, who in 1876
decorated Trinity church, Boston. His really distinguished work is marred by cruel conditions of
light, but it still marks a great moment. La Farge
built up a company of eager young helpers, Francis D.
Millet, Francis Lathrop, Kenyon Cox, among others,
and taught them the decorator's trade. More important yet, he naturalized among us the Renaissance
manner which he had learned from direct study of the

old masters as well as through Delacroix. At the outset he attained a color and grace that established a standard. His serene and versatile talent was only partly devoted to decoration. Intermittently he produced the most gracious designs, by preference historical—"Things as they might have been," he used to say to me. None of these is finer than the great Ascension in the New York church of that name which was finished in 1887. It is a most characteristic and skillful composite, the figure composition being taken almost bodily from a well-known Assumption of Palma Vecchio's school, and the landscape being based on a sketch made in Japan. Yet it is a complete and original creation and perhaps the finest religious decoration America has produced. In slighter vein La Farge did charming work in the Whitelaw Reid and Cornelius Vanderbilt houses, and in his feeble old age he put through by sheer force of mind and will the fine panels at Baltimore and St. Paul. No man did more for mural painting in America through the training of others, but his work in its clear relation to Delacroix and the great Venetians retains a solitary character.

In 1878, only two years later than the decoration of Trinity church, W. M. Hunt, the friend and adviser of La Farge, was asked to paint two lunettes in the Assembly chamber in the Albany Capitol. Hunt was trained in the school of fine painting under Couture, and sobered through association with Millet. He chose for symbolism and allegory, the

Barque of the Discoverer and the Flight of Night. Both had a fine conventional energy. Paul Baudry's opera decorations may well have been in his mind. Hunt's panels were set in unfit surroundings and in a few years were covered up in the reconstruction of the badly built room, only to perish utterly through later rebuilding. They were fine things in an academic way and served a most useful purpose in showing that America had artists professionally competent to design and execute monumental decorations.

Meanwhile, largely under the influence of that great minded architect, Charles F. McKim, private houses were being decorated. We have noted La Farge's work of this sort. Elihu Vedder began in the Collis P. Huntington House, in New York, the sort of work he perfected in the Bowdoin Art Gallery and the Library of Congress. It is a wholly symbolic art, plastic and impressive, austere in color, markedly rhythmical in pattern. Its precedents are in that Italy which has been Vedder's home of election, but again the brooding, sensuous quality is Vedder's own. Taking no account of the modern dogmas of flatness and blondness, it has not had its due praise. But I do not know a hall that is not richer for a Vedder decoration, richer both to the eye and to the mind; and I think the future will value the work more highly than the present does.

Within a matter of four years from 1893 the decorations of the Columbian Exposition had flowered and perished, the decoration of the Appellate Court in

J. S. SARGENT: THE SACRAMENT

JOHN LA FARGE: THE ASCENSION

New York, and of the Congressional Library had been completed, and the decoration of the Boston Public Library had been nobly begun. At the same time theaters, concert halls, and even hotels and railway stations were offering their walls to the artist, and office buildings were soon to follow. The development between 1890 and 1900 was merely on the material side one of the remarkable moments in the history of art, and the product suffered naturally from a somewhat mushroom growth. I cannot trace even in outline a movement excellently sketched in Samuel Isham's book, and critically analyzed in Edwin Blashfield's. It would be a pure subjectivity to extol personal favorites.

I wish rather to express my admiration for the sane professionalism that such veterans as Blashfield and Kenyon Cox have maintained, my admiration too for their capacity for growth. Both, somewhat against prevailing notions have stood firm for the place of symbolism and allegory as an enhancement of narrative and history. A fine example of the method is Blashfield's Washington Resigning His Commission, at Baltimore. It is valuable to keep the spirit of imagination alive in a positive age. How inevitably enhanced feeling seeks metaphor and symbol! Edwin Abbey, in the Boston Public Library the naïve illustrator of Malory, in the Pennsylvania Capitol renewed the mixed mood of reality and symbolism in which the warmer hearted decorators have ever indulged. Edward Simmons's pendentives at St. Paul are extraordinarily fine creations in the same traditional vein.

Yet there are many ways. And I have nothing but appreciation for the sterling historic designs of Turner, Millet, Reid, Simmons. Akin to these is the topical decoration, with daily toil as its theme, Van Ingen's record of the digging of the Canal at Panama. Frederick Dana Marsh's admirable pictures of mechanics' work in the Engineer's Club, New York, the late John W. Alexander's History of the Book in the Congressional Library. Of such is the fine prose of mural painting.

Alongside of these topical and traditional modes we find a delicate and learned eclecticism which is represented in Siddons Mowbray's library decorations for the University Club, New York, and John Sargent's extraordinary series on the History of Religion in the Boston Public Library. Mowbray's skillful adaption of the gilded relief, and coffering, and figure painting of the Borgia apartments certainly makes a harmonious room. Yet it has an exotic feeling, and arouses hazardous comparisons with the original at Rome.

From this defect Sargent's decorations are entirely free. They are immensely learned and in a measure composite, but the blend is so fine and potent that the particular ingredients no longer matter. Mr. Sargent was fortunate in controlling the decoration of the entire room. Half the ineffectiveness of our mural painting, as Mr. Blashfield has pointed out in his book, results from the failure of the artist to control

the minor decoration. In the hall of the Virgin and
Astarte, despite refractory architectural conditions, a
great harmony rules. Mr. Sargent will doubtless be
criticized for what is his greatest originality. After
the fashion of the primitive Spanish altarbacks, he has
thrust up the gold in relief as the dominant, under-
weaving it with a sharp contrast of scarlets and blues.
In the vault where are depicted the mysteries of the
rosary he has hidden away in oval and quatrefoil
compositions of the greatest beauty and tenderness.
Such a passage as the Boy Christ rushing to His
Mother is, I imagine, new to art. El Greco would
envy the invention. The complexity, the tendency to
obscure what most artists emphasize is baffling. It is
absent in the lunettes representing Israel, and the
three of the Last Judgment. One is grateful for such
an invention as the Messianic Era, with the superb
and radiant action of the Angels of the Gates—grateful that it is frankly announced.

Yet before joining in the obvious criticism of the
vaults, I ask myself, where else on this side of the
water can I experience such splendor? Where on the
other can I equal it? Certainly in few enough places,
possibly in the matchless baptistery at St. Prassede
at Rome, or at Ravenna. And for this impression of
splendor I am so grateful, that I shall not complain if
amidst it I happen almost incidentally upon images of
deepest tenderness and passion. These decorations
are so rich whether as decoration or narrative that
they will require time and knowing.

Their very eclectic and archæological character is merely an emphasis of qualities still pretty general in our mural painting. Few men have the audacity to strike out as A. B. Davies did in his semi-cubistic decorations for a private music room. This very successful adventure is rather isolated. The general note is still rather that of a sound professionalism than of a notable inventiveness.

THE REACTION AGAINST IMPRESSIONISM

THE REACTION AGAINST IMPRESSIONISM

Seurat, Van Gogh, Gauguin, Cézanne

WE may take the year 1895 as the turning point from Impressionism to those new movements, which, largely dominated by Cézanne, are comprised in the term Post-Impressionism. In 1895 the French Ministry of Fine Arts grudgingly accepted for the Luxembourg Caillebotte's bequest of Luminist paintings. But most of the Cézannes were weeded out of the Caillebotte gift, and he gained nothing from the complaisance of the Institute. So his friend and later biographer, the dealer, M. Vollard, promptly organized the first comprehensive exhibition of Cézanne's work. In those rugged and ragged canvases lay in germ pretty nearly all the experimentations and aberrations that were to mark the next quarter century. At the moment only J. K. Huysmans caught the meaning of the show. He wrote what may be the final judgment on the eccentric Master of Aix: "An artist with abnormal retinas who in apperceptions exaggerated by his peculiar eyesight is discovering the approaches to a new art."

The art of Cézanne represents in its purest and most pregnant form the reaction against Luminism, but before entering on that large theme, a word is necessary on certain other dissidents from Monet's theory and practice.

Even the Neo-Impressionists who ostensibly were merely carrying forward the work of Monet, by reducing to a science the methods of *"la peinture claire,"* were largely its critics. Especially Georges Seurat, some of whose most notable canvases appeared as early as 1884, in the first Salon des Indépendants, announced a return from the art of time-of-day to that of the Museums. While working out the procedure of dotting in color to its ultimate and self-defeating perfection—for so he only achieved a most complicated and difficult method of producing tone—Seurat in his practice hit straight at the dazzle and flimsiness of the Impressionists. Even more he eschewed their chance-caught arrangements in favor of dense and carefully studied compositions built solidly not only in pattern but also in mass. Seurat took festal Paris for his theme, became its admirable illustrator in humoresque and at time subsatirical mood.

And this everyday quality of illustration in such canvases as Le Chahut and those devoted to the circus, makes it difficult for the layman to appreciate Seurat's extraordinary gifts as a composer—the depth of his rhythms, the fastidiousness of his patterns, and withal his command of the æsthetic of the third dimension. All these perfections merely seem so many queernesses to an untrained eye. A trained appreciation will find the most piquant relish in Seurat's

Louvre

SEURAT: LE CIRQUE

search of grave and noble design at the suburban fair and in the music hall. He is at once so gay and so serious! Possibly these are gifts of youth. Seurat's Sunday at the Grande-Jatte was exhibited with the Indépendants in 1886, his twenty-seventh year, and his handful of canvases ending with Le Chahut of 1890 were completed within the remaining five years before his early death. No strenuously inventive artist has even been at ease with his art in his early thirties, and Seurat had no time to learn how to conceal his effort—in short to mature. It is evident that the great decorator in him was only partly realized. A full generation after his death he is an influence on the young men who are seeking to regain the nearly lost art of fine composition.

The year Seurat died, 1891, Piérre Bonnard and Émile Bernard made their first appearance with the Indépendants. They were men in the early twenties, enamored of the new "bright painting" but also enamored of the art of the museums. With somewhat less tenacity than Seurat, they have carried forward his experiments in figure composition and in division of color. Bonnard in his bathing scenes attains with the glow of flesh in sunshine great clarity and monumentality. He is more genial than Seurat, nearer to Renoir and the eighteenth century tradition. Bernard, a thoughtful and rich composer in his own right, has been unfairly overshadowed by his mad friend and correspondent, Vincent Van Gogh. It is perilous to fly with a comet; men remember only the blaze.

VAN GOGH: CYPRESSES

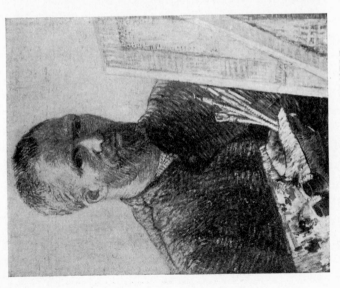

VAN GOGH: PORTRAIT OF HIMSELF

We have been dealing with that criticism of Impressionism which grew out of its own practitioners. We have now to consider the far more radical dissent of such men as Van Gogh, Gauguin, and Cézanne. And since their painting gave rise to the most extravagant theories it is well to insist at once that, save Cézanne, who, too, was a theorist only in a very limited sense, these men were not doctrinaires at all, but simply artists of independent bent deeply conscious of the defects of Impressionism and variously fumbling for a better method of expression. All three, as compared with such quasi-scientific types as Pissarro, Monet, Seurat and Signac, were professed emotionalists and while they were not conscious of any unity of purpose, in fact disapproved all around of each other's works, Expressionism is the word that best reveals their common aim. The more usual term Post-Impressionism has only chronological significance and might well be discarded.

But Cézanne, Van Gogh, and Gauguin, being all pre-destined expressionists, by the good right of having been born respectively crank, madman, and outlaw, were so more or less unconsciously and without programme. In this they differed from their successors of Henri Matisse's type, who have ritualized the cult of individual expression. These earlier and simpler predecessors wished merely to make very strong and emphatic pictures deeply charged with personal emotion, instead of correct and studied renderings of natural appearances. They all appealed from the notation of weather and time-of-day to the weather that each of us carries inside of him and the time that is measured only by heart throbs.

Vincent Van Gogh was born in Holland in 1853, the son of a Protestant pastor. The boy was solitary, and refra⸱ ory to all education save that of wide and desul ry reading. By his twenty-fifth year he had already broken himself seriously upon life, had failed a. a sa esman of prints, as a school teacher, as a wa dering evangelist to the Belgian miners, had stud ed for the ministry, and been criticized for "an unfor unate excess of zeal." Meanwhile his human compa sion, amid other aberrations, had drawn him to the morbid in exaltations in which piety and sensuality kept unnatural company. He was past thirty befo e he settled to painting and, characteristically, exce t for casual contact with his kinsman, Anton Mauve, and later with Cormon, at Paris, self-trained. He g ew slowly under the influence of Millet, whose vigo ous and humble themes were congenial, and these early studies of peasants and landscapes in charcoal or dark pigments show much power.

By 1886 he found Paris, where under the influence of Delacroix, Cézanne, Monticelli, and the Japanese woodcut masters he adopted wholeheartedly the new "bright painting." Meanwhile he had been for years a pensioner of his younger brother Theodore, whose devotion alone made possible Vincent's brief, incandescent career. In the street scenes and cabaret scenes and portraits painted at Paris between 1886 and 1888,

Van Gogh's bizarre power had already asserted itself. These were pure lyrical expressions hacked out with broad strokes of a brush charged with pure color. The line writhed across the canvas, giving a vivid sense of motion and direction but a weak and approximate notion of forms which in the haste and fury of the creative act were often violently distorted. Alongside the ugly constructional streaks, the canvas was left bare, the whole thing looked harrowed in the pigment, rather than painted, and was, withal, most sonorous in its abstract color and gripping in its lyrical attack upon the sensibilities. Nothing could be farther from the discretion of the time-of-day school. We have to do with a new symbolism for frenzy in abstract splendors of color and denatured forms; we have to do with a swift and transient pang of creation, with an agony quickly wreaked and exhausted, with so many orgasms of a spirit always near the breaking point.

It was at Arles-in-Provence, whither Vincent in 1888, his 35th year, had betaken himself for greater reverberations of sunlight than Paris afforded, it was at sun-smitten Arles that the breaking point came. Between the pictures which he painted in the asylum and those which date from before and after his overt madness there is no perceptible difference. All show an exasperation of vitality; the gentle olive, the stately cypress take up a swirl which comes from or passes into a vortical sky. In portraits, the loaded streaks of orange and cinnabar rise and fall over the

bony structure like a heavy textile shaken from be-
neath; the whole is a topographical survey of faces
generally ravaged with sinister feeling. At about this
time Cézanne saw Van Gogh paint and told him quite
brutally the simple truth that he "painted like a
madman." We should add "like a madman of
genius," for Vincent lived ever in that confusing bor-
derland where the lyrical muse and madness are wont
to consort. The year of his first breakdown, 1888,
he exhibited three of his Parisian poesies with the
Indépendants, and at thirty-five began to enjoy a certain esteem. For two years still he painted at Arles
then returned to Paris, only once more to break and
to perish by his own hand. The year was 1890, his
thirty-seventh. His work had all been packed into
the last six years of a life ever more rapidly lurching
into insanity.

In such a career there is much for amazement, much
for admiration and more for pity. Certain essential
explanations are lacking. As we have to do with a
diseased brain in Van Gogh, we probably have to do
also with a diseased retina. What the critic calls
creative distortion may have been something near his
actual vision of the world, but of this we are not
certain. What made the career significant for posterity was its uncompromising individualism—here at
last was the theoretical free and isolated personality,
here was a genius quite untainted by education and
tradition, here was the pure uprush of elemental
sensibility, which had been sought for ever since

Rousseau preached the little worth of civilization
and the pricelessness of passion. And so poor Vincent
within ten years of his death was to become a portent
and precedent, and his work exemplary for many who
quite on the safe side of madness were to practice
complacently the art of the emotional crisis.

Renoir here shall guide us when he remarks that
"the true painter loves to play with his canvas
delicately. Here Van Gogh failed. I hear you say,
what a painter! Yes, but the brush has never caressed
his canvas lovingly!" In short the lyric cry of Van
Gogh is always in danger of becoming mere noise,
but some miracle intervenes and holds it within the
realm of music—a music often harsh and barbaric
with a most direct appeal to the nerves. Such was his
art—that of an extraordinary and tragic human
animal seeking apart from the checks of reason full
emotional expression. And naturally those who have
built the art of painting solely upon the human animal
have sought their warrant in the mad painter-poet,
whose naïve expressions, in an age that has reg-
imented the passions themselves, remain in their
kind unsurpassed and probably unsurpassable.

That precious quality of movement which is so
strong in Van Gogh's art is nearly lacking in that of
his whilom associate, Paul Gauguin, whose lucidly
calculated and highly decorative painting has a
fairly Byzantine immobility. This is what might be
expected from the character of the two men. Van
Gogh was a mad poet, a true lyric; Gauguin was a

VAN GOGH: CANAL BRIDGE

GAUGUIN: HAYMAKERS, BRITTANY

more or less theatrical rebel in the conventional
romantic tradition. There is a sort of squalid Byronism in his entire career—in his ruthless waiver of
proximate duties, in his spectacular promenading of
his discontent amid exotic civilizations, in his brutal
dissoluteness, and finally in that chivalric championship of the helpless Marquesans which hastened his
end. All this for good or evil is highly Byronic. So
was Gauguin's pontifical manner as an artist-critic,
so the sardonic bitterness of his correspondence, and
even in his painting, the breadth, the oratorical quality of his effects, the brusquenesses, the absence of
modulation and atmosphere, the barbaric and slightly
artificial glamour of his mood and color—all this may
seem to ally Gauguin with Byron—the decorator
with the rhetorician. Both are saved for art by the
tragedy that ever underlies the pose, by unfulfilled
aspirations, by rare and unexpected lovelinesses,
simplicities, and understandings.

Paul Gauguin, after about seven years of exper-
iment as an amateur, at thirty-five quit a prosperous
business as a broker, and two years later forsook his
wife. He had already exhibited in the Salon and
with the much derided Impressionists, owned Cézannes, had made himself a mediocre Luminist painter
under the advice of Camille Pissarro. In solitary
studies in Brittany, in 1886, he developed his personal
style. It was fostered by the simple profiles of huts,
and boulders, by the looming masses of the *menhirs*,
by the rugged contours of rudely cut Calvaries. He

renounces the envelope once so assiduously studied, the color divisions, the finely adjusted tones, and offers now the nudity of a few carefully assorted objects, their assertion in colors chosen for emphasis and not copied from nature, the frank exaggeration of contour—a method recalling the abstract splendors of mosaic, and possibly owing something to the technically quite similar color prints of Japan. As his vision clarified and his art became more his own, he fell increasingly into poverty. Memories of his childhood in South America, and of his Navy days drew him to the tropics, and a brief and unsuccessful trip to Martinique, in 1887, preluded his ultimate escape to the South Seas. Again he sojourned in Brittany, where disciples sought him, visited Van Gogh at Arles, and left him insane, held his first individual exhibition under the auspices of Theodore Van Gogh, in 1888, and retreated once more to Brittany.

Here he perfected his method and his theory. The method was that of pattern in arabesque defined by contours like that of cloisonné enamel; the theory was that of color equivalences for an entire visual experience. We cannot express light by contrast nor feeling by the colors we actually see—but pure color may symbolize both light and emotion. This doctrine of equivalence was strengthened by his association with the Symboliste poets, who against the Parnassians, as Gauguin against the Impressionists, denied that art began in observation and ended in representation. Syntheticism was the word which

Gauguin and his associates at Pont Aven gave to their endeavor. Émile Bernard claims the invention of the peculiar methods of the Synthesists—the *cloisonné*, the untroubled and unmediated areas of sonorous color, and probably he is right as regards Gauguin. But the "invention," by merely substituting frank colors for tones, might have been drawn from any mural painting of Puvis, and represents an almost inevitable adventure in any colorist who seeks to work by conventions and symbols rather than by representations.

It was the flight to Tahiti in 1891, Gauguin's forty-eighth year, that brought the new æsthetic of Pont Aven before the most alluring and fitting subject-matter. Without this episode, there would be little to say of Gauguin in any general survey of painting. But in the South Seas he had wherewithal to fill and soothe his irritable vision—the silhouette of brown or golden forms against the forest shadows, the jewel-like geometrical splotches where tropical leaves and fruits and flowers glowed in emerald or amber against blue sky, the massive bulk of horses and hounds, the crisp white edge of a curling wave seen between glooming tree-trunks, and everything inter-penetrated with a sense of animal peace and calm, of passion without misgiving or tragedy, rising sap and throbbing blood almost equally inconscient and both moving towards decay and death—such was the vision that this deeply corrupted Parisian caught and fixed in a handful of the most remarkable canvases of our time.

From the great decoration on the Mystery of Human Destiny now at Montpellier, to those little heads which have a faunlike gentleness, we have to do with most distinguished vision and invention. It was as if Gauguin made atonement for his own satanic pride in the expression of such gracious humility and calmed his own stormy lusts in the contemplation of passions that moved below consciousness in a kind of innocence.

But the years at Tahiti and later in the Marquesas were unhappy. In vain he led the savage life. He remained the Parisian, humiliated by poverty, avid of fame. He returned to Paris in his fiftieth year, 1895, and for a couple of years achieved at least notoriety. Then he retreated once more to the South Seas, but not before incurring the shameful disease that carried him off at fifty-five, in 1898. His last act was a magnanimous one—the defence of the poor natives of the Marquesas against the *gens d'armes*. He had the qualities as well as the defects of his Byronism.

On the whole Gauguin is a very isolated and exceptional painter,—a rare creator of moods, a fine inventor of decorative patterns. Eclectically he had drawn from many sources—the conventions of Egyptian bas-relief betray themselves in his compositions. A real progressive, Cézanne, disowned him for his lack of structure. A gifted insurgent of purest Romantic type born too late, Gauguin dead escapes classification among his contemporaries, just as he found no place among them in life. He was a better painter, had a finer taste than either Van Gogh or Cézanne, was a more accomplished and complete figure as a craftsman, but he lacked the lyrical energy of the one and the dogged probity of the other. The fragmentary influence of Van Gogh and Gauguin, who represent respectively a naïf and a sophisticated lyricism, was to be consolidated and imposed upon an entire generation by their older associate, who had no music in his soul at all, Paul Cézanne.

Cézanne, although unwittingly the sponsor of the recent intellectualistic extravagances in painting, was in his own eyes simply an Expressionist—one desiring to find forms for strongest emotions. He divided his painter contemporaries into eunuchs and males, and naturally took his place with the latter. His emotion was a kind of shock experienced before nature, he never improvised, he speaks of it modestly as his "*petite sensation.*" That reflective quality which was really dominant in him he rarely mentions. He writes rather of force—"Nothing but the creative force, *id est* the temperament, can carry any one to the goal which he should attain." Here Cézanne joins hands with Delacroix, whom he deeply admired, and with Henri Matisse, concerning whom he is silent. But his temperament lacked what usually sustains initial emotion, discursive imagination. Without the *motif* before him he was impotent, and the *motif* itself evoked a shifting series of problems which were at once a fascination and a torment. Both in life and art he felt frustrated. A shy and suspicious nature, ne was also a timid and halting craftsman. "I have my little sensation," he told Vollard, "but I do not succeed in expressing myself; I am like a man who should have a gold piece without being able to use it." And again, after thirty years of solitary and assiduous work, he says: "I feel that I grow clearer before nature. Unhappily it is always very difficult for me to realize my sensations. I cannot achieve the intensity which reveals itself to my senses; I have not that magnificent richness of color which enlivens nature. However, considering the color sensations that I have, I regret my advanced age. It is sad not to be able to give many specimens of my ideas and sensations."

This utterance suggests everything that is important in Cézanne,—his misgivings as an executant, his proud sense of the value of his own vision, his assertion of its intellectuality, of its essential truthfulness and nearness to nature, and finally his consciousness of a peculiar power of color. Before telling the very simple tale of Cézanne's life and training, we should interrogate his pictures. They fall into four groups— portraits, compositions of nudes, landscapes, and still-lifes. Of these an unaccustomed eye will usually accept only the still-lifes. These arrangements of fruit and kitchen or tableware have the greatest succulence of texture and depth of color. They seem as they glow from within to gain size and monumentality—these apples and pots and pans. They excite and appease, adding, as it were, to our own visual

GAUGUIN: TAHITIAN SCENE

CÉZANNE: CARD PLAYERS

capacity. Painted in full light and color with a minimum of structural shadow they illustrate more completely than Cézanne's more imposing works his doctrine that "where there is fulness of color there should be fulness of form." Taken literally, as Émile Bernard has pointed out, the statement is false and nonsensical; or at least it is valid only for red apples and the like. No elaborate composition can be fully realized as form except through consenting to some waiver of color both in the darks and the lights. The mere clash of juxtaposed colors in full saturation may result in coruscation or in decoration; it will never deeply touch the plastic sense. That is the privilege of line and of black and white—tone and values.

Cézanne's intention was to avoid the closer registration of values and construct by boldly selected color indications of greatest brilliancy. This road he pursued falteringly. Much of his color is discreet enough, russets and greens, and grays, while his pearly water colors which are executed more straightforwardly than his oil paintings often are meticulous in balance of values of neutral tones. Doubtless much of the fumbling quality of Cézanne—"his timid and conscientious stroke" as Van Gogh, who was neither timid nor conscientious, puts it—comes from the fact that he was attempting the impossible. To return to the oil paintings, what will strike him who first sees the landscapes or the composition of nudes is their rough and sketchy character. Rugged contours repeat themselves inaptly or overrun their forms, little rubbings of green or brown seem to occur casually on the canvas with raw spaces between. The whole effect, taken superficially, is of slightness and heavyhandedness. There are no fine passages, nothing that can be excerpted.

Look more carefully at these rough and fragmentary indications, and they will begin to build a world; the writhing contours, the blots and smudges, will combine in a ponderous rhythm. The eye is led far back over houses and cliffs and orchards to stretches of sea beyond which hangs a mountain range under a palpable half-dome of blue sky. What time-of-day is it? The question always in order in Impressionist painting never arises in Cézanne's. It is what is always seen in sunlight or in forest shadow, the residual important thing that remains after the accidental appearances have been thought away. Cézanne always worked from nature and except the still-lifes no picture of his ever closely resembled its subject-matter. What he sought was a significant mental substitute for the mere appearance—indications that should give the truth of structure more sharply and completely than the thing itself. On study, then, the Cézannes reveal the most patient and cautious of eyes and hands. The rubbing that puts a boulder or the great trunk of a tree in place looks like a careless smudge of a thumb. More likely it has been enriched and revised a dozen times over many years.

Since Cézanne was simply trying to express his

temperament, or, technically, to find color equivalents for his ideated sensations, and since his temperament and sensations were often confused, he made many failures, and he knew it.   In disgust he often left his canvases on the sketching ground, hurled them into convenient trees, committed them to the fire.   He has always been and remains, despite the infinite talk about him, a painter's painter.   That means that the artist discerns something rare and precious in Cézanne's intentions even where they have failed of complete expression.

Cézanne once told Vollard that his aim was "to do Poussins before Nature."   Here was a quite impossible aim; the prolonged and considerate reflection that go to make a Poussin cannot be conducted under the changing and confusing conditions of painting in the open air.   But at least the words express Cézanne's ambition to make considered creations, to eschew time-of-day, intervening atmosphere, specific irradiation—all that his former Impressionist associates held dear.   He came late to art, after desultory studies in literature, in his thirties, moved in the circle of Zola and Manet, and had exhibited in the first three shows of the Impressionists.   He was passingly influenced by Delacroix, whom he always admired, and more slightly by Courbet, but his real training, which hardly began before his fortieth year, was in the exasperation of the daily struggle to clarify his own sensations before the *motif*.   He ceased to exhibit with the Impressionists in 1877, and from then on lived mostly at Aix-in-Provence, a quiet family man at peace with church and state, standing off from a world that wanted "to put a hook in him," living comfortably on his inheritance, hoping for official honors which never came, agonizing daily between hope and despair in the unending struggle to transcribe his *petite sensation* into the true truth about the *motif*.

What this true truth was he never fully told, but the hints that he let drop to his few friends give us a glimpse of it. First he wished to express the *motif* not in terms of its surface but in terms of its essential structure. Here analysis showed that all structure is comprised in a few geometrical forms. He wished to tell the truth not in terms of the visual object but in mental terms and terms of painting. The language of the truth as thus conceived is the abrupt little planes that push and thrust on his canvas and build up forms far more extensive and more solid than themselves. In theory the method suggests Manet's use of the *tache*. In practice it is entirely different. The planes are not mosaicked, but isolated. They irradiate and project structural values across voids in which they meet the balancing of other strokes and planes. In simpler terms, we have to do with clashing indications always implying motion and direction, and of very long range. The work is an ordered series of succinct gestures and never a description. Indeed it is always a distortion of the mere appearance of the *motif*. Cézanne must find the forms that express the

CEZANNE: PROVENCAL LANDSCAPE

CEZANNE: NUDES

ideas and sensations aroused by the object, and he must mediate between the object as it appears and the object as it is known to be. Such mediation of course is the problem of every artist who is not a mere recorder.

Cézanne merely carried the usual compromise a shade farther in the direction of distortion. He is said to have had also a vivid sense of the distortions and illusions that are occult in nature itself. Forms warp each other. Curves bend adjacent straight lines and vice-versa, angles repel or attract each other. These are well-known facts in optics which painters have usually disregarded. Cézanne seems to have been very sensitive to these distortions and to have exaggerated them in his canvases. It corresponded to his notion of a dynamic world. The notion, I need hardly insist, is scientific. Nothing is really inert, just so much bulk; everything is in stress and vibration. Cézanne's expression of the dynamic of structure is his most precious contribution to landscape painting. Not that it is exactly novel. Every great landscapist has felt the implications of motion in Nature. Ruysdael tingles with motion, so does Rousseau. But no other artist, unless it be El Greco, has sought such sparse and intellectualized symbols for this great fact of a universe in dynamic balance.

The apparent inferiority of the man to his ambitions and gifts is baffling. And Cézanne's world supplied few corrections or outlets for his timid, irascible, petty, and great spirit. Moreover his intel-

ligence was inferior to his task, and he grew in a
time when the education of the artist was at its lowest
level. His task required saturation with the anatomy
and physiology of man, plants, and the earth. His
intuitions of these facts were extraordinary but often
insufficient. Again he never achieved the craftsmanship that befits the great artist. He is like a Michelangelo approaching the unhewn marble block with
sandpaper and a file. As compared with the great
artists Cézanne lacks centrality, but he is one of the
greatest of provincials and will be remembered
honorably among painters whose zeal for research
obscured, if heroically, their balance and judgment.
He is the Paolo Ucello of our times.

In the Salons d'Automne of 1904, 1905 and 1906,
the last three years of his life, Cézanne exhibited
freely and amid the accustomed derision began to
receive favorable criticism. "I wish that Zola were
here now that I'm coughing up (*crache*) *chef-d'œuvres*"
he said to Vollard. In place of Zola's persistent and
offensive condescension, he was now offered the
wonder and admiration of scores of young men
studying mass, geometrical abstraction, and creative
distortion in his works. Indeed it is one of the
greater paradoxes of the history of art that all the
fanaticisms of the past twenty years have sought
their justification in the cautious and patient achievement of the master of Aix. He was after all a fanatic,
but of a fanaticism singularly adapted to his moment.
Thus his relation to the revolution now in progress in

painting is that of Rousseau to the French Revolution. Two men "feeble in life" have developed in death the most extraordinary vitality. Both for a certain ruthless primitivism and incapacity to see beyond their respective penpoint and brush deserve the appellation of "magnificent monster," which Charles Morice did not hesitate to lay upon the grave of Cézanne. It well expresses a dæmonic force that bequeathed to the world not merely so many unfinished works, but also imposed upon posterity so many urgent and plastic intentions.

The germinal ideas of Cézanne may be formulated as follows:

Creative Distortion: This means the departure from actual appearance that the artist makes either to express his emotion or to emphasize as against what the eye sees in the object what the mind knows to be there. We may call these distortions Expressive and Factual. A word on each.

Expressive distortion is simply the artist's alteration or deformation of appearances to express the emotion he feels before them. It has the same relation to pictorial plain statement, representation, that irony, hyperbole, or metaphor have to literary plain statement or description. Van Gogh, Gauguin, and Cézanne all distorted appearances freely to gain keener emotional effect. Here they merely asserted the normality of what had always been an admitted license, or perhaps they merely extended and advertised what all artists had practiced as a professional secret.

Artists who work under high emotional pressure without compensating inhibitions are invariably distortionists. Botticelli was, so was Michelangelo, so was Blake, so was Daumier. Short of such overt and flagrant substitution of the forms of the artist's feeling for those of nature, all painting involves considerable departures from truth of appearance. The mere perspective of any well made picture is seldom that of nature. The omissions, transpositions, and substitutions that have been made in a realistic picture, an apparently literal transcript of nature, would surprise both the artist and layman. For the layman is naturally ignorant of these inevitable procedures, whereas the artist takes them for granted and practices them unconsciously. But in the older painting extreme distortion was regarded as at best a license of eccentric genius, and the minor distortions were either ignored or tolerated on condition that the layman should not find them out. He seldom did.

What Cézanne, Van Gogh, and Gauguin did was simply to give a greater extension and theoretical warrant to expressive distortion, to apply it to color as well as to form, to discredit the authority of natural appearances over the artist. They furnished the precedent for the Expressionists, Henri Matisse, Van Dongen, Segonzac, Modigliani, Marie Laurencin, and others, who merely took one step further when they denied all authority to appearances and based their art solely on lyrical self-expression.

Factual distortion of a systematic sort is almost

Cézanne's personal invention, but not quite so. It took six centuries, the space between Giotto and Manet, for the European artist to make sure of what he saw. In the meantime his art was a compromise between what he saw, confusedly, perhaps, and what, less confusedly, he knew actually was in nature. Thus in the sense that only in recent times have pictures been close to actual appearance there has always been factual distortion. When Veronese in his grandiose Marriage of Cana makes the figures on the inner side of a great table on nearly the scale of those on the outer side, this is an expressive distortion in so far as it serves his decorative purpose to avoid confusing differences of scale, and a factual distortion so far as he and the spectator know that the far-away figures only seem to diminish. El Greco, whose influence on Cézanne is strong, illustrates this twofold distortion more signally. The warped and elongated anatomy of his figures is highly expressive of his own ecstacies, but the distorted and syncopated strokes also give a stronger plastic relief to skull and limbs than any painting more regardful of surfaces and respectful of appearances affords. In short El Greco tells the truth that interests him by ignoring or perverting the truth that does not; such truths as texture, atmospheric envelopment, exact dimensions do not count for him in comparison with truth of motion and projection.

Now the problem for the artist has ever been how far he should base his work on appearances, how far

on knowledge. The best artists had made the compromise simply and unconsciously on general grounds
of taste.   The whole progressive endeavor of the
nineteenth century was to purify the artist's vision
from the contamination of knowledge, to render appearances accurately.   Cézanne simply swung the
balance back towards knowledge.

Now imagine successors who take no account of
appearances at all, but admit only knowledge into
their painting, and suppose such knowledge to be
conveyed by Cézanne's formula that the "cube, the
cone, and the cylinder" are nature's fundamental
shapes—then you would have the Cubism of Gleizes,
Metzinger, Bracque, and Picasso. And indeed Cubism
is simply a fanatical intellectualistic reaction against
the generally anti-intellectualistic programme of Impressionism.   Its derivation from Cézanne's intellectualism is patent.   It merely substitutes for the
single aspect of an object, multiform mental assertions about the object considered in all its aspects.
Cézanne in making factual distortion not a matter of
tact but of duty and conviction led the way to the
declivity whence later his cylindrophile disciples
rolled down into a rationalistic dead sea.

Imagine Cézanne's vivid sense of implicit motion in
apparently motionless things, enlarged and transformed into a vivid curiosity about the flux of life—a
phenomenon eloquently re-emphasized by the philosopher Henri Bergson in the early years of this century—imagine the flux as the subject-matter of art—

then you would have Futurism as practiced by
Severini, Balla, Russolo, and others. It would, on
the technical side, merely have to convert the "simultaneity" of the Cubists, their multiform data in
space, into terms of motion—simultaneity of time.
So the Futurists also derive at one remove from the
dynamism of the solitary master of Aix.

Cézanne, then, is the key to modernist painting. I
fancy he would regret his eminence and look with
misgiving through the doors he opened. In particular he would suspect the professions of "temperament" in the Expressionists and feel its absence
in the Cubists. A certain responsibility for both
the impulsivist and intellectualist aberrations of the
last twenty years must certainly go to the eccentric
bourgeois of Aix who in almost savage isolation, by
sheer force of work and thought became both the
Voltaire and the Rousseau of the revolution of the
art of painting.

If I have treated at disproportionate length the
work of Van Gogh, Gauguin and Cézanne, it is because
their art goes far to explain the confusing radical
movements of the day. And also a rather full discussion of their art seemed necessary since our attitude
towards them necessarily colors our attitude to their
successors. If these men seem very great artists to
us, if, not to go behind the last century, we can set
them beside David, Delacroix, Ingres, Millet, Daumier, Puvis, Renoir, Degas, the case for their followers is strong. If they seem to us merely minor artists

of exceptionally interesting type, then the expansion of their practice into a school will seem on the face of it an aberration. Especially the student of Modernism in painting must come to terms with Cézanne. Is he just an interesting character and a stalwart experimentalist, or is he a great artist? The answer to these questions is crucial. Whatever the answer, his importance for our age cannot be gainsaid. He marks in a century that had progressively renounced the rationale of art a return to reason. Unhappily neither his character nor his work was calculated to make reason amiable. Deep calls unto deep; the crank multiplies his kind. Cézanne's generally sound views were largely belied by the eccentricity and inadequacy of his practice. His mannerisms and foibles, however, became gospel for the uneasier and abler young men of twenty years ago, and the double revolution under the watchwords of liberty and discipline achieved only a liberty at which he would have shuddered and a discipline which he would have utterly renounced.

MODERNIST MOVEMENTS IN THE TWENTIETH CENTURY

MODERNIST MOVEMENTS IN THE TWENTIETH CENTURY

THE new movements which announced themselves strongly about the year of Cézanne's death, 1907, may be roughly divided as impulsivistic or intellectualistic. Impulsivism, or Expressionism, is merely the climax of that romantic individualism which had guided the art of the nineteenth century. The value of the individual resides in his emotions. He now expresses them more sharply and swiftly because all the residual if diminishing checks imposed on the older impulsivism by the taste and common sense of the public, by the reason and second thought of the artist himself, by the habit of consulting and respecting natural appearances—because all these checks have been whistled down the wind. After a century and a quarter, the prophetic exclamation of Mephistopheles, "Feeling is the whole thing," *"Gefühl ist alles,"* is fully realized. All the more vigorous youth, the wild beasts, *les fauves,* as the censorious call them, march under that banner. Henri Matisse, most typical and prominent of Expressionist painters, has written of his own art:

"What I seek beyond all else is expression. . . . I am unable to distinguish between the feeling which I have for life and the manner in which I render it."

353

Here is implied a creative spasm necessarily of brief duration in which feeling and execution blend in a passionate blur to produce the work of art. It must be such as can be achieved before the creative *élan* ceases. It is no longer a question of the days that Manet spent before a single canvas, nor that of the three or four hours in successive days that went to the fixing of Monet's impressions. It is now a question of hours or even of minutes. The work is slashed out in great tingling strokes—gestures determined by the fury of the unconscious mind. The canvas writhes with curves that are distortions of the actual forms, and sings with baldest assertions and discordances of color. Even if there were any desire to imitate nature—and Expressionism indignantly repudiates the endeavor—there would be no time to do so. Nature is at most only the detonator of the emotionally charged bomb which is the artist, and the work of art is only the imprint of the vigorously flying fragments of a personality.

The Impressionists had striven to regain the innocence of the eye; the Expressionists seek the more complete innocence that attaches to a soul intact from guidance as regards society, nature and the rational part of its own possessor. If we consider this ambition in the light of history, it is merely an accentuation of our old friend the lyrical fallacy—the chief gift of Romanticism to æsthetic theory: that is, because feeling is the beginning and indispensable mover of the work of art, it is the only thing of value.

More than fifty years after Edgar Allan Poe had asserted that the only true poem is the short poem— the lyric, because it alone can be carried through in a single gush of emotion, the young painters took up the teaching. What has resulted is so many pictorial lyrics, or, more prosaically, thousands and tens of thousands of big and blatant sketches, often hideous, sometimes morbid, more frequently perhaps burlesque—in short as compared with the older lyricism of the violin, the bleating and snorting lyricism of the saxaphone. It was not for nothing that jazz music, the moving picture, and Expressionism grew up together.

It is not the time to renew the unending debate concerning the relation of impulse and reason in artistic creation. It may be enough to remind the reader that when the early Romanticists exalted the rôle of passion in art, they were less describing their own practice than reprobating the Empire style, in which pedantry had ruled, from which passion was absent. They never meant what Poe meant, what Matisse professes, what Kandinsky elaborates in his book, "The Art of Spiritual Harmony"—that creative passion is brief and orgasmic. On the contrary, they stood with the old masters and with their own rivals of the academic schools in the faith that a creative impulse can be maintained through pains of thoughtful execution, can be tempered and refined by the artist's self-criticism without losing strength or authenticity, can be recovered in its integrity after

intervals of rest and reflection. In this Delacroix
would have agreed with Ingres, and Daumier with
Puvis, and Gérôme with Besnard. Indeed these men
all valued immediate lyrical expression, which in
their sketches they practiced most ably, less highly
than an expression which, without losing its emotional content, had found its ultimate form under the
direction of judgment and taste. In short Mephistopheles' *Gefühl ist alles*—the bribe which a cynical
rationalist successfully dangled before a Romanti-
cist—would no more have gone down with Mephistopheles' best portraitist, Delacroix, than it would
with Faust himself after experience had purged off his
Romantic green-sickness.

Evidently the Expressionist ideal practically limits
the education of the artist to the fostering of strong
emotions, of the value of which he himself is the sole
judge. If, as Matisse has very precisely said, the
emotion and its rendering are one and the same thing
and indistinguishable to the artist himself, there can
be no question of studying technic. The wind of
passion bloweth whither it listeth and breathes and
carves its own forms upon the shifting yet plastic
sands that are the materials of the artist.

Claude Monet once drily remarked that "With
doctrines one doesn't paint pictures." Evidently
there must be some sort of preparation for the
creative detonation even of the purest Expressionist.
He must lay in materials against the not impossible
pang. He is very likely to cultivate his emotional

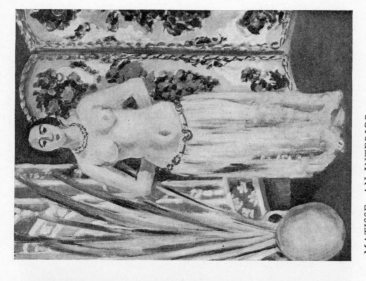

MATISSE: AN INTERIOR

MATISSE: PORTRAIT

capacity by observing the work of fellow Expressionists, indeed of all who have created in joyous
innocence. High among those are the Congo blacks
who have fixed their fears and obscenities in ebony
images nearly as enduring as bronze. Indeed there is
such a monotony about the pure spontaneity of the
Expressionists that their most benevolent critic can
only conclude that the movement has paradoxically
developed an academism of its own, merely substituting for the academism of civilization that of
barbarism.

Henri Matisse is so much the premier Expressionist
that an estimate of his art serves fairly well for that
of his group. Fundamentally he seems to me a fine
draughtsman gone wrong. He is a master of his own
sort of drawing and equally a master with the line
or the blot. His line is tight and minutely descriptive
in the rare instances where he wants it to be so, but
generally it is loose and dynamic, the preoccupation
being with the larger truths of mass and balance. At
his best his drawing has extraordinary *bravura* and
equal truthfulness. I remember a little crouching
nude in the Armory Show of 1913. An unbroken
thick line told the whole story of torso settling into
thighs and thorax bending into abdomen. The little
study, an affair of two minutes, would have stood up
beside a Hokusai.

This is possibly the limit of Matisse's vision and
power, for the paintings are garish and unsteady,
splotched with conventionally sharp colors, like a

tomato salad with mayonnaise, which are exciting
without being really decorative. At best the work
achieves a whimsical sort of caricaturism—the Young
Sailor, M. Pellerin, the Madras Bonnet, the Girl with
the Green Eyes. For twenty years and more he has
been painting in this fashion, very variously and
often amusingly, without achieving a notable work
in color, betraying no sign of development or maturity. It is the penalty of any counsel of pure lyricism
that one cannot grow old gracefully on it.

Of his younger compeers Segonzac seems to me the
most powerful. His work is extravagently over-
assertive but dense and purposeful; it has the qualities
of its temperamental coarseness. Marquet is the
most accomplished. His simplifications are exquisitely calculated, his color highly decorative and
structural. To the landscape methods of Cézanne he
has added amenity. With less vivacity Marchand
evinces a similar taste, while Vlaminck's work,
though of slighter structural value and less orderly,
is freshly felt and highly decorative. The German
Kandinsky has gone further from nature than the
French Expressionists, depending on abstract cloud-
like forms and blots to produce what according to
their degree of elaboration he calls improvisations,
impressions, or compositions. They are all sup-
posed to have musical implications as he has inter-
estingly explained in his book, "The Art of Spiritual
Harmony," and they suggest analogies with the new
music such as Debussy's, which deals only with

nuances. Of the numerous young American Expressionists Marsden Hartley is perhaps the most
able. He has passed through Luminism and a phase
akin to Cézanne, to an Expressionism of an unctuous
Segonzaclike sort, with episodes of a cubistic
order. In short he has painted joyously like half-a-
dozen talented young insurgents and always with a
certain *beauté de diable*. The whole hardly constitutes
an *œuvre*. The highest average level of Expressionism
to-day is perhaps found in Germany, and particularly
in Munich. No figure is really outstanding, but
dozens of fresh and not a little impudent talents
capitalize their youth to fair artistic purpose. A
visit to the Glaspalast at Munich leaves one little to
remember, but sends one away distinctly cheerful.
But there is little richness or knowledge in their
gayety. They represent the defects of a recently
and too quickly civilized race which takes in lyrical
debauches its moral holidays from the oppressiveness
of its grandiose materialism.

Evidently the Expressionists have merely hardened
into a dictum, Monet's practice of "painting as the
bird sings." Even among birds the doctrine is defective. There are birds which sing badly.

Alongside the pure impulsivists, Expressionism has
developed certain talents of a more reflective sort,
for the expulsion of mind from art is really more
difficult than would seem. Like love, when you have
closed the door on it, it comes in by the window.
The common bond between talents as various as that

of Henri Rousseau, "Le Douanier," André Derain,
F. E. Tobeen, André Lhote, with Picasso and Severini
(in their latest phase) is the struggle for a stronger and
more novel emphasis of form. Except in the naïf,
Rousseau, feeling is entirely secondary to plastic effect.
There is in all an insistence on the roundness and
bulk of the forms which finds its nearest precedent in
Seurat. Rousseau merely painted away at his
imaginary tropical forests and at his holiday scenes
until they got the substance and seriousness of a well-
made embroidered sampler. In his desire to make
strong he is akin to Cézanne, of whom he probably
had never heard. He was born in 1844, exhibited from
1886 with the Indépendants, painted really as an
amateur, and acquired prestige in his last ten years,
and died in 1910. As the fashion swung towards
the bizarre, he acquired vogue and received on Sun-
days. His is a beguiling talent with a touch of Blake,
a stronger infusion of Dickens, and, converted into a
modest poetry, the mental agility and perspicacity
of a Parisian bourgeois.

Picasso, Severini, Derain and Tobeen are talents of
a very self-conscious and resolute sort devoted to the
investigation and creation of a new grammar of form.
In this endeavor they represent the most legitimate
succession of Cézanne, though they generally ignore
his capital precept that form and color are in plenitude
together. Instead these men are what an older
criticism would call tonalists, contriving the most
ingenious and subtle relations of tone, often nearly

monochrome, in order to give the strongest assurance
of mass.   Being intellectualists, their bond with
Expressionism is merely superficial.   Indeed the relation comes to little more than the habit of distortion,
and again the distortions of the group we are considering are by no means the result of passionate
gestures, but of the most careful calculation.   We
really have the substitution of very emphatic abstrac-
tions for the actual forms, but the abstraction retains
much of the character of the form from which it
derives and is always easily legible.   The procedure
comes to a more strenuous practice of selection and
elimination and distortion than we have had in the
past.   The sacrifice of texture and local color is more
or less inevitable in this work, and naturally, since the
aim is to embody a permanent mental aspect, specific
illumination and time-of-day yield to artificial and
highly calculated lighting.   Severini in his recent
book, "Du Cubisme au Classicisme," advocates a
return to Piero della Francesca, and it is of that
admirable artist that I am at times reminded when I
admire the broadly emphatic modeling of Derain and
the similarly powerful pale blues and greens of Picasso's recent landscapes.

Whatever real novelty and promise there may be in
the Modernist painting seems to me to lie with these
men.   They have added to Cézanne's higher impact
of color upon the eye a higher impact of coördinated
tones.   I see no great masterpiece among their works
(perhaps I am too near them) but I see many grave

and delightful compositions which, keeping the dignity of the tradition, have their distinct novelty. I am not convinced that the degree of abstraction represented in these masters is really desirable in painting or correspondent to our way of thinking and feeling. The whole issue is whether we need to be liberated from the realistic tradition or merely from a rather stupid sort of conformity to it. If we are, however, to abandon the representative tradition, without entirely abandoning common sense and established standards of taste, then these men are the pathfinders. Their watchword is construction. One may find the programme in André Lhote's excellent little booklet on Seurat. So far the actual constructions do not seem to warrant the sacrifice of versimilitude required to attain them. But the endeavor is a serious one and will bear watching.

Most of the group we have been considering have passed through Cubism. And indeed that was a bridge which an intellectualist painter of the early years of this century was likely to cross. Cubism grew out of Cézanne's predilection for the simpler geometrical forms in design, and first was used as a decorative expedient by such young painters as Albert Gleizes, Jean Metzinger, Georges Bracque and Pablo Picasso. The forms were blocked out in so many planes and often partly veiled by a sort of net. For convenience of study, Dürer, Luca Cambiaso and others had considered the body as so many cubes, cylinders, and cones. Imagine such sketches squared

PICASSO: A WOMAN

PICASSO: PORTRAIT OF MLLE. G. S.

for enlargement and one has the formula of decorative Cubism. Gleizes' Man on a Balcony, Picasso's Mandolin Player are of this sort, with however a difference. For this decorative Cubism soon hardened into a general theory. One may get it with difficulty from the books of Guillaume Apollinaire and of Gleizes, or more intelligibly in Willard Huntington Wright's excellent book on Modern Painting.

The theoretical Cubists merely turned upon the prevailing Expressionism the criticism which Cézanne had applied to Luminism: namely that both were deficient on the intellectual side, conveying only the merest fraction of what the artist knew about his theme. The Cubists held also that painting had been kept in an incipient stage through accepting the apparent limitations of a plane surface, on which only motionless and coexistent objects can be set, and these in a single aspect. I am painting the model. Why impoverish my picture by presenting one what I see of her as I paint, that is 180 degrees of her. I know the other 180 degrees. I may know as well her horizontal and vertical sections. It will be well to indicate them on the canvas. Besides, economy is in order. Both sides of her head are alike. It is enough to give the contour of one side, in full face, and in order to show that the head has a back to set beside or upon the frontal half-contour also the contour in profile. Now I am achieving "Simultaneity," showing what one learns by walking around the model and remembering the varying aspects, and this is not merely simultaneity but also "mental enrichment of the visual impression." This enrichment can be carried far. Suppose the model, like Trilby, is a *blanchisseuse du fin.* I can convey that in various ways. If it is important, I can superimpose upon my already numerous sections that of a floating laundry, or I can symbolize it more delicately by painting in, or pasting on, a wash-list, or by interlacing with my superimposed sections the letters spelling the name of some favorite laundry soap.

What I have written hardly caricatures the theory and the procedure of Cubism. What actually resulted was the most bafflingly complicated mechanical drawings, often highly ingenious, usually rendered in monochrome or with reduced color. It is a world of slipping and sliding planes—these portraits and groups of Picasso and his associates. One gets similar vertiginous sensations by looking at a big steam engine through a loophole too small to let the whole mechanism explain itself, or, as a friend once more happily put it, by standing on a railroad bridge and watching several trains passing each other in different directions. The movement had much vogue in Paris from about 1910 to the War. In its decorative aspects it influenced the English painter-illustrator Nevinson and such talented young Americans as Walter Pach, Charles Demuth and Arthur B. Davies. A residuum of the decorative devices there is still in industrial design, in illustration, and in painting of the type of Derain's and Lhote's. But Picasso, the most versatile of its practitioners, has passed out of the movement, similar desertions have followed and the movement is effectively dead. The Ex-Cubists generally, in the tone of one mentioning an outgrown love or a discarded religion, profess to have experienced a valuable discipline in their Cubist endeavor. Naturally they are the judges.

At least Cubism has the interest of having pushed to its logical absurdity the intellectualist conception of painting. Intellectualistic exercises that are legible only to their creator may be of highest importance to him; they hardly concern the critic or the lover of art.

Futurism, again a discarded aberration, is only interesting for its incidental philosophical and historical implications. It got its name and programme from the clever Italian journalist critic, Marinetti, in 1908. His cult was that of a ruthlessly iconoclastic energy, growing out of his disgust with the idea that Italy is only a sort of museum. On the side of politics we may say that Futurism forecast and fostered the new Italian Nationalism of Mussolini and his *Fascisti*. On the side of art, with scorn of the past, went admiration of the new. Machinery, clamor, power— these are the themes of the Futurist.

Conceiving the world as simple flux—a Heracleitan notion eloquently revived by Bergson—the Futurist has merely to suggest its whirl. The spectator is to be drawn into the picture, to feel that he moves with it and in it. Time and motion are to be brought into painting. That simultaneity in time and space which the Cubist symbolized merely, is now to be actually represented. Dynamism is the favorite word in the various Futurist manifestos from 1910 to 1912. Everything in the picture must dance and move. The actual procedures of the five Italian artists who signed the Futurist platform were quite various. Balla merely painted the many twinkling legs and tails which one sees in a spaniel as he runs. The result was amusing but not calculated to sweep the spectator into the onrush of the picture. Russolo invented effective geometrical symbols. Thus a wedge flying in space denoted indifferently Revolution or the Dynamism of a Motor Car. Severini, the ablest of the group, wove a gay and baffling tapestry out of samples of what might be experienced in an evening at the Bal Tabarin. One had bits of musical instruments, hints of set tables, women's shoulders, dancing-slippers—in short, a very vivacious example of those samplers with which Cubism had already provided us. Boccioni, a sculptor, made his figures move by considering them as composite columns of which the drums have been shifted out of place by an earthquake. It is a procedure which the clever British artist, Stephen Haweis, was later to adapt to painting in his slipped contours. So it went with the Futurists.

The movement passed like the rest. To discuss it is hardly necessary today. Yet since it rested on a sort of philosophy of the flux, we may at least note the fallacy of the theory that the artist, the picture, and the spectator should move together in one dynamic rhythm. One who is completely in and of any flux would of course have no way of knowing his felicity. Something must be at rest if only to permit the motion to be perceived. The artist must be enough out of the picture to produce it, and the spectator must be in at least a different motion from any outside moving thing, including a Futurist picture, if he is to realize that there is any motion at all. Evidently the Futurist programme was conceived in that warm and expansive blur which is said to be favorable to artistic creation. Whatever was real of it passed into the new Italian Nationalism. In art nothing much happened save another reason for the illegible picture and a new demonstration of the fact that the freedom of the artist may only mean his right to act foolishly.

Synchromism has so much passed that M. Coquiot has dropped its manifesto from the later edition of his book, "Les Indépendants." Yet Synchromism had at least the merit of closing a doctrinal controversy that had lasted for a century, by a convincing reduction to the absurd. It was, I believe, in 1910, that Macdonald Wright and Morgan Russell exhibited *chez Bernheim jeune*, and published their programme. Their aim was the complete purification of the art of painting. It must cease to borrow from appearances and live solely on such resources as are proper to itself. These resources are simply areas of color. The task of the artist is to learn color and to produce the effects which are proper to color, without recourse to illustrative features—that is to recognizable objects of any sort.

So this young American and young Canadian re-studied color, and established their scale of colors that advance or retreat.　In short they were really repeating the Futurist endeavor to obtain move-ment, but of course movement of an abstract sort and free from these irrelevant illustrative features which Futurism had too much affected.　The Synchromist pictures were swirls of pure color—tartan patterns cunningly reorganized to produce vortical depths. By Willard Huntington Wright, brother of the painter, these polychrome whirlpools were described as cosmic abysses and as the final and culminating invention in painting.　Within a few years the critic had perceived that the consummation of the art of painting in Synchomism must also mark its end.　Since, if paint-ing is simply to play with effects of space and implica-tions of movement in color, it is foolish to use motion-less pigment when you can use actual colored light in motion.　In short the color organ had arrived and the picture must go—*ceci tuera cela.*　So the second thought of Mr. Willard Huntington Wright, in "The Art of Color."

All the same, painting continues to survive.　There are signs that the painter is sick of movements, bored with his own liberty, and in search of a discipline. Expressionism still rules among the young, but they now vaunt less their originality than their legitimacy. To be in the tradition is now the cry.　For years the charming eclectic painter Maurice Denis has been preaching it and writing it.　It is the cry of André

PICASSO: LANDSCAPE

SEGONZAC: DRAWING, LANDSCAPE

Lhote.   Severini a short ten years ago, a frenetical
Futurist, is now appealing to the compass and rule,
to geometry of design, to fixed color proportions, and
exquisite calculation—classicism.   Matisse's compositions are still like arrangements of peppermint canes,
but they are now quiet and proper peppermint canes,
no longer savagely distorted.   Long ago, Derain
passed out of Cubism towards roundnesses and balances through which one glimpses Ingres and Poussin.
Picasso having successively and ably exploited the
vein of Steinlen, of Puvis, of Cubism, is again back
with Ingres.   Modernist pictures are becoming discreet, almost cautiously monotonous in color, and
they generally deal with recognizable subject-matter.
After a century of struggle for purity, the old compromises reassert their inevitableness.   Common-
sense and tradition have once more become the
respectable watchwords, though they still appear
rather faintly in works of painters whose speaking
acquaintance with either is of quite recent date.

Reviewing the uprush of emotionalistic and ration-
alizing individualism in the past twenty years—it
appears rather as a destructive than as a constructive movement.   It has enlisted many fine talents—
the capacity of men like Othon Friez, Segonzac,
Picasso, Marchand, and Derain, seems to me incon-
testable, but it has provided these talents only with a
development as capricious as incomplete.   It has been
a period of wasteful expansion, of reckless abandon-
ment of the past.   Indeed the weakness of the move-

ment has been that it was, deep in the artist's consciousness, less a struggle for liberation than a protest against prevailing styles. There was much reason in the protest, but it produced in the new artists a mood of mere negation. Most of them, while ostensibly expressing themselves, were really flouting traditions the value of which they failed to understand. It seems to me clear that the greatest artists of the end of the last century and the beginning of this are not the modernists but those who have followed the traditions of Puvis, of the Luminists, and even of the older Academism. Renoir, Degas, Besnard, Simon, Cottet, Blanche, Forain, Maurice Denis, Le Sidaner, Ménard, André in France,—this is the tradition. In comparison the Modernists have attained nothing of the coherence or authority of a school.

The new movements have at least done the service of putting to the test of practice ideas that had been only verbal. When Delacroix appealed to the freedom of the artist and for the purity of painting, he had no prevision that the artist would ever regard his freedom as an exemption from all outer discipline, or that a hint of natural appearance in a picture should ever be regarded as an impurity. It took only about sixty years to drive the liberating counsels of early Romanticism to their logical and absurd extreme. It really amounts to a peeling off process, as if one should successively throw away the layers of an onion in the hope of disengaging the ultimate form and fragrance, the quintessential onion ordinarily concealed by a specious exterior both from gastronomes and from painters of still-life.   It is plain that the process would have its drawbacks.   There might be nothing at the center, or nothing much.

So I think it was with that prolonged and finally accelerated peeling-off process by which painting was purified.   Delacroix and his disciples merely renounced the academic authority of the moment, appealing to better traditions; in that, he did well.   Courbet and his Realists joined Manet in renouncing the mind's eye.   One paints only what one sees.   The restriction was right enough for men of Courbet's and Manet's make-up, but unfortunate as a general programme. With Monet and the Luminists, the artist renounced his memory.   This moment marked joyous discovery and also a disastrous disregard of tradition with a deep impoverishment of painting on the mental side. The early Expressionists in their endeavor to put more mind and feeling into art asserted their right to distort natural appearances.   But they still respected nature.   The younger Expressionists of Matisse's generation practically put nature out of the studio window, asserting an unlimited right either of distortion of appearances or of creation in which appearances were not consulted at all.   The Cubists completed the banishment of natural appearances from the art of painting, substituting therefor a mental world of geometrical derivatives.   The Futurists endeavored to set this geometric-mechanical world in motion, thus rejecting the static idea of the picture and competing partially with the cinema. Finally the Synchromists threw overboard everything recognizable in the picture and attempted to build abstract spaces and movements in arbitrary color areas. Painting had become a frozen Catherine Wheel.

We have a successive elimination of academic authority, imagination, memory, fidelity to nature, and nature itself. It would seem as if the last sacrifice had been made; but no. In all these rejections and in the most grotesque experiments the painter had retained his seriousness and self-respect. This too went by the board in a brief moment after the War when the Dadaists bade the artist create in a mood of joyous bluff, meanwhile mocking himself and his world. The oft-repeated demonstration is complete once more—the latter end of expansive Romantic individualism is Romantic disillusionment and Romantic Irony.

The moment seems ripe after so many subliminal uprushes of undisciplined individualism for "a subliminal uprush of common sense." Irving Babbitt has been hopefully predicting it for twenty years, and so far as the painters are concerned it is plain that the ablest painters to-day would welcome a discipline.

But the fond adventure towards purity which we have seen in bankruptcy in our days should not be regarded as merely the wrong feeling and wrong thinking of a few individuals. The Time-Spirit imposed it. It was an inevitable reaction of the artist

to the new conditions imposed upon him by democracy—conditions of unprecedented isolation and hardship. Up to the reign of democracy, the public and
the patron had ordinarily told the artist what he
should do. The painter's task was like that of the
architect to-day, to produce a work of art by means
of or in spite of conditions laid down by a client. It
was a wholesome and a helpful relation, and the best
pictures in the world were thus painted, under what
virtually was coöperation between painter and
patron. But such a relation was posssible and
tolerable only so long as there was a considerable
likemindedness between artist and public. People
must at least want pictures enough to go to the man
who makes them and tell him what they want—to
repose in the artist the confidence they repose, say
in the tailor. The fact that such a relation seems
queer to-day shows the lack of any sound relation
between artist and public.

When the heads of scores of art patrons fell in the
French Revolution, and everywhere the old aristocracy sank in wealth and prestige, the painter had
abruptly to cope with a new public. The new industrial and commercial wealth lacked the, however
limited, traditional taste of the aristocracy it had
displaced, and naturally had no taste of its own.
Nor was it given the opportunity to form a taste for
itself. Its taste was carefully guided by the new and
active forces of dealerdom. Nobody, except rarely
the dealer, now told the artist what to do; he worked

in isolation, to express his soul, on the off chance that his soul when expressed should be saleable and gain him a living. Meanwhile it was not merely more difficult for a painter who had attained competence to find a supporting public, but it was also increasingly more difficult to attain competence at all. The instruction of the schools fell to nearly zero by 1890. Nobody knew which of the many technics was the better. The painter had to teach himself, and, as is usually the case, had a bad teacher. Of course Renoir and Cézanne had pointed out that the museums were the teachers. But this is true only in a limited sense, and the temper of the art students was averse from such study. Meanwhile, further to confuse matters, Romantic æsthetic had imposed upon the artist with a liberty, which was of little use to him and generally a positive embarrassment, the duty of displaying an absolute originality. The favorite word in Parisian criticism of the '80s and '90s is *inédit*.

Now see the predicament of the artist under the new democratic conditions of patronage. His evident short road to success was sycophantism—to cultivate the great dealers and their clients. The alternative was to win through poverty and neglect to a fit patronage. This was the course of Millet, of Rousseau, of Renoir. But heroic resignation to misunderstanding and neglect is as rare among artists as among men generally. It can be more readily maintained upon an adequate private income, such as Manet, Puvis, Corot, and Cézanne enjoyed, than without. The long struggle, hoping against hope, is not for everybody. It is a hero's part. So the artist who was neither a sycophant nor a hero often became consciously or unconsciously a sort of rebel, building up in isolation compensating delusions against the hardness of his lot, scorning the bourgeois immoderately, hardening into his own mental habits without fit fellowship or helpful criticism. Under these conditions men readily yield to what Lord Bacon graphically calls "the fallacies of the cave."

Despite Mr. Whistler's flippant assertion that "art occurs," it occurs, usually only under the right patronage. Probably about the same proportion of babies are potentially great painters at one moment and another. But whether these babies become great painters or not depends very much on the kind of education and encouragement they get. Democracy has failed completely in the direct education of the artist and has not as yet developed any steady and enlightened patronage of art, leaving what is the privilege of every reasonably prosperous person to the rare enlightened dealers or to the museums. The hopeful side of our generally discouraging survey is the energy of the museums throughout the world in giving instruction to the public. This is at least a new fact, a democratic solution for a democratic problem. How far such instruction will reach is as yet uncertain, for the endeavor is only some twenty years old.

So far as Expressionism and its collateral movements imply an entire change in the artist's relation to nature, they seem to me simply wrong. What has changed is the material conditions that affect the artist; his spiritual problems remain very much what they have always been. Nature is still the painter's nearest friend. His is a visual art. Expression apart from what he has seen or remembered of his seeing is generally artificial and false, and of little value if genuine. Besides the only conceivable ground of communication between artist and patron is a common stock of visual memories. Only the artist who paints solely for himself can afford to ignore nature.

There has been no real gain in the new liberty to distort. The good artist has always freely made the omissions, transpositions, and special emphases that seemed necessary to the coherence of his work. Normally he seeks to convey with fidelity, not everything that he has seen, but something he has seen with vividness and joy. Even a Blake transcribes his hallucinations faithfully.

Nor has the old, old problem of pictorial compromise between the thing seen and what is known about it changed simply because we possibly see more acutely than our predecessors. It is a dilemma which as before can only be settled by taste. And these new movements which have run true to a saying of one of their ablest champions that "nothing is so unimportant as taste and civilization" have not made good their case. The Congo has not superseded the Acropolis.

It remains a somewhat urgent problem of democracy to provide enough taste to go around, for taste and standards are ever minority products of an intellectual aristocracy.

Since art grows out of the emotional-mental experience of its creator, the problems of æsthetics and of simple right living lie near together and frequently overlap. The art of painting has suffered from the unbounded individualism of the last century, just as manners, literature, business, industry, and politics have suffered from the same cause. To succeed as a person and an artist, the painter has had to assimilate some older and tried discipline, adapting it to his personal needs. This has been also the problem of the man in the street—to attain in an age of license a morality which transcends that of the police court. Mr. Brownell in one of his recent books has admirably redefined the famous and usually misunderstood saying of Buffon—"le style c'est de l'homme." It does not mean that style gushes inevitably out of the man —which is the standard Romantic misinterpretation, but that style belongs to the man, that he controls it. The heights of art as of simple right living are only reached through a very constant, patient and delicate exercise of judgment, and the saying of Leonardo still is true that "When the work surpasses the judgment of the worker (i. e. rests merely on emotional overflow) that worker acquires little, and when the judgment surpasses the work, that work never ceases to grow better, unless avarice prevents it."

To establish a fine judgment in a recklessly expansive age is the problem of the painter and of pretty nearly every thinking mortal. Evidently it must first be re-enthroned in individual souls. Only then will there be any hope in collective efforts looking toward a restoration of authority to such old-fashioned notions as taste and civilization.

INDEX